**GUIDE TO COMMODITIES**

## OTHER ECONOMIST BOOKS

Guide to Analysing Companies
Guide to Business Modelling
Guide to Business Planning
Guide to Cash Management
Guide to Decision Making
Guide to Economic Indicators
Guide to the European Union
Guide to Financial Management
Guide to Financial Markets
Guide to Hedge Funds
Guide to Investment Strategy
Guide to Management Ideas and Gurus
Guide to Managing Growth
Guide to Organisation Design
Guide to Project Management
Guide to Supply Chain Management
Numbers Guide
Style Guide

Book of Business Quotations
Book of Isms
Book of Obituaries
Brands and Branding
Business Consulting
Business Strategy
Buying Professional Services
Doing Business in China
Economics
Emerging Markets
Marketing
Megachange – the world in 2015
Modern Warfare, Intelligence and Deterrence
Organisation Culture
Successful Strategy Execution
The World of Business

Directors: an A–Z Guide
Economics: an A–Z Guide
Investment: an A–Z Guide
Negotiation: an A–Z Guide

Pocket World in Figures

# GUIDE TO COMMODITIES
Producers, players and prices,
markets, consumers and trends

**Caroline Bain**

THE ECONOMIST IN ASSOCIATION WITH
PROFILE BOOKS LTD

Published by Profile Books Ltd
3a Exmouth House
Pine Street
London EC1R OJH
www.profilebooks.com

Copyright © The Economist Newspaper Ltd, 2013
Text copyright © Caroline Bain, 2013

All rights reserved. Without limiting the rights under copyright reserved above, no part of this publication may be reproduced, stored in or introduced into a retrieval system, or transmitted, in any form or by any means (electronic, mechanical, photocopying, recording or otherwise), without the prior written permission of both the copyright owner and the publisher of this book.

The greatest care has been taken in compiling this book. However, no responsibility can be accepted by the publishers or compilers for the accuracy of the information presented.

Where opinion is expressed it is that of the author and does not necessarily coincide with the editorial views of The Economist Newspaper.

While every effort has been made to contact copyright-holders of material produced or cited in this book, in the case of those it has not been possible to contact successfully, the author and publishers will be glad to make amendments in further editions.

Typeset in EcoType by MacGuru Ltd
info@macguru.org.uk

Printed in Great Britain by Clays, Bungay, Suffolk

A CIP catalogue record for this book is available from the British Library

Hardback: 978 1 84668 896 6
Paperback: 978 1 84668 895 9
e-book: 978 1 84765 843 2

The paper this book is printed on is certified by the
© 1996 Forest Stewardship Council A.C. (FSC).
It is ancient-forest friendly. The printer holds FSC chain of custody SGS-COC-2061

# Contents

| | |
|---|---|
| Acknowledgements | vii |
| Introduction | 1 |
| **Part 1 Market fundamentals** | **5** |
| The economics of commodities | 7 |
| Commodities as financial assets | 18 |
| **Part 2 Base and precious metals** | **27** |
| Aluminium | 29 |
| Copper | 41 |
| Gold | 53 |
| Other precious metals | 65 |
|     Silver | 65 |
|     Platinum | 70 |
|     Palladium | 75 |
| Lead | 79 |
| Nickel | 90 |
| Tin | 101 |
| Zinc | 112 |
| **Part 3 Energy** | **123** |
| Coal | 125 |
| Natural gas | 136 |
| Crude oil | 147 |

**Part 4 Agriculture** 161
Cocoa 163
Coffee 171
Fibres 178
    Cotton 178
    Wool 185
Maize 191
Rice 200
Natural rubber 209
Soybeans 217
Sugar 225
Wheat 235

Glossary 245
Sources of statistical information 253
Index 257

# Acknowledgements

I would like to thank Jessica Godden, who not only helped to compile and check commodities data but was also a great source of encouragement. Thanks also to my colleagues at the Economist Intelligence Unit (EIU) for their support and for giving me the opportunity to undertake this book. I am especially grateful to the experts on commodities that contribute to the EIU commodities publications – they have taught me a lot.

Finally, thanks to everyone at Profile Books for their help, guidance and enthusiasm, and especially to Penny Williams for her meticulous eye during the editing process.

# Introduction

WE LIVE OUR LIVES surrounded by products made, in part at least, using the world's natural resources – from the clothes we wear and the food we eat to the cars we drive, the houses we live in and the electronic devices we use. We depend on commodities, and commodity consumption increases with per-head incomes as countries become more developed.

Steadily rising, although at times volatile, prices in the past decade have underlined the economic importance of commodities and how dependent we are on them. The price of gold has soared to new peaks as currencies have endured a crisis of confidence; demand from China has pushed metal prices up; instability in the Middle East and North Africa has had its effect on the oil price; and food prices have been increasing in parallel with worries about whether there is enough to feed the world.

The exploitation and refinement of natural resources have been an integral part of human and economic development. The discovery of metals and subsequent experiments that determined their potential use were the catalyst for leaps in economic development and productivity. For thousands of years, people have been exchanging and trading natural resources – agricultural products in particular – largely in marketplaces throughout the world. Traders would often go far afield to bring back goods that were not produced domestically and so would command a high price. The first formal commodity exchanges started to emerge in the mid-19th century to meet the growing demands of a rapidly industrialising United States.

Commodities have a number of unique qualities. They are typically uniform in quality and lack product differentiation. For this reason, and unusually, there is a global price or benchmark for most commodities. Industrial commodities are usually used as inputs in the production of other goods and services, following some refining process on the raw material after extraction. Agricultural commodities are also often refined or processed in some way and are used as ingredients to make food and feedstuffs or textiles. Thus commodities are rarely bought directly by consuming households but are typically intermediate goods bought by manufacturing companies.

In its broadest sense, the word "commodity" can be used to describe any traded good (it is usually used for goods rather than services, but can be applied to both). Historically, it was also used to describe something of quality or value, but this interpretation has become largely obsolete – although it does still apply to some precious metals. In recent years, the word has spawned a number of verbs, including "commodify" and "commoditise". The former is to make something commercially viable, while the latter is more about reducing the power of producers as goods become hard to differentiate.

This book focuses on the narrower, or perhaps purer, definition of commodities: natural resources or raw materials, whether mineral or agricultural. It looks at trends in the consumption and production of, and markets for, these goods, and at how prices have changed over the years and how they are likely to change in future. In short, it is a comprehensive guide that provides a concise explanation of everything that people need or will find helpful to know about commodities.

## About this book

This book discusses commodities primarily from an economic perspective. Chapter 1 outlines the main economic issues, such as the finite nature of some commodities, whether natural resources bring economic benefits and what determines price movements. Chapter 2 expands on the recent growth in commodities as an investment asset, outlining the main financial instruments and looking at why investors would want to invest in natural resources and raw materials.

Parts 2 to 4 cover the three main types of commodities: industrial (primarily base metals, but also some precious metals), energy and agricultural. As far as is possible, coverage of the principal commodities in each category follows a consistent pattern and includes their characteristics, how they are used, the main consumers and consumption trends, the main producers and production trends, where the commodities are traded, price developments and the broad outlook.

The book concludes with a glossary of terms and a list of the main sources of statistical information and research.

**PART 1**

# Market fundamentals

# The economics of commodities

TYPICALLY, COUNTRIES NEED INCREASING AMOUNTS of industrial raw materials (particularly base metals) and energy as they industrialise and urbanise, and then decreasing amounts when they have reached a certain level of development and are becoming more service-sector oriented. This has undeniably been the pattern of commodity consumption in the United States and Europe. Figure 1.1 shows the quantity of steel production in the United States and China between 1970 and 2010, reflecting their different stages of development. Commodity prices and demand were weak or falling as economic growth at the time was largely concentrated in the developed world, particularly the United States, and was increasingly being driven by growth in the service sector rather than manufacturing or construction. While recent history suggests the theory holds, it is a crude maxim for estimating future trends in commodity consumption and production as it suggests that all countries will follow the same route to economic development.

In the past decade there has been rapid economic development in the developing world, particularly in China. These countries need to build transport networks, electricity grids and housing, so global commodity demand has soared. Furthermore, China opted for the traditional industrialisation route, in the process becoming the world's manufacturing centre and the largest consumer of nearly all industrial commodities (with the notable exception of oil).

FIG 1.1 **Steel production per head in the US and China, 1970–2010**

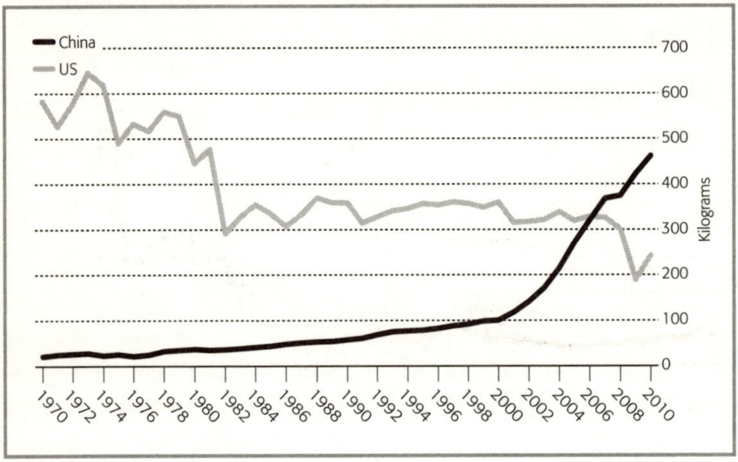

Kilograms

Sources: China's National Bureau of Statistics; US Census Bureau; World Steel Association

## Another supercycle?

One theory that is often used to describe the recent surge in commodity demand is that we are in the midst of another commodity supercycle, one of those long waves – maybe 15–20 years or even longer – in which we move from a trough in commodity prices to a peak and back to a trough again. Typically, such waves are characterised by a fundamental or structural change in the global economy or by wars, revolutions or major technological innovations, for example in transport or communication.

Figure 1.2 shows *The Economist* industrial raw materials commodity price index going back to 1862 in nominal terms. Periods of commodity price inflation are highlighted. They coincide with structural change in the global economy starting with the industrialisation of the United States, the reconstruction of Europe and Japan after the first and second world wars, the oil shocks of the 1970s and 1980s, and ending with the industrialisation of China.

The analytical framework for supercycles was developed and expounded by two economists, among others, working separately, Nikolai Kondratiev in Russia and Joseph Schumpeter in the United

FIG 1.2 ***The Economist* industrial raw materials commodity price index**

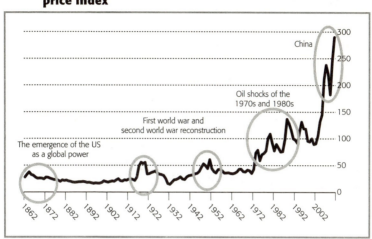

**Source:** *The Economist*

States. Kondratiev outlined long waves or cycles spanning 40–60 years using commodity prices, interest rates, industrial production and external trade. His cycles involved a steady increase in economic activity coupled with low interest rates and rising prices. However, an inflexion or turning point is reached where asset price bubbles start to form, interest rates rise and economic growth slows. A final phase of the cycle involves recession or depression and an unwinding of the excesses of the earlier economic boom.

Within a supercycle you can have periods of short-term volatility, often in response to some exogenous (that is, outside the variables being considered) or unpredictable factors such as the weather or war, which can change the otherwise overriding trend in commodity prices. Schumpeter's work focused on these shorter cycles within the large supercycle.

The theory, as applied to commodities, suggests that a structural or fundamental change in the global economy – say, a war or a revolution or a major innovation in transport or communications – leads to soaring demand for natural resources. Supply fails to meet the unanticipated increase in demand, and prices rise. Supply of raw materials then plays catch-up with demand. With most industrial raw materials, such as metals or energy, it can take years to bring new supply on stream, so there is a period of relatively high prices. By the time supply starts to meet demand, consumption may be tapering off, because following a period of rapid expansion demand growth starts to stabilise at a more sustainable level.

While economists undeniably like a theory to explain what is going on in the global economy, the theory – if you accept it – does serve a purpose. Investment decisions, particularly in the mining and energy industries, are based on a long-term outlook for demand and prices. Furthermore, countries that are rich in natural resources need to be aware of likely trends in commodity prices. However, it is easy to look back and analyse a 30-year period of high commodity prices, but much more difficult to look ahead and determine the next peak or trough.

Sceptics of the supercycle theory argue that periods of high prices are just a cyclical phenomenon, akin to the wider cycles based on fiscal and monetary policy followed by all economies. In looking at the recent decade of booming prices, it could be argued that excessively loose monetary conditions generated inflation and led to a bull market in commodities.

## "Peak oil"

Another theory used to explain commodity market developments, but with a less benign outcome, focuses on the oil market and the fact that oil is a finite resource. It evolved from a paper published in 1956 by M. King Hubbert, a geologist working at a Shell research laboratory in Houston, Texas. The theory is that annual world oil supply has peaked and will be in terminal decline from now on leading to permanent upward pressure on oil prices.

Any finite resource such as oil, copper or coal follows a bell-shaped production curve, so that at some point a peak is reached and thereafter production declines. The decline mirrors the rise in production and is based on the extent of available reserves.

Implicit in this theory is that the world will engage in a scramble for these ever scarcer resources that will lead to conflict and even wars. Until recently, it was claimed that Hubbert had successfully predicted the rise and subsequent fall of American oil production, but this can now be disputed. American oil production has started to rise again, albeit primarily from unconventional sources, and is expected to increase steadily over the next ten years. Furthermore, Hubbert's assertion that American oil production would peak in 2000 proved to be false.

One of the problems with the peak oil theory has been that both technology and prices were held constant in the original model. High oil prices and technological advances have made the extraction of oil from unconventional fields technically possible and economically viable. Breakthroughs in technology are also making it possible to exploit conventional resources that were previously impossible to extract.

Nevertheless, there is increasing awareness that many industrial raw materials are finite resources, which has led to increases in the recycling of metals and efforts at energy conservation. The peak oil theory is perhaps the most extreme manifestation of security of supply fears related to the world's relationship with commodities (see below).

## Security of supply fears

Geopolitical tensions throughout history can often be traced back to efforts to secure natural resources, and the rise of resource nationalism (countries seeking to ensure that national resources are not exploited by foreign powers or multinational companies) has added to worries about a reliance on imported natural resources. Since the second world war, many countries have sought to be as self-sufficient as possible; this was evident in the 1950s development model in South America and still prevails in China, which seeks self-sufficiency in most basic foods. Compounding these "security" fears is the fact that many natural resources – notably all hydrocarbons and metals – are finite. Standard trade theory may suggest that countries should produce the goods in which they have a comparative advantage and then trade with other countries, but nation states feel vulnerable when they have to import what they consider essentials.

As a result, both food security and energy security are highly politicised and, in the case of the latter, have been an active component of foreign policy in some resource-scarce countries. In the past decade, countries exporting agricultural commodities have imposed trade restrictions when they have had bad harvests; Middle Eastern countries with limited water supplies have bought tracts of land or invested in countries with agricultural potential; and China has made massive investments in resource-rich countries, particularly in Africa. These are all attempts to ensure supplies of essential natural resources for domestic consumption. Fears about disruption to supply can have a strong influence on commodity prices.

## Producer action

The often geographically concentrated nature of supply of many of the world's resources, for example the massive silver and copper belt spanning the Americas and the tin-producing region of South-East Asia, means there is considerable scope for the small number of producers to be powerful players in determining prices. During the 20th century, however, numerous attempts by producing countries to set prices, such as the International Coffee Agreement and the International Natural Rubber Agreement, fell apart. The only cartel-like body that has managed to survive and wield considerable power in the market is the Organisation of Petroleum Exporting Countries (OPEC), which now accounts for about 40% of global oil supply.

OPEC tries to set a target for output that it deems will meet oil-market needs but not lead to a fall in prices (unless oil prices are soaring unsustainably). The organisation has had a chequered history and mixed success. It cannot penalise member states that flout their targets and choose to free ride on the prevailing OPEC policy, and only one member state, Saudi Arabia, has the capacity to act as a swing producer and raise its output significantly in order to affect prices. Another problem is that producers can dictate only one side of the commodity trade: supply, a relatively blunt tool.

## Are resources a blessing?

Resource-poor countries may fret about being reliant on the need to import what are deemed "strategic" goods, but economic history suggests that it is not always a blessing to be a resource-rich country. On the face of it, countries with sought-after resources have an advantage. They can use the resources for their own economic development (without fears about supply) and export the remainder, ideally at an attractive price. However, some of the wealthiest countries in terms of natural resources are the weakest in terms of gross national income or development.

One of the reasons for this is that the resource sector can crowd out the rest of the economy. Valuable resources, particularly if they attract a high international price (such as oil in recent years), may mean there is less incentive to develop other parts of the economy. Furthermore, the rich vein of commodity exports, and possibly the foreign investment that the country's resource attracts, may lead to exchange-rate appreciation, making the country's other exports less competitive and encouraging imports (again removing the incentive for developing domestic capacity). Another problem is that, aside from agriculture, the resource sector can be a small employer (mining, forestry and energy), and thus the sector does not contribute significantly to wider economic growth. During the 1970s, this phenomenon was labelled "Dutch disease" by *The Economist* in an article examining the decline in the Netherlands' manufacturing sector as a result of exchange-rate appreciation following a massive natural gas find in the 1950s.

Developing countries also worry that the economic benefits of the exploitation of their resources will go disproportionately to the foreign firms whose expertise is necessary to exploit them. Hence the rise of "resource nationalism" and an awareness of the pitfalls of being commodity rich, which has led many resource-rich countries to operate large sovereign wealth funds, keeping excess liquidity out of the domestic economy and preventing all the receipts from going into government current expenditure. Efforts are also being made to invest windfall revenue in human and physical capital.

A further problem for resource-rich countries is starting to be addressed. In the past, countries that produced raw materials just exported them and the profits went mainly to those towards the end of the chain: intermediaries, traders, processors or retailers. This was the case particularly with some agricultural commodities; for example, West Africa exported cocoa beans to Europe and the United States and all the grinding and blending (or adding of value) took place in the destination countries. This trend was sometimes exacerbated by difficult access to importing countries as a result of tariffs (on higher valued-added goods), a proliferation of standards or public support policies including subsidies. Now processing is increasingly taking place in the countries that produce the raw materials.

## What determines the price of a commodity?

The cost of producing a commodity provides a floor for prices. In particular, producers look at the marginal cost of production – the total cost of producing an additional unit of output – to determine whether a project is viable. If the price of a commodity falls below the marginal cost of production, producers can be expected to scale back output. However, in reality producers sometimes continue to produce the good, hoping that the price will rise, or there are market distortions – such as subsidies – which mean production will continue.

The macroeconomic approach to commodity prices is broader, seeing price as a function of demand and supply and the behaviour of inventories (stocks). For example, if stocks are falling, there is typically upward pressure on prices as it suggests demand is growing faster than supply. Falling stocks also make the market more vulnerable to an unanticipated disruption to supply. If the demand for a commodity increases relative to its supply, the equilibrium price (or market-clearing price – the one at which both buyers and sellers are happy with price and quantity) moves up.

In theory, demand should have a positive relationship with economic growth and rising incomes but this is not always the case (see Figure 1.3). Demand is not always met; there may be demand for ever larger amounts of copper, for example, but the price may be too high or supply may be insufficient. To predict the level of consumption, we need to know something about the price elasticity

FIG 1.3 **Demand curve**

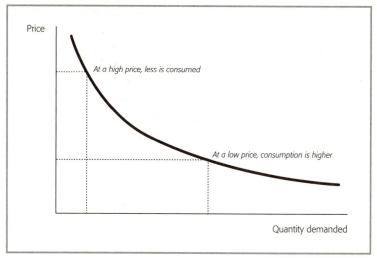

of demand (the responsiveness of consumption to a change in the price). As prices rise, will consumption start to wane or will it stay constant (called perfect elasticity of demand)?

This has been much discussed in recent years as commodity prices have risen. Typically, if a good is seen as a staple or a necessity, the price elasticity will be low, but what is considered a necessity in the United States (gasoline, for example) may be considered a luxury in other parts of the world. Other factors that influence price elasticity include the availability of (presumably cheaper) substitutes and the duration of the change in price. For example, a short, sharp spike in the price of fuel is unlikely to lead to a change in habits or consumption levels, but an enduring increase in prices might lead to permanently lower consumption.

Another relationship to be considered is income elasticity of demand. Do rising incomes lead to higher, lower or unchanged consumption of a good? Although you would expect higher incomes to lead to increased consumption, for commodities such as basic grains it could mean that consumption shifts in favour of more expensive foods, such as meat.

The supply side is also difficult to predict. Agricultural and some mining industry output can be affected by unpredictable weather or, in the case of agriculture, the prevalence of disease. Geopolitical events, labour unrest and changes in government policy on taxes, trade or ownership can disrupt supply. The speed of supply response should also be considered. Producers of some agricultural products (sugar, soybeans) can respond quickly, within a season, to a change in demand or price; other agricultural commodities take longer (a coffee or rubber plantation). In mining and energy sectors, it can take a decade for production to come on stream. These industrial commodities face additional constraints including the need for skilled labour and high capital investment in developing the necessary infrastructure.

There is also uncertainty over stock levels, mostly to do with a lack of transparency over size and quality. Countries may build strategic reserves or stockpiles in some commodities, and if the level of their stocks is not divulged, physical consumption of the commodity will appear much higher in a country than it is. Stocks, however, can be stabilising in that they can smooth out the availability of a commodity when there are one-off disruptions to supply.

It is no longer possible just to assess the market fundamentals in order to determine the likely trend in a commodity's price. The dramatic rise in investment interest in commodities means that other factors have to be considered, including:

- global liquidity levels (high liquidity or loose monetary policy is generally believed to lead to higher commodity prices);
- the value of the dollar (most commodities are priced in dollars and thus the two typically have an inverse relationship, as commodities can, for example, provide a hedge against dollar weakness);
- movements in alternative assets (bonds, stocks);
- interest rates (unlike most financial investments, commodities do not pay interest – if interest rates are low, returns on other investments will be low and it will be easier for commodities to outperform other asset classes);

- investor behaviour or sentiment (investors are sometimes accused of following the herd);
- changes in the commodity-related financial products available;
- the oil price (other commodity prices sometimes follow the behaviour of the oil price).

Over the past century, commodity prices fell in real terms. One reason for this was that global growth was being driven by already well-developed economies. Unfair trade practices favouring the developed world, such as high tariffs, could also have been a factor. However, after years of low prices and underinvestment, when the surge in demand that was part and parcel of China's industrialisation during the 2000s came, commodity producers were not ready to meet it and so prices rose strongly. While demand and supply fundamentals undeniably appeared to have justified the recent price rises, the extent of the rise was compounded by investment inflows into commodity markets.

# Commodities as financial assets

**THE EARLY COMMODITY TRADING EXCHANGES** were dominated by agricultural commodities, and until recently these exchanges were largely the preserve of producers and consumers of the raw materials, who might buy or sell forward to hedge their risk.

Historically, the only viable way to invest in commodities without buying or promising to buy the physical asset was indirect, typically through ownership of the debt and/or equity of companies operating in the sectors involved in production and/or distribution. However, this involved more than just the risk associated with commodity exposure, as a buyer was taking on a specific corporate risk. For example, zinc prices might be rising but a zinc mining company could still be performing poorly if its costs are too high, its governance is poor, its particular zinc mine is not performing well, the mine is located in a country with an unfavourable business operating environment or circumstances such as bad weather or labour unrest disrupt supply. The investor was also taking on financial market risk. Mining company shares might fall in an equity bear market even while commodity prices are rising.

The difficulty of investing in commodities meant that for years commodity markets remained thinly traded and thus vulnerable to price volatility and even market manipulation because of the lack of depth in the market. However, as commodity prices started to rise and the number and complexity of financial products mushroomed during the late 1990s and 2000s, instruments to invest more directly in commodities markets increased and the cost of trading fell. Another development was the increasing number of commodity exchanges: there are now at least 70 exchanges around the world trading commodities futures, although many have only a limited offering and trading volume is low. As a result, it is no longer sufficient to look at the demand and supply profile of an individual commodity to determine whether its price will rise or fall; macroeconomic factors, such as interest rates, exchange rates and global liquidity trends, which drive investor sentiment, must also now be considered.

Much of the recent expansion in commodity trading has been in over-the-counter (OTC) markets (where there is no official exchange or trading floor and transactions are carried out by telephone or through an electronic platform) and thus has been only lightly regulated. Trading has surged in the past decade, with the number of commodity futures contracts traded globally rising from 418m in 2001 to 2.6 trillion in 2011, according to UNCTAD data.

However, periods of spiralling commodity prices in recent years and the 2008 financial crisis have led to concerns about the influence of speculators in the market and efforts to increase regulation. There have even been calls for a complete ban on investment trading in politically and socially sensitive agricultural commodities. There are concerns that food-price volatility and high energy costs are having a negative impact on low-income or poor households, thus making it more difficult to reduce global poverty levels.

In 2010, the G20 (group of finance ministers and central bank governors) announced that "food security" was a priority. Subsequent reports from the G20 Study Group found that financial investment in commodities has led to price distortions, with prices not reflecting the demand and supply fundamentals. A tendency by investors to follow each other (the "herd" mentality) exacerbates the dislocation. In 2011 the G20 endorsed efforts directed at greater regulation of commodity derivative (futures) markets, and the US Commodity Futures Trading Commission (CFTC) and the European Commission plan to implement tighter regulation of commodity futures markets in 2013–14. This is likely to lead to less OTC trading in commodities and more trading on formal exchanges. There are also likely to be limits on the size of the stake a single investor can hold in a particular futures contract.

## Futures markets

The first commodity financial instruments to evolve were forward and futures markets, which were designed to give greater certainty to producers on the price they would get for their crop or metal. They also helped consumers to budget by enabling them to lock in a price for their raw materials. In recent years, financial investors who have no need of the raw material have also been buying commodity futures, boosting liquidity in the markets. A futures contract is specific, detailing the exact properties of the good and where it is stored. The futures exchanges also operate warehouses.

By buying futures in a commodity, investors are placing a bet on the expected price at a certain time. If the shape of the futures price curve (see Figure 1.4) is downward sloping, the expected price of a commodity in three or six months' time is lower than the current spot price and the market is said to be in backwardation. In this situation, producers might choose to run down stocks, fearing that they may get a lower price in the future. If the futures price curve is upward sloping, that is, expected prices in six months' time are higher than the spot price, the market is said to be in contango. It is often said that futures markets play a price discovery role for the physical markets.

The total return available to investors from an investment in commodity futures has three components, sometimes known as "spot, roll and return":

- Spot return. This is the change in the spot price of the underlying commodity.
- Roll return. The return associated with selling a nearby futures contract (the futures contract that is closest to its settlement date) before its expiry and reinvesting the proceeds in a further-dated futures contract. The return on that transaction is positive when the futures curve is in backwardation or negative when the futures curve is in contango. If the futures curve predicted exactly what the future price would be, there would be no loss or gain for the investor.
- Collateral return. Futures contracts do not require all of the value of the contracts to be paid up front – a smaller amount,

FIG 1.4 **Futures prices**

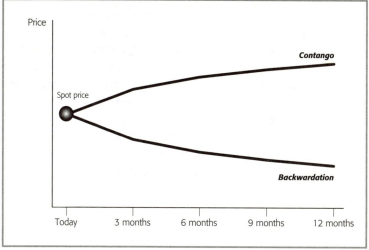

called "the margin", is paid instead. Investors can chose to invest the remainder of the value of the investment in an alternative instrument (usually treasury bills, but sometimes cash) during the term of the contract. The collateral return is the return from this other investment. For example, when you choose to invest $1,000 in oil futures, you may only pay a margin of 10%, that is $100 upfront for the right to buy in the future. An investor may chose to invest the remaining $900 in a treasury bill that pays interest to make some additional money as well as to ensure that he has the means to pay for the futures investment when the time comes.

The choices are such that investors do not have to seek all the returns from a commodity investment; they may just buy futures or perhaps look for unfunded (no collateral) exposure to commodity futures prices.

## Investment is now much easier

It is still difficult to invest in the physical market for commodities, but investors are probably not too concerned. Apart from gold, a return is difficult to achieve on the spot price, as commodities have to be stored at a cost and delivered at a cost. The cost of storing agricultural commodities is particularly high. Furthermore, the opportunity cost of storing commodities rises with interest rates because you cannot earn interest on commodities, making them less attractive compared with other financial assets. For the investor who still wants exposure to commodities, a number of proxy methods have been evolved, primarily involving commodity futures.

Perhaps the most significant catalyst for change in recent commodity market history was the development of commodity indices. These typically track a basket of commodity futures prices, although the methodologies underpinning the indices can vary widely. The indices can be distinguished by their breadth of coverage (number of commodities), the weights assigned to the different commodities within the index and their "rolling mechanism" (this is the means by which the futures contracts are rolled as they expire). Most indices roll their positions on a monthly basis, but some investment banks have launched enhanced indices whereby they seek to invest in different contracts along the futures curve (nearby or longer-dated futures) in a bid to optimise the rolling mechanism.

There are many commodity indices. Some are not designed for investment purposes, such as:

- FAO Food Price Index;
- World Bank commodity price indices;
- IMF commodity price indices;
- Central Research Bureau commodity price indices;
- *The Economist* commodity price indices.

The benchmark commodity indices for investment include:
- S&P GSCI (Standard & Poor's and Goldman Sachs Commodity Index);
- DJ-UBS (Dow Jones-UBS Commodity Index);
- Rogers International Commodity Index.

These companies do not, however, have one benchmark index. Indices have been developed for specific parts of the commodity markets, enabling investors to make allocations to a particular commodity or commodity subset, for example the S&P livestock index. Another variation on the traditional commodity index can involve timing or a methodology on the rolling of futures contracts so that persistent losses from a contango curve can be avoided, for example the S&P GSCI enhanced index.

Investing in commodity indices provides efficient access to the markets, but it is passive. In other words, it is not the sort of investment that is blamed for commodity asset price bubbles. Index investors do not hoard commodities to sell at a later date at a higher price and they do not alter demand for a commodity. With this sort of passive investment, allocation to specific commodities is stable and is independent of the shape of the futures curve.

As it is difficult for smaller investors to trade in commodity futures markets, a number of investment vehicles have emerged to help them. These primarily take the form of exchange-traded products (ETPs), in particular exchange-traded funds (ETFs) or exchange-traded notes (ETNs). ETFs can invest in a commodity index, or in a particular commodity or in a basket of commodities. In recent years, investment in ETPs has largely been to gain exposure to precious metals and agricultural commodities, rather than base metals.

An ETF is simply a fund that holds a specific set of underlying assets. Shares in an ETF trade on a stock exchange like a regular corporate share. Historically, ETFs in a commodity index were a passive investment with holdings mirroring the index, but recently more actively managed ETFs have been launched. With these active investments, the fund manager will seek to improve on the return from the index.

An ETN is a note or bond that an investor can buy from a financial institution. The return on the note will be linked to the return on an underlying asset, such as a commodity index. An ETN is a riskier investment than an ETF as it also involves risk attached to the financial institution – that is, whether it will be able to honour its note.

## More complex instruments

Perhaps to counter the passive nature of index investing, commodity-linked structured products were launched. A structured product usually has a fixed income (bond) component (that at least guarantees the return of part of or all of the original investment) and a derivative (or option) on the underlying asset. With commodity-structured products, the underlying asset is a commodity future.

The popularity of structured products grew strongly during the 2000s but has since faltered, partly because of the bad press they received in the wake of the global financial crisis in 2008. The uncertain prospects for the global economy and commodity demand have also undermined investment in recent years.

## Why invest in commodities?

Investment in commodities boomed over the past decade, despite the volatility in prices. The textbook reasons for investing in commodities centre on the benefits of portfolio diversification and the role of commodities as a hedge against inflation. For example, the prices of commodities often rise in response to a catastrophic event, such as drought or geopolitical tension, while other assets, such as equities, typically fall.

Other investors may have a macroeconomic belief that suggests commodity prices will rise, such as the peak oil and supercycle theories (see the preceding chapter on the economics of commodities). More practical reasons for the recent increase in investment in commodity markets include the lower costs associated with trading and the increasing number of financial commodity products available (although this was in itself a response to investors seeking greater access to commodity markets).

## Portfolio diversification

For an asset manager, it was argued that holding commodity assets would provide a hedge against macroeconomic or market events that would affect most other financial assets in a similar fashion. Between 1971 and 2007, commodity markets posted positive returns in six of the eight years when returns on the S&P 500 stockmarket index were

FIG 1.5 **S&P 500 composite index (equities) and S&P Goldman Sachs commodity price index**

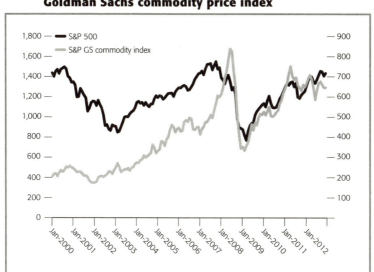

**Sources:** Standard & Poor's; Haver Analytics

negative. Commodities were deemed to outperform both equities and bonds during market downturns. However, the huge increase in commodity investment has started to erode the diversification benefits. Commodity markets have become more sensitive to portfolio rebalancing by investors, which has made them more correlated with other financial asset markets, including equities (see Figure 1.5).

Furthermore, in recent years commodity markets have been trading in a similar fashion to other financial markets – equity markets in particular – rising when global growth prospects appear to improve or monetary policy is eased in an effort to boost economic growth. This could be a temporary phenomenon generated by the unusual times and the diversification benefits may be restored as monetary policy starts to normalise. One theory is that when demand trends are driving prices (strong demand leading to higher prices), commodity markets will be correlated with equities; but if the market is being driven by supply developments (for example, a drought causing wheat prices to rise), commodity prices will move differently.

## Commodities as a hedge against inflation

If inflation is increasing, commodity prices are likely to be increasing. Indeed, they may be the cause of the rising inflation rate. Stockmarkets, however, generally fall as inflation rises, largely because of the likelihood that central banks will tighten monetary policy to curb inflation, leading to slower economic growth. Indeed, historically equity markets have been weak following, for example, an oil price shock and the subsequent monetary tightening.

Some investors steer well clear of commodity investments, arguably for good reasons, as the thinness of markets meant that prices could be manipulated. This is no longer such a risk but prices remain highly volatile.

# PART 2

# Base and precious metals

# Aluminium

ALUMINIUM IS THE MOST ABUNDANT metallic element in the Earth's crust. It is found in large quantities in bauxite, an ore that contains aluminium oxide or alumina. Alumina has to undergo a complex smelting process that results in aluminium, the metal. Aluminium is lightweight but strong and these qualities are making it an increasingly attractive alternative to steel, particularly in cars. Its other properties include good conductivity, resistance to corrosion, elasticity and a low melting point (which makes it easily recyclable). It has a wide range of end-uses in, for example, the electronics industry, transport (particularly aircraft and vehicles), construction, cooking utensils and food packaging.

## Bauxite: reserves and output

Bauxite typically contains about 30–35% aluminium and is mined primarily in tropical parts of the world. Guinea has the world's largest known reserves, followed by Australia and Vietnam (see Figure 2.1). Bauxite is plentiful and any supply shortages that emerge will be for economic (lack of profitability) or political (resource nationalism) reasons. However, in recent years, consumers have complained about a lack of availability of high-grade bauxite. Bauxite output rose by 6% year on year in 2011 as a result of increased production in Brazil, China, Guinea, India, Jamaica, Suriname, and Venezuela; Australia is currently the world's largest producer. In 2007, China overtook Australia as the world's largest alumina producer even though it has only limited bauxite reserves (about 3% of the world's reserves).

FIG 2.1 **Bauxite reserves, 2010**

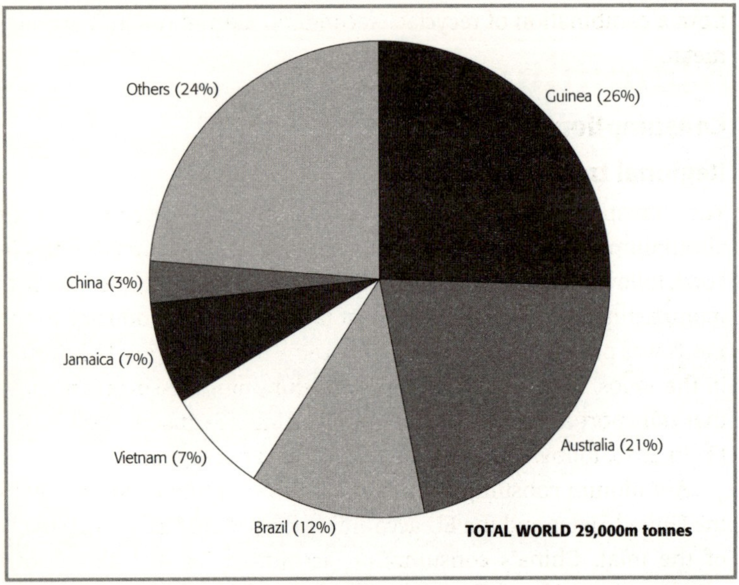

- Guinea (26%)
- Others (24%)
- Australia (21%)
- Brazil (12%)
- Vietnam (7%)
- Jamaica (7%)
- China (3%)

**TOTAL WORLD 29,000m tonnes**

**Source:** US Geological Survey

## Processes and products

Alumina is extracted from the bauxite ore in a refinery using the Bayer process and is then smelted to produce primary aluminium. As a rough rule of thumb, 4–5 tonnes of bauxite produce about 2 tonnes of alumina, which is used to generate 1 tonne of aluminium. The production of aluminium is highly energy intensive (about 14,000kwh of electricity is needed to produce 1 tonne of aluminium) with the result that many smelters are located in energy-rich countries. The aluminium smelters use the Hall-Héroult process to produce ingot products (rolling slabs, extrusion billets, primary foundry ingots and remelt ingots) that are generally shipped in domestic or international trade for further processing – often within the same company – into semi-finished products such as sheet, extrusions, wire rod and castings.

Semi-finished products are used in the packaging, transport, construction, engineering and power industries, and are traded mainly within regional markets. Such products are usually made from a combination of recycled (secondary) aluminium and primary metal.

## Consumption and trade
### Regional trends

The transport equipment industry is the largest consumer of aluminium in all forms, accounting for about 25% of consumption in 2008, followed by building construction (23%), packaging and electrical manufacturing (14% each). The most rapidly growing industry in the 1980s was packaging, but transport became the main growth industry in the 1990s. Data from the European Aluminium Association show that transport accounted for 37% of aluminium consumption in the EU in 2010, followed by building at 26% and packaging at 16%.

Aluminium consumption stood at just 18.7m tonnes in 1991, with the United States and the EU accounting for 30% and 22% respectively of the total. China's consumption accounted for just 5% of total consumption. Aluminium consumption subsequently grew at an annual average rate of 2.9% between 1992 and 1999 before accelerating to annual growth of 6.2% in 2000–07.

The principal driver of this growth was China, through urbanisation, infrastructure development, manufacturing growth and rising domestic vehicle ownership. China's apparent aluminium consumption growth was a robust 11.2% year on year in 2011 preliminary data suggest that it grew by a further 11% in 2012. (Apparent consumption includes aluminium that goes into stocks or is not used; real consumption is aluminium that is physically used.) Strong growth has also been recorded in India, Brazil and parts of South-East Asia.

Global consumption contracted by 7% in 2008–09, but strong growth has since resumed. In 2011, consumption of aluminium was 42.4m tonnes (see Table 2.1), with China accounting for 42% of the total, the United States 9.6% and the EU 16.7%. In Europe, consumption fell by nearly one-third in 2008–09, leaving only Germany, Italy and France among the top ten aluminium consumers in the world. European consumption has since recovered, led by Germany's successful manufacturing industry. In the United States, consumption also fell sharply in 2008-09 and fell again in 2011 as the American automotive industry was hit by disruptions in the global automotive supply chain. Consumption bounced back in 2012 in conjunction with a recovery in vehicle production. However, consumption is still estimated to have been 17.1% lower than in 2007.

TABLE 2.1 **Leading aluminium-consuming countries**

|  | 1991 | | 2000 | | 2011 | |
| --- | --- | --- | --- | --- | --- | --- |
|  | '000 tonnes | % of total | '000 tonnes | % of total | '000 tonnes | % of total |
| China | 938 | 5.0 | 3,499 | 14.0 | 17,629 | 41.6 |
| US | 4,137 | 22.1 | 6,161 | 24.6 | 4,060 | 9.6 |
| Germany | 1361 | 7.3 | 1,491 | 5.9 | 2,103 | 5.0 |
| Japan | 2,432 | 13.0 | 2,225 | 8.9 | 1,946 | 4.6 |
| India | 430 | 2.3 | 602 | 2.4 | 1,584 | 3.7 |
| South Korea | 384 | 2.0 | 823 | 3.3 | 1,233 | 2.9 |
| Brazil | 354 | 1.9 | 514 | 2.1 | 1,077 | 2.5 |
| Italy | 670 | 3.6 | 780 | 3.1 | 971 | 2.3 |
| Russia | – | 0.0 | 748 | 3.0 | 685 | 1.6 |
| France | 728 | 3.9 | 782 | 3.1 | 584 | 1.4 |
| Others | 7,310 | 39.0 | 7,434 | 29.7 | 10,526 | 24.8 |
| Total | 18,743 | | 25,059 | | 42,398 | |

**Source:** World Bureau of Metal Statistics

## Trade

Demand in the former Soviet Union collapsed after 1990 and remains lower than in the 1980s, boosting export availability. Since 1992 Russia has become the world's largest exporter of primary aluminium and accounted for 26% of total exports in 2011. Canada is the next largest exporter with 11% of the market, with China some way behind with a 3.5% market share (see Table 2.2).

TABLE 2.2 **Leading exporters and importers of primary aluminium, 2011**

|  | Exports | | | Imports | |
| --- | --- | --- | --- | --- | --- |
|  | '000 tonnes | % of total |  | '000 tonnes | % of total |
| Russia | 5,582.7 | 26.1 | US | 2,695.7 | 13.0 |
| Canada | 2,486.1 | 11.6 | Japan | 2,692.7 | 13.0 |
| Netherlands | 1,895.2 | 8.9 | Germany | 2,554.9 | 12.3 |
| Australia | 1,680.3 | 7.9 | Netherlands | 2,070.6 | 10.0 |
| Norway | 1,428.9 | 6.7 | South Korea | 1,317.6 | 6.4 |
| China | 766.1 | 3.6 | Italy | 1,046.7 | 5.0 |

**Source:** World Bureau of Metal Statistics

Trade in aluminium has been falling as a share of world consumption from a peak of 66% in 2004 largely because China is self-sufficient. Exports accounted for 50% of total consumption in 2011. Imports of primary aluminium are typically duty-free but trade in semi-finished and finished products is more restricted. The exception to this is the EU, which imposes a 6% tariff on imports of primary aluminium.

## Production and stocks

### Refined production and smelting capacity

Aside from China, the greatest expansion in aluminium smelting capacity in recent years has been in energy-rich regions or countries with low-cost electricity such as Canada, Australia, Russia, Southern Africa and the Middle East. Nevertheless, it is China that has recorded the largest expansion in capacity, based mainly on coal-fired electricity.

China accounted for 41% of total aluminium production in 2011 and its output grew by 26% and 11% year on year in 2010 and 2011 respectively. Output was also growing at an average annual rate of 10% for much of 2012. Chalco, the state aluminium company, controls a large block of production, but there are numerous small smelters that are owned by local government and private interests. In recent years, the government has sought to curtail the expansion of the aluminium sector as China is a net exporter of aluminium and because of the energy-intensive nature of production – the sector is estimated to account for about 6% of China's electricity use. The government has raised export tariffs and lowered value-added tax rebates, which, coupled with rising power and labour costs, is leading to a fall in the price competitiveness of China's aluminium (as well as hitting corporate profitability). Notwithstanding the government's efforts at consolidation, production has generally followed the trend in prices, reflecting the large number of small, marginal producers who raise production when prices are high. China's 20 largest smelters account for about 70% of China's capacity and about 30% of world output.

Until 2000, the United States was the world's largest producer of primary aluminium, owing to low-cost hydroelectric and coal-fired power (see Table 2.3). Since then problems with the availability and cost of power, as well as difficulties with alumina supply, have led to smelter closures so that in 2011 it accounted for less than 5% of global output and is a large importer of primary metal.

In Europe, consumption now greatly exceeds production – aluminium casting and semi-fabricating are labour-intensive operations and there has been considerable migration of activity to lower-wage countries – and dependence on imports is increasing. Norway and Iceland significantly expanded primary aluminium production in the 2000s, helping to meet the EU's large import requirement. The EU also imports from former colonial countries in Africa under duty-free import arrangements, supplemented by traditional exports from Russia to neighbouring EU member countries. High energy and raw material prices since 2005 have again brought into question the viability of primary aluminium smelting in western Europe, as have stringent legislation on reducing carbon emissions and the adverse economic conditions.

One region that has seen a significant expansion in aluminium production capacity is the Middle East, in particular countries in the Gulf Co-operation Council (GCC), and projects in progress suggest that their share of total output will increase. Production in the United Arab Emirates expanded by 31.4% in 2011 to just under 1.8m tonnes; in Qatar production reached 408,000 tonnes in 2011, compared with

TABLE 2.3 **Leading aluminium-producing countries**

|  | 1991 | | 2000 | | 2011 | |
| --- | --- | --- | --- | --- | --- | --- |
|  | '000 tonnes | % of total | '000 tonnes | % of total | '000 tonnes | % of total |
| China | 962 | 4.9 | 2,794 | 11.4 | 18,062 | 40.5 |
| Russia | – | 0.0 | 3,247 | 13.3 | 3,992 | 9.0 |
| Canada | 1,822 | 9.3 | 2,374 | 9.7 | 2,983 | 6.7 |
| US | 4,121 | 21.0 | 3,668 | 15.0 | 1,984 | 4.5 |
| Australia | 1,229 | 6.3 | 1,762 | 7.2 | 1,945 | 4.4 |
| UAE | 239 | 1.2 | 536 | 2.2 | 1,765 | 4.0 |
| India | 504 | 2.6 | 649 | 2.7 | 1,660 | 3.7 |
| Brazil | 1,140 | 5.8 | 1,271 | 5.2 | 1,440 | 3.2 |
| Norway | 858 | 4.4 | 1,026 | 4.2 | 1,202 | 2.7 |
| South Africa | 169 | 0.9 | 683 | 2.8 | 808 | 1.8 |
| Others | 8,610 | 43.8 | 6,409 | 26.2 | 8,727 | 19.6 |
| Total | 19,653 | | 24,418 | | 44,568 | |

**Sources:** World Bureau of Metal Statistics

145,700 tonnes a year earlier; and Saudi Arabia is developing a bauxite mine and smelter operations (with a capacity of 740,000 tonnes per year) that are expected to come on line in 2013–14. Typically, electricity costs are highly subsidised in the GCC, significantly boosting the profitability of aluminium production.

India, which has ample reserves of bauxite and domestic coal, is also trying to raise aluminium production. However, there has been environmental and public opposition to the development of bauxite mines and India is struggling with domestic coal production and power supply.

## Secondary production

The secondary aluminium industry comprises remelting operations that recycle specific grades of scrap, such as aluminium cans, to produce rolled and extruded products, and smelters that turn scrap into ingot for castings. Some large aluminium companies participate in remelting, but many have left the secondary aluminium industry, which is dominated by small independent companies.

There has been rapid growth in demand for castings, but the profitability of secondary smelting fluctuates depending on the availability and price of scrap. In 2011, secondary production accounted for nearly 20% of total aluminium production. The United States dominates secondary production, accounting for 35% of total production in 2011; western Europe accounted for a further 30% and China for 13.6%. Secondary aluminium smelting uses only about 5% of the energy required for primary smelting, so it is likely to be encouraged as part of efforts to reduce carbon emissions and conserve energy.

## Stocks and related issues

Although aluminium is a strategic metal, government stockpiles are insignificant and have no influence in the market. The most active government purchaser in the past was South Korea's Supply Administration, acting as a conduit for material to smaller domestic consumers. Periodically central and provincial governments in China purchase aluminium ingots as a support for domestic producers. These are then sold back to the market when prices are deemed attractive.

Commercial stocks of aluminium were high in 2011-12, partly because low interest rates made it cheap to hold stocks and partly because of sluggish demand growth. However, much of the metal was held by banks and traders and tied up in warehousing deals. The deals rely on a combination of low interest rates, financial incentives and the fact that spot aluminium was trading at a large discount to longer-dated futures. If interest rates start to rise, these stocks could be released. An additional problem is significant delays in accessing stocks. In 2012 the London Metal Exchange (LME) raised the minimum rate at which its biggest warehouses must deliver (to 3,000 tonnes/day from 1,500 tonnes/day previously) and increased the rental costs for users to store aluminium. However, reportedly there were still long delays in releasing stocks, so that it can take months to obtain metal stored in, say, the Dutch port of Vlissingen, the Malaysian port of Johor and the American port of Detroit.

## Principal corporate players

Many of the largest companies in the aluminium industry are integrated businesses, with operations at most stages from bauxite to semi-finished products. In the mid-2000s, there was widespread consolidation among the world's leading aluminium-producing companies, particularly in Russia and China. The result is that four large companies – Chalco (China), Rio Tinto (UK/Australia), UC Rusal (Russia) and Alcoa (United States) – now control about one-third (2011) of the world's aluminium production (see Table 2.4).

Despite the emergence of Western-style integrated companies in Russia and China, the huge rise in production by smaller enterprises in China has increased the capacity of independent producers and reduced the share of the largest companies. The 12 largest producers now control only 56% of world capacity.

TABLE 2.4 **Leading aluminium-producing companies, 2011**

| Company | Country | Output, '000 tonnes |
| --- | --- | --- |
| UC Rusal | Russia | 4,127 |
| Rio Tinto Group | UK/Australia | 3,829 |
| Alcoa | US | 3,669 |
| Aluminium Corporation of China (Chalco) | China | 3,127 |
| Norsk Hydro | Norway | 1,705 |
| Dubai Aluminium | UAE | 1,386 |
| China Power Investment Corporation | China | 1,381 |
| BHP Billiton | Australia | 1,249 |
| Shandong Xinfa Aluminium and Electricity Group | China | 1,016 |
| Aluminium Bahrain | Bahrain | 881 |

**Source:** Bloomberg (data compiled by CRU Group)

## The aluminium market

Although much metal is moved within integrated company systems, primary aluminium is widely traded. Market pricing has been made transparent by the LME, which has traded primary aluminium since 1978. Although metal is still sold directly between producers and consumers on prices fixed for various periods, the setting of those prices is now overwhelmingly influenced by the LME quotations, particularly the 3-months future quotation.

The LME quotation refers to aluminium in ingot form, import duty unpaid, in LME warehouses around the world. To receive physical delivery of the particular qualities of duty-paid metal that they require, consumers normally pay an additional charge (premium) above LME prices. There are also further charges for shapes and alloys other than 99.7% pure ingot. Since the late 1990s the pricing of semi-fabricated aluminium products has also moved steadily towards a method of pricing based on the LME price of primary aluminium plus a conversion charge. This has replaced specific negotiated prices for semi-fabricated products.

Aluminium is now traded on a number of exchanges around the world, notably the Shanghai Futures Exchange and the New York Commodity Exchange (COMEX) and also exchanges in Singapore, Rotterdam, Japan and Malaysia.

## Price trends

Prices of aluminium soared from an annual average of $1,898 per tonne in 2004 to a peak of just over $3,200/tonne in early July 2008. However, the onset of the global financial crisis caused aluminium prices to plummet, with a low of $1,253/tonne reported in the first quarter of 2009. At this level aluminium producers were making a loss and subsequent cuts in output coupled with a bounce-back in consumption led to steady increases in aluminium prices during the remainder of 2009 and into 2010–11. But jitters about financial stability in the euro zone and global economic growth more generally coupled with weak automotive production meant that prices slipped again in the second half of 2011. Automotive production was particularly weak in 2011 because of the negative impact on global supply chains

## FIG 2.2 Aluminium stocks and prices

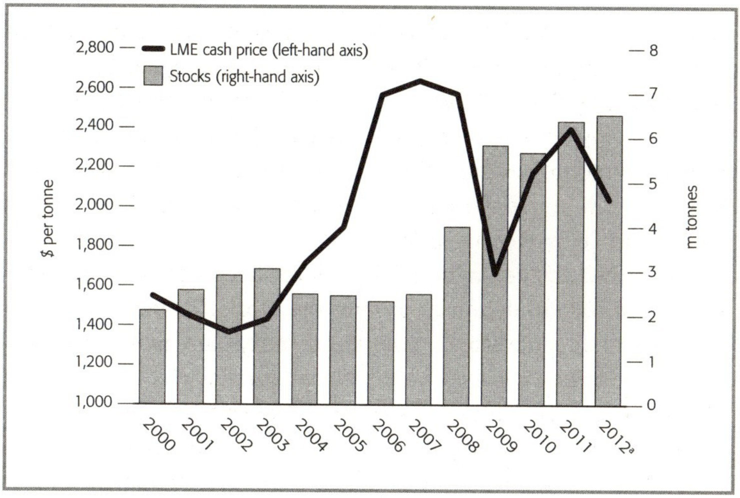

[Chart showing LME cash price (left-hand axis, $ per tonne) and Stocks (right-hand axis, m tonnes) from 2000 to 2012a]

a EIU estimates.
**Sources:** London Metal Exchange; World Bureau of Metal Statistics; International Aluminium Institute

of the damage caused by the March earthquake in Japan and severe flooding in Thailand later in the year.

Prices started to recover in early 2012, peaking in February before starting to slip once more, falling below $2,000/tonne in May. They rose above this critical level in September as part of a general rally in commodity prices, but fell back below $2,000/tonne in October. Prices oscillated around the $2,000/tonne level for the remainder of the year, so in annual average terms prices fell by 15.8% in 2012 (see Figure 2.2). The cause of the downturn was generally attributed to rising production in China at a time of weak demand.

## The future

- Demand for aluminium will be supported by steady growth in car ownership in countries such as China and India. Alongside its use in construction, consumer goods and packaging, the metal's lightweight properties will ensure that it will be in considerable demand in the production of lightweight, fuel-efficient aircraft and cars. Its easy recyclability will also make it a greener option for end-users.

- The energy-intensive nature of aluminium production means that production is likely to become more polarised in energy-rich countries. It is also likely to move to lower-wage regions of the world. This combination suggests EU production is in structural decline.
- The policy of the Chinese government is to discourage such energy-intensive activities as smelting and to rely more on external sources of metal for the domestic semi-finishing industry. It has declared its intention to close 800,000 tonnes of obsolete aluminium capacity and to restrict its primary aluminium consumption to no more than 24m tonnes/year by 2015. However, progress on these goals is likely to be gradual as recent history suggests that every upturn in metal prices will prompt some new projects in China.
- High energy costs and environmental issues are limiting output growth both in China and globally. These restrictions and the high cost of inputs (both energy and bauxite) mean there will be an increased focus on boosting the use of recycled aluminium instead of refining new metal.
- Limited bauxite supply could constrain aluminium supply as importing countries are dependent on a few main exporters. In 2012, Indonesia (which accounted for 80% of China's bauxite imports in 2011) imposed a 20% tax on bauxite exports that led to a sharp drop in exports.

# Copper

COPPER WAS PROBABLY the first base metal to have its properties recognised and to be used extensively by humans. Copper is versatile: it is malleable and ductile; it has superb alloying characteristics; it is resistant to corrosion, strong, durable and recyclable; and it is an excellent conductor of heat and electricity.

## Extraction, processes and reserves

Copper occurs naturally in the Earth's crust and is extracted by both open-pit mining (the majority of copper mines) and underground mining. Around 80% of copper mine production is in the form of concentrates (copper sulphide minerals typically containing around 30% copper before concentration), requiring smelting and refining. In 2011, world copper smelter production reached 15.8m tonnes. SX-EW (solvent extraction and electrowinning), in which smelting is replaced by leaching, is a process that allows refined metal to be produced at the mine without further processing. It is usually used with copper found in oxides and has become increasingly popular in recent years, partly because it costs less. In 2011 SX-EW accounted for 17% of refined copper, but it is not applicable to all types of ore and copper recovery rates are lower.

Secondary copper smelters use scrap copper as their feed and are estimated to have accounted for around 18% of refined production in 2011, according to the International Copper Study Group (ICSG), compared with around 15% in 2006-09. China, which imports most of its scrap, is the world's leading secondary producer, accounting for 57% of total secondary output of 3.3m tonnes in 2011. ICSG data show

FIG 2.3 **Copper reserves, 2010**

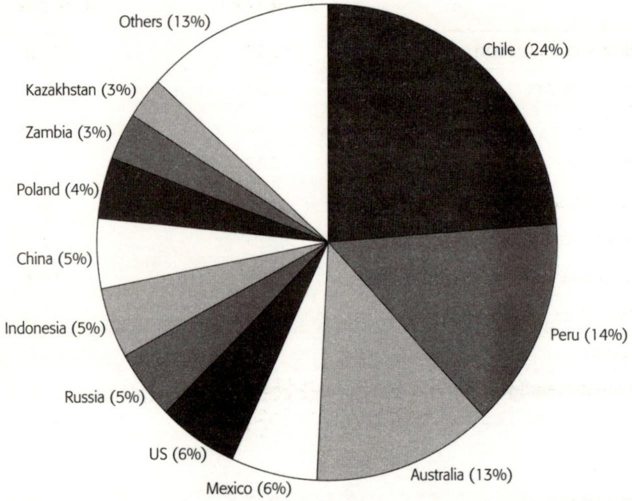

- Chile (24%)
- Peru (14%)
- Australia (13%)
- Others (13%)
- Mexico (6%)
- US (6%)
- Russia (5%)
- Indonesia (5%)
- China (5%)
- Poland (4%)
- Zambia (3%)
- Kazakhstan (3%)

**TOTAL WORLD 630m tonnes**

**Source:** US Geological Survey

that secondary copper smelters recorded growth in output of 7.2% in 2011, compared with 2.9% growth in output of primary smelters.

Known copper reserves stood at just 340m tonnes in 1990, compared with the latest estimate in 2010 of 630m tonnes (see Figure 2.3). Global reserves are still at best estimates – they expand with improved technology and favourable economics, but can decline with extraction. The Americas hold the bulk of the world's copper reserves, but recent high prices have encouraged countries in other parts of the world to seek copper deposits and have them geologically surveyed.

## Products and uses

Copper's largest end-use is in construction, principally building wire and plumbing, which accounted for about 33% of consumption in 2009 according to the ICSG. However, construction's share of

TABLE 2.5 **Copper end-uses, 2009**

|  | m tonnes | % of total |
|---|---|---|
| **Building & construction** | **7,264** | **32.9** |
| Electrical power | 5,273 | 23.9 |
| Plumbing | 1,336 | 6.0 |
| Architecture | 327 | 1.5 |
| Building plant | 193 | 0.9 |
| Communications | 5,273 | 23.9 |
| **Infrastructure** | **3,266** | **14.8** |
| Power utility | 2,541 | 11.5 |
| Telecom | 725 | 3.3 |
| **Equipment manufacture** | **11,569** | **52.4** |
| Industrial | 2,742 | 12.4 |
| Automotive | 1,590 | 7.2 |
| Other transport | 967 | 4.4 |
| Consumer & general products | 1,814 | 8.2 |
| Cooling | 1,330 | 6.0 |
| Electronic | 768 | 3.5 |
| **Total** | **22,099** |  |

**Source:** International Copper Study Group

consumption has been falling, the high cost of copper through much of the 2000s being one factor that accelerated the substitution of copper by plastics in plumbing applications. Aluminium, which has similar properties to copper, can also be substituted in some applications. Related to the construction industry, infrastructure is another major consumer of copper, especially for power cabling, accounting for 15% of consumption in 2009 (see Table 2.5).

Copper also has many crucial applications in electrical and general engineering, coinage and transport. Copper wire is used extensively in the manufacture of electronic equipment, as are some types of sheet and strip. Copper and its alloys still dominate in the production of connectors, but in telecommunications, where new technologies require high-speed data transmission, copper faces competition from fibre optics. Furthermore, wireless communication, which eliminates physical connections altogether, is advancing rapidly.

Aluminium radiators have largely displaced copper in the automotive industry, but use of copper here has started to recover, partly through the introduction of a lightweight alloy radiator and even more by the increased use of electronic components in modern vehicles.

Copper is also benefiting from environmental legislation and the promotion of renewable energy systems. Approximately ten times more copper is required per megawatt of effective capacity for wind turbines than for coal- or gas-fired power stations.

## Consumption and trade

### Uses and trends

In Europe and the United States, building and construction account for the bulk of consumption. In Asia, electrical and electronic production is more important, but as countries develop, infrastructure and construction are also absorbing larger amounts of copper.

Over the past decade, demand for copper has been led by Asia. Between 2000 and 2010, China's consumption growth averaged 16% per year. Its surging demand for copper is a result of urbanisation and rural electrification: power generation capacity accounts for up to half of China's copper consumption. With increased prosperity, demand has been rising for air conditioners and refrigerators, electrical appliances and other copper-intensive consumer durables, including motor vehicles. Equally important is the growth of exports; China is a leading producer and exporter of most of these items. Although not quite matching China's breakneck speed of expansion, the annual average rate of growth of India's copper consumption has also been an impressive 7% over the same 2000–10 period. This compares with contractions in EU and American average annual consumption of 1% and 4% respectively during the same period.

China accounted for 40% of total consumption of copper in 2011, dwarfing the second largest single consumer, the United States, which accounted for about 9% of total consumption (see Table 2.6).

TABLE 2.6 **Leading copper-consuming countries**

|  | 1991 | | 2000 | | 2011 | |
| --- | --- | --- | --- | --- | --- | --- |
|  | '000 tonnes | % of total | '000 tonnes | % of total | '000 tonnes | % of total |
| China | 590 | 5.5 | 1,928 | 12.7 | 7,915 | 40.4 |
| EU | 3,081 | 28.8 | 4,371 | 28.8 | 3,325 | 17.0 |
| US | 2,058 | 19.2 | 2,979 | 19.6 | 1,745 | 8.9 |
| Japan | 1,613 | 15.1 | 1,351 | 8.9 | 1,003 | 5.1 |
| South Korea | 343 | 3.2 | 862 | 5.7 | 784 | 4.0 |
| Latin America | 445 | 4.2 | 628 | 4.1 | 620 | 3.2 |
| Taiwan | 399 | 3.7 | 628 | 4.1 | 457 | 2.3 |
| India | 96 | 0.9 | 240 | 1.6 | 402 | 2.1 |
| Others | 2,070 | 19.4 | 2,204 | 14.5 | 3,360 | 17.1 |
| Total | 10,695 | | 15,192 | | 19,611 | |

**Source:** World Bureau of Metal Statistics

## Trade

Chile remains by far the dominant exporter of all types of copper, accounting for 36% of refined exports, 32% of concentrate and 55% of blister in 2011. Exports from Africa have increased sharply in recent years in tandem with rising mine supply, and in 2011 Zambia was the second largest exporter of refined copper after Chile, accounting for nearly 8% of total exports (see Table 2.7).

The pattern of imports is somewhat more dispersed, but the concentrate import trade is dominated by Asian countries, led by China (32.1% in 2011) and Japan (23.1%), with China having overtaken Japan as the world's largest import market in 2009. In addition to rapidly increasing domestic production of refined copper, China supplements this with substantial imports. Inflows, however, have become increasingly price sensitive, with Chinese buyers destocking at times of high prices and restocking when prices fall. This pattern of behaviour has been exaggerated in recent years by state buying for strategic reserves.

TABLE 2.7 **Leading exporters and importers, 2011**

|  | Exports | | | Imports | |
| --- | --- | --- | --- | --- | --- |
|  | '000 tonnes | % of total |  | '000 tonnes | % of total |
| Chile | 2,981 | 35.7 | China | 2,836 | 36.6 |
| Zambia | 640 | 7.7 | Germany | 735 | 9.5 |
| Japan | 437 | 5.2 | US | 649 | 8.4 |
| Peru | 345 | 4.1 | Italy | 615 | 7.9 |
| Poland | 328 | 3.9 | Taiwan | 461 | 6.0 |
| Russia | 325 | 3.9 | South Korea | 347 | 4.5 |

**Source:** World Bureau of Metal Statistics

## Production and stocks
### Mine production

Copper exploration revived in response to the 2002–08 bull market, but companies continued to favour growth by acquisition. As a result, there have been few major discoveries and new projects over the past decade. The credit crisis and collapse in copper prices that started in the second half of 2008 exacerbated the problem.

Chile has been the largest copper miner since 1982, when it overtook the United States. In 2011 it produced 5.3m tonnes and accounted for 32% of total production (see Table 2.8). State-owned Codelco is the largest producer, although Escondida, the country's largest mine, is privately owned (by BHP Billiton of Australia and Rio Tinto of the UK/Australia, among others). Chile's copper belt continues north into Peru, Mexico and the United States and these four countries dominate world production, accounting for about 50% of the total in 2011.

In the 1960s and 1970s the Central African copper belt, encompassing Zambia and the Democratic Republic of Congo (DRC), was one of the leading copper-producing regions of the world, accounting for 15–20% of world output in its heyday. With high prevailing prices in the past decade, the region started to attract investment again, particularly from China, and production is now recovering. According to the World Bureau of Metal Statistics (WBMS), output in the DRC had risen from just 26,000 tonnes in 2002 to 440,000 tonnes in 2011, while Zambia's production had risen from 308,000 tonnes to 784,100 tonnes in the same period.

China is another large producer of copper at 1,267,000 tonnes in 2011, but this still falls far short of its needs and it is the world's largest importer of both copper and refined copper.

TABLE 2.8 **Copper mine production**

|  | 1996 | | 2003 | | 2011 | |
| --- | --- | --- | --- | --- | --- | --- |
|  | '000 tonnes | % of total | '000 tonnes | % of total | '000 tonnes | % of total |
| Chile | 3,115 | 30.7 | 4,904 | 34.1 | 5,263 | 32.4 |
| China | 440 | 4.3 | 604 | 4.2 | 1,267 | 7.8 |
| Peru | 485 | 4.8 | 843 | 5.9 | 1,235 | 7.6 |
| US | 1,920 | 18.9 | 1,124 | 7.8 | 1,138 | 7.0 |
| Australia | 550 | 5.4 | 830 | 5.8 | 957 | 5.9 |
| Zambia | 340 | 3.3 | 347 | 2.4 | 784 | 4.8 |
| Russia | 520 | 5.1 | 665.1 | 4.6 | 725 | 4.5 |
| Canada | 690 | 6.8 | 557 | 3.9 | 566 | 3.5 |
| Indonesia | 525 | 5.2 | 1,003 | 7.0 | 526 | 3.2 |
| Mexico | 340 | 3.3 | 356 | 2.5 | 440 | 2.7 |
| Poland | 475 | 4.7 | 503 | 3.5 | 427 | 2.6 |
| Others | 750 | 7.4 | 2,629 | 18.3 | 2,913 | 17.9 |
| Total | 10,150 | | 14,365 | | 16,242 | |

**Source:** World Bureau of Metal Statistics

## Mining constraints

The copper-mining industry faces a number of constraints, some of which affect miners of other minerals and some of which are specific to the copper industry. In particular, falling ore grades are a problem, especially in the more mature copper-mining regions in Chile and the United States. In Latin America, and also in Indonesia, there have been falls in output because of strikes and projects have been delayed because of environmental or local community concerns. High energy costs have also lowered profitability as mining operations are typically energy intensive. Uncertain operating environments have created additional difficulties with periodic changes in tax and regulatory regimes by more nationalist governments.

Notwithstanding the constraints – which have been a significant factor in the strength of prices in recent years – additional supply is on its way. In Zambia there are a number of projects that are expected to add 315,000 tonnes per year (t/y) of additional output by 2014; in the DRC ramp-ups at Mutanda (Glencore) and KOV (Katanga Mining) should add around 150,000 t/y; and in Botswana, Discovery Metals has confirmed the commissioning of its 36,000 t/y Boseto mine. Other significant mine commissions in 2012 and 2013 are Oyu Tolgoi in Mongolia, Jabal Sayid in Saudi Arabia and Salobo in Brazil.

## Refining: countries and companies

The four largest refined-copper producing countries accounted for 54% of refined output in 2011: China for 26.4%, Chile for 13.7%, Japan for 6.7% and the United States for 5.3%. These four producers and the EU account for two-thirds of total production (see Table 2.9). Recent and proposed additions to capacity suggest that China will be increasing its share of total refined production over the next few years; its output (primary and secondary) grew by 14.5% in 2011, according to official data, and by an estimated 8% in 2012.

In 2011, the largest eight companies producing copper accounted for 40% of total output. Chile's Codelco is the world's largest producer of refined copper followed by Freeport-McMoRan Copper & Gold (United States), BHP Billiton (Australia) and Xstrata (Switzerland). Four of the world's ten largest refineries, however, are in China (see Table 2.10).

## Stocks and related issues

Reported stocks of copper averaged a healthy 4.7 weeks of consumption between 1992 and 2002. But as demand from China gathered pace

## TABLE 2.9 Leading refined copper-producing countries

|  | 1991 | | 2000 | | 2011 | |
| --- | --- | --- | --- | --- | --- | --- |
|  | '000 tonnes | % of total | '000 tonnes | % of total | '000 tonnes | % of total |
| China | 560 | 5.2 | 1,371 | 9.3 | 5,197 | 26.4 |
| Chile | 1,228 | 11.5 | 2,668 | 18.0 | 3,092 | 15.7 |
| EU | 1,432 | 13.4 | 2,333 | 15.8 | 2,708 | 13.7 |
| Japan | 1,076 | 10.1 | 1,437 | 9.7 | 1,328 | 6.7 |
| US | 1,995 | 18.7 | 1,790 | 12.1 | 1,031 | 5.2 |
| Russia | – | – | 824 | 5.6 | 910 | 4.6 |
| Others | 4,396 | 41.1 | 4,381 | 29.6 | 5,432 | 27.6 |
| Total | 10,688 | | 14,805 | | 19,698 | |

**Sources:** World Bureau of Metal Statistics; International Copper Study Group; EIU

## TABLE 2.10 Leading copper refineries

| Refinery | Country | Owner | Capacity, '000 tonnes |
| --- | --- | --- | --- |
| Guixi | China | Jiangxi Copper Corporation | 900 |
| Chuquicamata Refinery | Chile | Codelco | 600 |
| Birla | India | Birla Group Hidalco | 500 |
| Jinchuan | China | Jinchuan Nonferrous Metal Co | 500 |
| Yunnan Copper | China | Yunnan Copper Industry Group (64.8%) | 500 |
| Codelco Norte (SX-EW) | Chile | Codelco | 470 |
| Toyo/Niihama (Besshi) | Japan | Sumitomo Metal Mining Co | 450 |
| Amarillo | US | Grupo Mexico | 450 |
| El Paso (refinery) | US | Freeport-McMoRan Copper & Gold | 415 |
| Jinlong (Tongdu) (refinery) | China | Tongling Nonferrous Metals (52%); Sharpline International (13%); Sumitomo (7.5%); Itochu (7.5%) | 400 |
| Las Ventanas | Chile | Codelco | 400 |

**Source:** Bloomberg (data compiled by CRU Group)

during the 2000s, stocks were drawn down and averaged just 1.5 weeks of consumption in 2004 and 2005. The global economic slowdown, by reducing consumption, allowed a recovery in stocks to around three weeks of consumption in 2009, but still historically low.

The copper market was close to a net balance in 2010 and 2011. However, reported stocks (not including metal in transit, in strategic stockpiles or in bonded warehouses in China) ended 2011 equivalent to just 2.7 weeks of total consumption.

Reported stocks do not tell the whole story, however, as they do not include countries' strategic reserves. Only a tentative estimate can be made of the size of China's state copper reserves. Furthermore, there are stocks held by corporate consumers that are not officially reported.

## The copper market

Copper is the most actively traded of the base metals. The London Metal Exchange (LME) is the dominant price setter along with the Commodity Exchange Division of the New York Mercantile Exchange (COMEX/NYMEX), which is the benchmark for the North American market. The Shanghai Futures Exchange is the main exchange in China. Prices are settled by a bid and offer process. These exchanges also offer futures and options contracts, and provide warehousing facilities that enable market participants to make or take physical delivery of copper in accordance with each exchange's criteria.

Monthly average LME and COMEX prices are widely used in contracts, with premiums for refined copper depending on quality and location. Concentrates are sold on the basis of LME or COMEX prices, minus charges for smelting and refining. Blister copper is sold in the same way as concentrate, without the deduction for smelting.

In December 2010 the first exchange-traded funds (ETFs) backed by physical holdings of copper were launched. Throughout 2011 appetite for the product was subdued, and after picking up in early 2012, holdings subsequently dwindled again. Despite the relative lack of initial interest in the physical copper ETF, other similar products are planned, two in the United States and one in South Korea. However, with LME stocks so low, opposition to these physical ETFs is growing

FIG 2.4 **Copper stocks and prices**

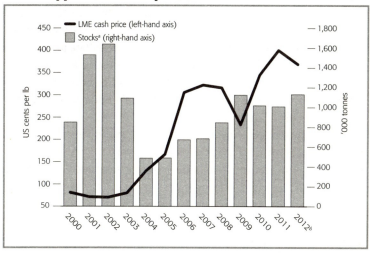

a Total reported Western commercial stocks; end-period. b EIU estimates.
**Sources:** Federal Reserve Board; London Bullion Market Association

on the grounds that they could artificially inflate prices, exacerbating tightness in the physical market by locking up stock that would otherwise be available to consumers. Nevertheless, in December 2012 the Securities and Exchange Commission in the United States approved a copper ETF, managed by JP Morgan.

## Price trends

Copper prices have been extremely volatile in recent years. In May 2006, the price of copper touched 400 cents per lb when industry stocks fell and set off buying by investment funds. A sharp sell-off followed, bottoming out in February 2007 at 237 cents/lb. By early 2008, prices had recovered to 400 cents/lb, and by July had reached a new all-time high of 407.6 cents/lb. Within five months copper had shed 69% of its value, and ended 2008 trading at just 127.6 cents/lb. This extreme volatility has continued, with copper prices rising by an annual average of 48% in 2010 as the global economy emerged from recession (see Figure 2.4).

Prices remained strong in the first eight months of 2011 before falling sharply in the general sell-off of the commodity asset class in September-October of that year. In 2012 prices struggled amid concerns about global economic growth in the wake of the sovereign debt crisis in the euro zone and uncertainty about economic growth in China. Average prices fell by nearly 10% in 2012. Despite the volatility and copper's close relationship with the economic cycle, the copper market is supported by strong fundamentals, with supply struggling to keep up with demand and stocks at uncomfortably low levels.

## The future

- Copper is essential to the processes of urbanisation and raising living standards in the developing world, ensuring that long-term demand will prove resilient. For example, China's State Grid Corporation is targeting a 77% expansion of capacity to 1.7 billion kilowatts by 2020, which will require large amounts of refined copper. However, it also makes the metal highly susceptible to cyclical trends in emerging-market growth.
- Mine production has been particularly vulnerable to unplanned disruption. Strikes, accidents, technical difficulties, low ore grades, planning constraints, tight credit conditions, political risks, and shortages of skilled personnel, equipment and other supplies have all hampered the timely start-up of new projects and the smooth operation of existing ones.
- There are potential shortages of power and water, both of which are used in, and are crucial to, the copper extraction or mining process, in key producing regions, in particular Chile, Southern Africa and China.
- Investor demand for copper is an important factor. There is now a close positive correlation between dollar weakness and investment fund interest in commodities.
- If prices remain high and stocks low, there will be rationing of copper, substitution with other metals where possible and the greater use of scrap.

# Gold

GOLD IS ONE OF THE RAREST METALS in the world and one of the oldest known to man. While gold has been much used for decorative objects, it also has industrial uses. Its properties include strong resistance to corrosion and good conductivity; it is also malleable and ductile. The softness that helps its malleability means that it sometimes needs to be alloyed with other metals (silver or copper) for additional strength. Gold is easily recyclable because of its low melting point. Its traditional role as a store of value has meant that, according to the World Gold Council (WGC), only 2% of all the gold that has ever been mined has been lost over time.

## Extraction, processes and reserves

Gold is mined in both open and underground pits, often alongside other metals, especially lead, zinc and copper. It is widely dispersed geographically, with no one region accounting for more than 20% of production. Gold deposits are usually found in riverbeds (placer deposits) or in cracks of rocks (lode deposits). Once the gold ore is extracted, it undergoes extensive and time-consuming processing to remove the gold from the carbon or oxides or sulphides that are also in the ore. The final stage of processing involves melting the gold into a "dore" bar, which is about 90% pure gold. These bars are then shipped to a refinery.

The US Geological Survey (USGS) estimates gold reserves (still in the ground) at 51,000 tonnes.

## Products and uses

Traditionally, jewellery-making was the primary end-use of gold. As recently as 1999, jewellery consumption at 3.2m tonnes accounted for 80% of annual gold consumption, but by 2011 its share had slipped to just 48% or just under 2m tonnes (see Table 2.11). Some of the decline in gold's use in jewellery has been a reflection of high prices in recent years as well as the weakness in Western economies since 2008. Whether for reasons of austerity or just fashion, there has been a move away from gold jewellery to cheaper costume jewellery.

The gap left by the fall in jewellery consumption has been more than filled by strong growth in investment demand for gold. This includes bars and coins as well as the gold held by exchange-traded funds (ETFs). Gold has a number of characteristics that make it an attractive investment – in particular, an attractive commodity investment – such as high liquidity and global acceptance or recognition (clear quality standards that can be checked), a high value relative to volume (making it easily transportable and reducing storage costs) and the fact that it is virtually indestructible. It is also scarce (especially when compared with fiat currencies – paper money issued by governments). On the negative side, however, relative to currencies, it does not have a body such as a central bank that can monitor its value and take action to support its price. Also interest cannot be earned on a gold investment.

An additional source of demand in recent years has been central banks, which had been net sellers of gold for decades but since 2010 have become net buyers. (Gold is still the world's third largest reserve asset behind dollar- and euro-denominated assets.) This is probably a reflection of concerns about the outlook for the dollar and the euro, in particular, with central banks seeking to diversify their reserve holdings.

Gold also has industrial uses (although because of its high price it is used only as a last resort when a suitable alternative is not available). It is used in the electronics industry in the manufacture of semiconductors, in particular, and circuit boards. It could be used in wiring because of its good conductivity, but aluminium and copper are typically used instead as they cost much less. Historically,

TABLE 2.11 **Gold consumption by type**

|  | 2002 | | 2011 | |
| --- | --- | --- | --- | --- |
|  | tonnes | % of total | tonnes | % of total |
| Jewellery | 2,662 | 78.9 | 1,963 | 48.3 |
| Net retail investment[a] | 353 | 10.5 | 1,487 | 36.6 |
| Industrial & dental | 358 | 10.6 | 464 | 11.4 |
| ETFs | 3 | 0.1 | 154 | 3.8 |
| Total | 3,376 | | 4,067 | |

a Gold bars and coins; does not include ETFs or other investment flows.
**Source:** World Gold Council

gold was used extensively in medicine and dentistry because of its biocompatibility with the human body, but the availability of much cheaper plastic or ceramic substitutes means it is losing its role in dentistry. Industrial and dental use of gold accounted for 11.4% of total gold consumption in 2011, according to the WGC, but it fell by 2.8% in that year and remained weak in 2012.

## Consumption and trade

India has historically always been the largest consumer of gold jewellery and gold more generally (see Table 2.12). Culturally, gold has been the principal store of wealth and spikes in consumption have tended to coincide with Indian festivals and/or the Indian wedding season. However, Indian jewellery consumption slumped in 2011 by 13.7% and remained weak in the first half of 2012. There were signs of a pick-up in consumption in the second half of 2012, but consumption fell for a second consecutive year. Meanwhile, China's consumption was growing strongly in 2011, up by 13.6% year on year, despite high prevailing prices. After a strong start to 2012, China's consumption started to weaken along with the slowdown in the wider economy, and it contracted over the year as a whole.

TABLE 2.12 **Gold jewellery consumption**

|  | 2001 | | 2011 | |
| --- | --- | --- | --- | --- |
|  | **Tonnes** | **% of total** | **Tonnes** | **% of total** |
| India | 615 | 20.4 | 567 | 28.7 |
| China | 203 | 6.8 | 545 | 27.6 |
| US | 389 | 12.9 | 115 | 5.8 |
| Russia | – | 0.0 | 75 | 3.8 |
| Turkey | 92 | 3.1 | 64 | 3.2 |
| UAE | 95 | 3.2 | 58 | 2.9 |
| Saudi Arabia | 163 | 5.4 | 56 | 2.8 |
| Indonesia | 98 | 3.3 | 30 | 1.5 |
| Italy | 92 | 3.0 | 29 | 1.5 |
| Japan | 51 | 1.7 | 21 | 1.1 |
| Others | 1,211 | 40.2 | 415 | 21.0 |
| **Total** | **3,009** |  | **1,974** |  |

**Source:** World Gold Council

High international prices, signs of a slowing economy and the weakness of the rupee (gold is priced in dollars) in the second half of 2011 and into 2012 curtailed demand in India. In contrast, in China a number of factors had been encouraging consumption, such as negative real interest rates (making bank deposits unattractive), government policies seeking to dampen the property market (previously an important investment vehicle for Chinese savers), new products that facilitated gold purchases, the deregulation of the local gold market and concerns about inflation.

In 2010–11 consumption of gold more generally was boosted by concerns about sovereign debt in the euro zone and America's fiscal woes. Confidence in what were previously considered safe assets was low as Greece hovered on the brink of default, the United States had its debt downgraded by rating agencies, and quantitative easing (particularly in America) was undermining the value of currencies.

Indeed, in 2011 Turkey started to allow banks to hold gold as part of their reserve requirements. However, the flight to gold was generally deemed destabilising and some of the largest exchanges – COMEX in America and the Shanghai Gold Exchange and Futures Exchanges – raised initial margin requirements on gold investment in a bid to take the heat out of the market. Sentiment towards gold soured somewhat in the second half of the year but investment consumption (including bars and coins) still rose by 24% in 2011, offsetting the nearly 3% fall in total gold jewellery demand.

## Production and stocks
## Mine production

Mine supply typically accounts for nearly 70% of annual gold supply (an annual average of 68% in 2000–10), a low amount compared with other commodities. As prices rose in the latter half of the 2000s, interest and investment in gold mining picked up, the higher price making smaller, less productive mines more attractive. Many of the junior mining companies that invested in more marginal mines suffered in the wake of the credit crunch in late 2008 and early 2009 but the gold price fared better than the prices of other commodity assets during this period.

Since then, gold mining has continued to struggle with a number of constraints, many of which are faced by the mining industry generally. In particular, labour unrest has severely hampered output in Indonesia and in Peru in recent years as miners have sought higher wages or improved conditions. Power supply has been an issue in South Africa as have falling ore grades, and the government's clampdown on safety and environmental regulations has hindered output growth in China.

In 2007, China overtook both South Africa and Australia to become the world's largest gold miner, a position it has retained with annual average growth in production of 7.5% between 2008 and 2011 (see Table 2.13). Meanwhile, the gold-mining industry in traditionally the world's largest gold producer, South Africa, appears to be in long-term decline, partly because of falling profitability as power and labour costs have risen but also because of ageing mines. After a weather-disrupted fall in output in Australia in 2011, growth resumed in 2012 and was expected to continue in the medium term owing to a number of new mines becoming operational.

Aside from South Africa, gold mine production is generally rising across Sub-Saharan Africa, particularly from smaller mines. New mines in Burkina Faso raised total production in the country by 95.5% in 2010 and 40.3% in 2011, and output from a number of new mines in Côte d'Ivoire increased total production by over 107.9% in 2011, albeit from a low base, to 11.1 tonnes. Production in Mali slipped back in 2011 but recovered and grew strongly in 2012, while expansion work in some of Tanzania's mines contributed to year-on-year growth in output of 10.3% in 2011.

TABLE 2.13 **Gold mine supply, 2011**

|  | **Tonnes** | **% of total** |
| --- | --- | --- |
| China | 361 | 14.1 |
| Australia | 258 | 10.1 |
| US | 232 | 9.0 |
| Russia | 189 | 7.4 |
| South Africa | 187 | 7.3 |
| Peru | 164 | 6.4 |
| Canada | 100 | 3.9 |
| Ghana | 88 | 3.4 |
| Indonesia | 74 | 2.9 |
| Others | 913 | 35.6 |
| **Total** | **2,566** |  |

**Source:** World Gold Council

## Secondary supply from recycling

Recycled gold or scrap accounted for about 28% of annual supply in 2000–10, but its contribution swelled to over 40% in 2008–10 as economic uncertainty led to some distressed selling and high prices further encouraged sales (see Figure 2.5). Scrap supply fell by 3.1%

FIG 2.5 **Gold supply, 2011**

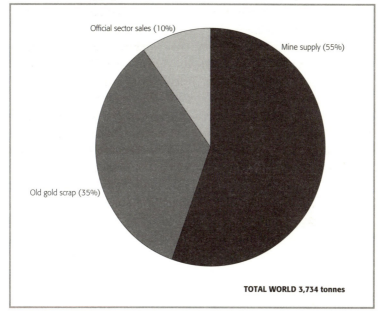

Note: There was no net producer hedging in 2011.
**Source:** World Gold Council

in 2011, according to the WGC. This would appear to be somewhat counterintuitive considering the high – and rising – gold prices, but it seems that many potential sellers resisted in anticipation of even higher prices. Another reason could be that easily accessible scrap supply had already largely been exploited. Furthermore, the overall stagnation of the market masks differing trends globally. Recycling was particularly strong in the United States and southern Europe (probably distressed selling) but fell in the traditional markets of the Middle East, India and East Asia.

## The gold market

Although gold has effectively been used as a currency or as a store of value for thousands of years, it began to be formally traded only during the 17th century in London. However, by the 19th century its importance had grown to such an extent that it became the basis for a global fixed exchange-rate system called the Gold Standard. It was also used to underpin a fixed exchange-rate regime known as Bretton Woods, from the mid-1940s until the system collapsed in the early 1970s. The breakdown of the Bretton Woods arrangement arguably undermined the perceived value of gold, but it also meant that gold was able to trade freely for the first time for some 300 years.

The gold market is larger and more liquid than almost all other commodity markets; in terms of volumes traded it is more like a large developed-country sovereign bond market. Historically, the majority of trading has taken place in over-the-counter (OTC) wholesale markets, where less information is available. London is the largest market, with significant trading also in New York, Tokyo and Zurich. Recent steps to move more commodity trading on to regulated exchanges (as a result of the 2008–09 financial crisis) are likely to result in less OTC gold trading.

The most internationally recognised benchmark for gold prices is the London Bullion Market Association (LBMA) twice-daily price fix – the result of a telephone call between representatives of gold-trading firms in London. However, gold is traded across the world with other important exchanges in Dubai, Shanghai, Vietnam, China, India and Pakistan as well as more traditional markets in the United States, Europe and Japan.

The first major exchange-traded fund (ETF), SPDR Goldshares, was initiated under the auspices of the World Gold Council in 2004. It is still the largest gold ETF, and as of mid-2012 was the sixth largest ETF in the United States. ETFs are a way for investors to gain access to the spot price of gold. Previously, they could invest in gold only indirectly, by buying either gold futures or gold-mining stocks. ETFs are regulated by exchanges and are widely available in Asia, South Africa, North America and Europe. They have widened the investor base for gold but have been criticised for offering investors an alternative to holding gold-mining equities, making it more difficult for miners to raise finance. They have also been criticised for taking supply off the market – some ETFs are backed by physical gold – at a time of rising demand, thus supporting prices. (Gold's high density and the ease with which it can be transported and stored make it desirable as a physical investment.) However, not all ETFs are backed by physical gold; some use gold futures as security.

The gold futures market is the largest commodity futures market after oil. Gold derivatives (futures and options) were the traditional way for miners to hedge against a dramatic movement in the gold price. However, the recent high prices have meant that almost all miners have closed their hedging books. Gold futures are still widely traded, however, particularly in the United States on COMEX and electronic trading platforms (CME Globex), the Chicago Board of Trade and the Tokyo Commodity Exchange; they are also traded in India and Dubai and on the Shanghai Futures Exchange.

There was a small amount of hedging activity during 2011, of a net amount of 10 tonnes for the year as a whole. Although the amount was small, it was notable for being the first positive net hedging figure in over a decade. However, net hedging turned negative again in 2012. In recent years, the market has been characterised by dehedging – the buying back of the gold that was previously sold in the futures market. Producers do this when they think the price will rise.

## Price trends

As with all commodities, textbook economic theory and market fundamentals (the demand-supply balance) can rarely predict exactly the trend in gold prices, but there are a number of relationships between gold and economic indicators that have held in the past. In particular, gold prices are typically inversely correlated with the dollar (see Figure 2.6). This reflects gold's property as a hedge against inflation as well as its appeal as a safe haven in times of dollar uncertainty. Furthermore, a falling dollar makes gold and other commodities that are typically denominated in dollars cheaper in terms of other currencies, increasing both demand for gold and the price.

Gold prices have also generally done well when other investment assets such as equities (in particular) or bonds are performing poorly; this is partly because gold demand does not have the direct link with the economic or industrial cycle that characterises base metal and energy demand.

FIG 2.6 **Gold prices**

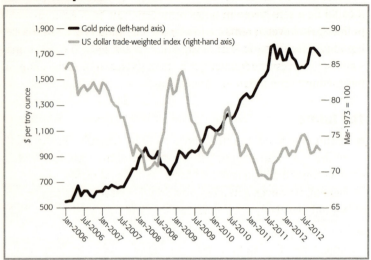

**Sources:** Federal Reserve Board; London Bullion Market Association

The appeal of gold is enhanced when interest rates are low. As holding gold involves only a capital return (no interest), it is less appealing as a savings vehicle if interest rates are high.

Gold is also perceived as a hedge against inflation, particularly hyperinflation, as it will retain its value as fiat currencies are debased. There is also no counterparty risk with gold – this was particularly relevant during the 2008–09 financial crisis when actual or perceived counterparty risk was high. Geopolitical risk is a further factor that can encourage the consumption of gold (and lead to higher prices).

Gold prices (using LBMA PM Fix) have risen on an annual average basis every year since 2001, when they slipped by 2.9%. Between 2002 and 2011, prices rose by an average of 20% a year. However, before this strong increase in prices, the value of gold had been falling in real terms since its previous peak in the early 1980s. Prices reached a trough in August 1999 at $252 per troy ounce.

After rising by 28% in 2011, gold prices lost momentum in 2012, although they still rose over the course of the year by 6.2% to an average of $1,668/troy ounce. Gold appeared to be following trends in industrial metals rather than benefiting from the perception that it could be a safe haven in times of uncertainty, both economic and political. However, it remained supported by ultra-low interest rates, liquidity injections – as part of quantitative easing (QE) programmes – and solid investor demand. QE, or the expansion of money supply, has medium-term inflation implications.

## The future

- If concerns about the creditworthiness of the euro zone escalate, or the American economy slows sharply or the American government fails to tackle its fiscal deficit, gold prices would benefit. However, a marked slowdown in developing countries would negatively affect gold demand and thus prices.
- A normalisation of global monetary conditions (that is, an end to unorthodox monetary policy such as QE) and eventual tightening would diminish gold's attractiveness as an investment vehicle.
- As one of the most actively traded commodities and the one with only limited productive use, gold may suffer unduly from efforts to prevent speculative trading. This could include ever higher reserve requirements in futures trading.
- There remains a substantial risk of another collapse in gold prices. If economic conditions worsen, investors could be forced to sell off their gold positions en masse to offset losses elsewhere, driving down prices. Conversely, should the global recovery gather pace more quickly than anticipated, investors may decide that gold prices have peaked and seek to take profits to invest them elsewhere, triggering a collapse in prices.
- Mine supply could become increasingly uncertain, particularly if gold prices fall or mining companies struggle with financing. This is particularly the case as mining costs are expected to increase in the medium term as a result of high energy costs, rising labour costs and potentially more expensive capital investment, as readily available sources of supply are depleted and ores become more difficult to extract.

- In the medium term, gold is expected to retain its industrial role; it is being used in a number of new technologies, particularly as an active catalyst in controlling emissions and in solar cells.

# Other precious metals

## SILVER

Silver is a shiny white precious metal. It has many of the same chemical properties as gold, and because it is more plentiful and cheaper its industrial uses are more extensive. Silver is ductile and malleable and has high electrical and thermal conductivity. Historically, it was also used in health products because of its antiseptic qualities. It is found in a pure form, as an alloy with gold or with various other ores (principally copper, lead and zinc). As a result, silver is often mined as part of a wider mining operation focused on gold or copper, for example.

### Consumption and uses

Silver has been used in jewellery and coinage for thousands of years and in decorative household items such as cutlery. Today the biggest market for silver jewellery is India. Silver is also used in electrical conductors, switches and circuit breakers, batteries, mirrors and photographic film. Recently, growth in demand for silver has come from the solar energy industry, particularly photovoltaic (solar energy) panels, which accounted for 5% of silver consumption in 2010, doubling to 10% in 2011. The solar energy industry benefited from attractive feed-in tariffs in the EU, but these are now being scaled down because of increasing fiscal austerity and the large subsidies involved. Nevertheless, other parts of the world are continuing to encourage solar-power projects. Indeed, in 2012 China raised its target for the contribution of solar-powered energy by 2015 from 15 gigawatts to 21 gigawatts.

FIG 2.7 **Silver consumption by sector**

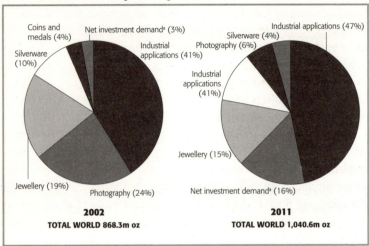

a Includes producer hedging activity.
**Source:** The Silver Institute

In 2011, industrial consumption of silver accounted for 47% of total consumption, while jewellery and net investor demand accounted for 15% and 16% respectively (see Figure 2.7). Industrial consumption slipped slightly in 2011, by 2.5%, largely owing to weak global economic growth. In 2007–08 industrial demand peaked at 54% of total demand, but since then investor demand has grown strongly (it accounted for just 0.1% of demand in 2003 and there was disinvestment of silver in 2002). As in the case of gold, physically backed exchange-traded funds (ETFs) were launched which expanded the investor base. However, ETF holdings started to fall in 2011 and by the end of the year had dropped by 8% to 15,750 tonnes. American silver mint sales, however, rose by 17% in 2011 to 39.8m troy ounces. These trends were reversed in 2012, with ETF holdings rising by a provisional 1,464 tonnes while American silver mint sales fell.

## Production

Mine supply accounted for about 73% of annual silver supply in 2011, with the remainder made up of scrap recycling and negligible amounts of official sales and producer hedging. Mine supply has been growing steadily, rising by 1.4% in 2011, the ninth consecutive year of growth. However, silver-mining companies face many of the same issues as their gold-mining counterparts, in particular disruption as a result of labour unrest and falling ore grades in many mines. Nevertheless, supply has continued to grow because of a number of new, relatively small mining projects and larger amounts of silver being extracted in the process of lead/zinc or gold mining.

Mexico, Peru and Chile accounted for 48% of total silver output in 2011 (see Table 2.14), helping to make Latin America the prime regional producer. Silver is geographically dispersed, though, with large producers in Asia (China, India), Australia, Europe (Turkey, Sweden) and Russia. The largest silver-producing companies include BHP Billiton (Australia), Fresnillo (Mexico), KGHM Polska Miedz (Poland), Pan American Silver (Canada) and Gold Corp (Canada) but no one company dominates and there are many smaller mining companies involved in silver exploration and production.

TABLE 2.14 **Leading silver-producing countries, 2011**

|  | m oz | % of total |
|---|---|---|
| Mexico | 152.8 | 20.1 |
| Peru | 109.8 | 14.4 |
| China | 103.9 | 13.6 |
| Australia | 55.2 | 7.2 |
| Chile | 42.1 | 5.5 |
| Poland | 40.8 | 5.4 |
| Russia | 40.0 | 5.3 |
| Bolivia | 39.0 | 5.1 |
| Others | 178.0 | 23.4 |
| **Total** | 761.6 |  |

**Source:** The Silver Institute

## The silver market

Investors can buy silver in the form of bullion (pure bars), coins and medallions or through ETFs on the New York, Toronto or London stock exchanges. Derivative products in silver are also available on the New York Stock Exchange. As the silver market is much smaller than the gold market, there have been instances in the past where a large buyer has tried to corner the market in an attempt to manipulate prices (most famously, in the late 1970s, the Hunt brothers), but no one has succeeded. The most commonly quoted benchmark prices for silver are the Handy & Harman price in the United States and the London Bullion Market Association fixing price.

## Price trends

Like gold, the silver price has been rising steadily over the past decade, primarily because of investor demand. Silver prices rose markedly in 2006 with the launch of what is the largest ETF, now managed by BlackRock (UK), and again in 2009 with the launch of two further ETFs in the United States and Australia. However, although silver has many of the same properties as gold, because silver is used more extensively in industry its price can be more influenced by the global economic or business cycle (unlike gold, whose price can rise in times of economic weakness). Nevertheless, silver prices (like those of gold) rose during the 2008–09 economic slowdown.

In 2011, prices rose again, although like those of most commodities they fell towards the end of the year. Reflecting its relationship with gold, silver futures were subject to the same increases in margin requirements that affected the gold market in 2011 amid concerns that the market was getting unsustainably inflated. In 2012 prices were weak for much of the year but strengthened in the final quarter of the year. Nevertheless, annual average prices still fell by 10.3%. Figure 2.8 shows the close relationship between movements in the prices of gold and silver and highlights the higher volatility in the silver price.

FIG 2.8 **Gold and silver prices (Jan 2006 = 100)**

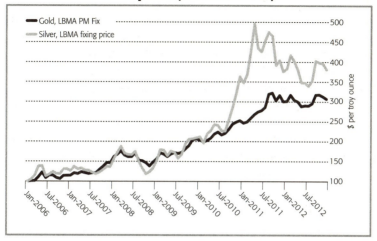

**Source:** Haver Analytics

## The future

- Silver's industrial uses, particularly in a number of new, green technologies, suggest that it will continue to enjoy strong industrial demand in the medium term.
- In recent years, growing investment demand has driven consumption. This makes the price vulnerable to a loss of investor interest, for example when monetary policy starts to tighten and interest rates to rise.
- Strong investor interest is leading to higher prices, potentially undermining silver's competitiveness in industrial uses. However, in some applications, there are no suitable substitutes for silver.

## PLATINUM

Platinum is a grey-white precious metal and one of the rarest elements in the Earth's crust. It is malleable and ductile, has a high melting point, is an excellent electrical conductor and is highly resistant to corrosion. Platinum occurs naturally in a pure form and also alongside nickel and copper ores. It was discovered in the early 18th century, with work on refining the metal and testing its properties starting in the 1750s.

### Consumption and uses

Platinum's main industrial use is in catalytic converters in diesel-powered cars, accounting for 38% of total consumption in 2011 (see Figure 2.9). Autocatalysts use precious metals to convert the noxious gases in vehicle exhausts into harmless substances. Slightly less than one-third of total consumption of the metal is in jewellery – platinum jewellery is particularly popular in China and India. Other uses are in electrical contacts, liquid crystal display (LCD) glass, petrochemicals, oil refining and laboratory equipment. Platinum is also used in dentistry and medicine.

Annual growth in consumption averaged 2.2% in 2003–08 before a sharp 15% drop in 2009 during the global economic slowdown. After bouncing back to 16% growth in 2010, consumption grew by a modest 2.4% in 2011, constrained by a sharp fall in investment demand and the weak automobile market in Europe. Because of the large number of diesel-powered cars in Europe (about 50% of the market), with platinum in their catalytic converters, the metal has been particularly hard hit by the downturn in this market. Offsetting this, however, are signs of growth in demand for diesel-powered cars and trucks in the United States; and the roll-out of the EU's Euro VI emissions legislation from January 2013 will boost demand in the medium term. More broadly, supply disruptions in the automobile market (see palladium) hampered growth in platinum consumption in 2011.

As platinum prices rose during the 1980s, a variety of platinum bars and coins appeared on the market, and the metal has increasingly been seen as an investment asset, with physically backed ETFs, similar to gold and silver. Investment demand fell by 30% in 2011

FIG 2.9 **Platinum consumption by sector, 2011**

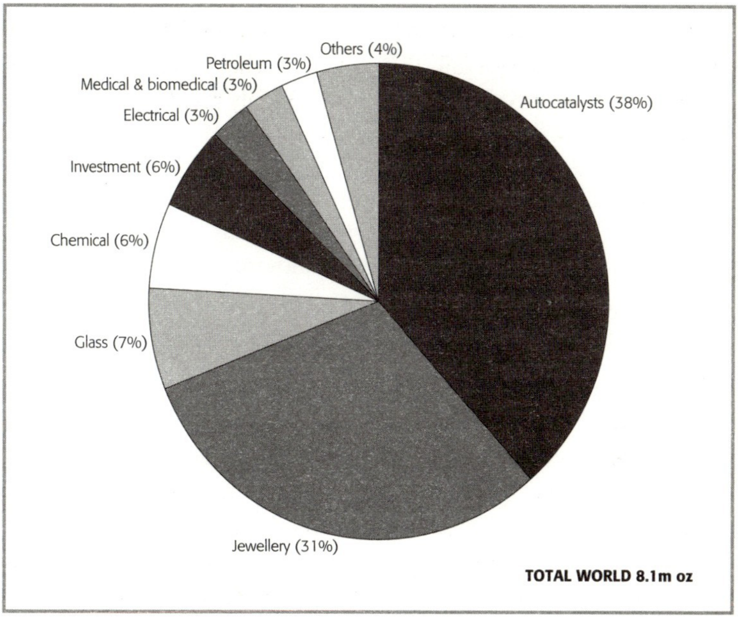

- Autocatalysts (38%)
- Jewellery (31%)
- Glass (7%)
- Chemical (6%)
- Investment (6%)
- Electrical (3%)
- Medical & biomedical (3%)
- Petroleum (3%)
- Others (4%)

**TOTAL WORLD 8.1m oz**

**Source:** Johnson Matthey

compared with 2010, but remained positive at 460,000 ounces. Platinum jewellery demand is price sensitive, and in 2011 there was a surge in Chinese buying as prices fell towards the end of the year.

## Production

Platinum supply grew by 7% year on year in 2011 to 6.48m ounces (see Table 2.15), boosted by some stock releases in South Africa and a 12% increase in scrap supply (or recycling). South Africa dominates production, accounting for approximately 75% of annual output of platinum, with 90% of that being sourced in the Western Bushveld region. As with gold, South Africa's share of production is starting to slip as a result of uncertain and expensive power supplies, declining ore grades and rising costs, notably wages. In recent years, labour disputes have hampered output, and in 2011 South African mine output of platinum fell by 3%. A further more marked fall is estimated in 2012 as strikes in August and September of that year will have led to lower annual production. Zimbabwe, however, increased platinum output by 21% year on year in 2011 as the new Unki mine became operational, and the country accounted for 6% of total supply in that year, compared with 3% in 2010. Russia, with its large nickel mines, is the second largest platinum producer, but the industry is beginning to suffer from ageing mines and lower ore grades.

Leading platinum mining companies are Anglo American Platinum and Impala Platinum, with mines mainly in South Africa.

TABLE 2.15 **Leading platinum-producing countries**

|  | 2002 | | 2011 | |
| --- | --- | --- | --- | --- |
|  | '000 oz | % of total | '000 oz | % of total |
| South Africa | 4,450 | 74.5 | 4,855 | 74.9 |
| Russia | 980 | 16.4 | 835 | 12.9 |
| North America | 390 | 6.5 | 350 | 5.4 |
| Zimbabwe | 0 | 0.0 | 340 | 5.2 |
| Others | 150 | 2.5 | 100 | 1.5 |
| Total | 5,970 | | 6,480 | |

**Source:** Johnson Matthey

## The platinum market

Platinum is traded on the New York Mercantile Exchange (NYMEX) and the London Platinum and Palladium Market; NYMEX also has platinum futures contracts. Like the other precious metals, platinum bars and coins can be bought by investors, and in early 2007 a physically backed platinum ETF was launched in Europe, listed on the London Stock Exchange. In 2009, a platinum ETF, linked to the existing London-based ETF, was launched on the Tokyo Stock Exchange. The response in Japan was fairly muted, but the launch of a platinum ETF on the New York Stock Exchange in January 2010 led to a surge of buying interest. Two more US-based platinum ETFs were launched in 2011.

FIG 2.10 **Gold and platinum prices**

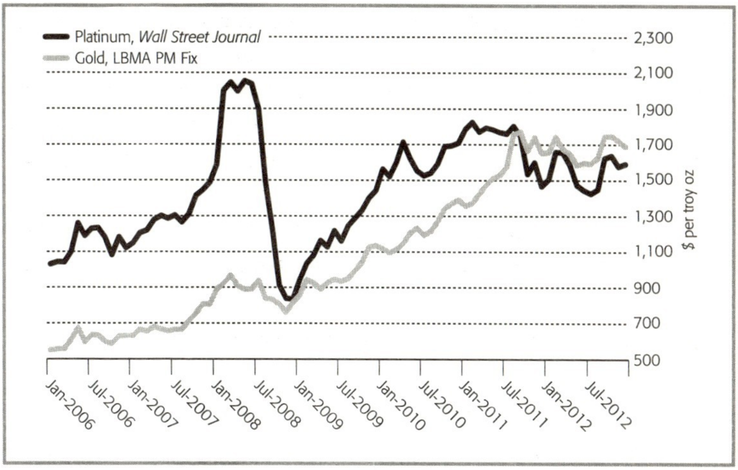

— Platinum, *Wall Street Journal*
— Gold, LBMA PM Fix

*$ per troy oz*

**Sources:** LBMA; *Wall Street Journal*

## Price trends

Platinum prices rose strongly throughout the 2000s, supported by strong physical demand in the industrial sector (as the global economy boomed) and by a surge in investor interest (boosted by new products encouraging investment). The price rose from just $433 per tonne at the beginning of 2000 to a peak of over $2,100/tonne in June 2008, before the onset of the global financial crisis led to a spectacular collapse (see Figure 2.10). Platinum was trading at just below $750/tonne by late October 2008. However, it then started to rise swiftly, to over $1,000/tonne in January 2009, and performed strongly thereafter. (The small size of the market – at least compared with gold – makes it particularly vulnerable to a loss of investor confidence or liquidity.)

While average prices were 7% higher in 2011 than in 2010, the platinum price started to fall sharply from August/September 2011 because of worries about financial stability in the euro zone and global growth more generally, falling to a two-year low of $1,364/tonne by the end of the year. From a fundamental perspective, the market was in surplus in 2011 with strong supply growth and only sluggish demand growth. In 2012 prices continued to weaken amid concerns about the outlook for the American and EU economies and mounting evidence of slower economic growth in some of the large developing countries, suggesting that demand from the automotive sector would be weak. Annual average prices fell by 9.9% in 2012.

The platinum price is considered in terms of its relationship with gold. In August 2011, the platinum:gold price ratio dropped below 1, having reached nearly 2 in the bull market in early 2008. Platinum prices remained weak compared with gold in 2012 and the ratio fell to lows not seen since the early 1990s.

## The future

- Like all the precious metals, platinum has become more vulnerable to investor sentiment in recent years, as investors account for an increasing amount of the consumption of the physical metal. This will lead to heightened price volatility.
- Volatile prices create considerable uncertainty for mining companies, given that it takes years to develop a mine and capital costs are typically high.
- The concentration of mining in a few countries makes the supply of the metal vulnerable to disruption.
- Developments in the automotive industry are crucial for the future of platinum. With palladium increasingly replacing platinum in some lighter diesel-fuelled cars in Europe, there is a possibility that platinum will find itself sidelined in its main market.

# PALLADIUM

Palladium is a rare steely white-coloured metal. It has many of the same properties as the other precious metals: it is ductile and malleable, has good conductivity, has a low melting point and is recyclable. It is also non-corrosive. However, palladium is the softest of the precious metals making it particularly suitable for fine decorative work. It is typically mined in "placer" deposits alongside platinum and other precious metals, including gold. It can also be a by-product of nickel mining.

## Consumption and uses

Its primary use, accounting for 71% of consumption in 2011 (see Table 2.16), is in autocatalysts in petrol-fuelled cars, but it is also used in the chemical industry, dentistry, electrical components and increasingly in jewellery. It is also bought and sold for investment purposes.

TABLE 2.16 **Palladium consumption by sector, 2011**

|  | '000 oz | % of total |
| --- | --- | --- |
| Autocatalysts | 6,030 | 71.4 |
| Electrical | 1,380 | 16.3 |
| Dental | 550 | 6.5 |
| Jewellery | 505 | 6.0 |
| Chemicals | 445 | 5.3 |
| Investment | −565 | −6.7 |
| Other | 105 | 1.2 |
| Total | 8,450 |  |

**Source:** Johnson Matthey

Annual growth in palladium consumption averaged 8.7% between 2003 and 2010, but fell by 13% in 2011 primarily because of a contraction in investment demand. Industrial use of palladium rose strongly, despite the difficulties faced by the automobile industry because of weak economic growth and austerity in Europe, weakening emerging-market currencies against the dollar, and the disruption to supply chains caused by the March 2011 earthquake and tsunami in Japan, and the serious flooding in Thailand later in the year. Furthermore, new restrictions (including tighter credit conditions) in China cut growth in car sales to 5% in 2011, compared with 33% in 2010.

## Production

Palladium reserves have been found in South Africa, Russia and North America. Palladium supply was largely unchanged in 2011. Russia is the largest supplier (including stock releases), accounting for 47% of total supply in 2011 at around 3.48m oz, and South Africa is the second largest, producing 2.56m oz in 2011 (see Table 2.17). North America is an important (and increasing) source of supply, and Zimbabwe has started to increase its production of the metal. However, annual supply data are sometimes distorted by Russia's policy on strategic sales from its stockpile. Sales continued in 2011 but at a lower rate, and in recent years speculation about the depletion of Russia's stockpile has had an impact on prices. Other sources of supply in the palladium market are scrap or investor selling from physically backed ETFs.

Leading mining companies include Anglo American Platinum, Impala Platinum and Lonmin in South Africa and Norilsk Nickel in Russia. Smaller players include Stillwater Palladium in the United States and North American Palladium in Canada.

TABLE 2.17 **Leading palladium-producing countries**

|  | 2002 | | 2011 | |
| --- | --- | --- | --- | --- |
|  | '000 oz | % of total | '000 oz | % of total |
| Russia: primary production | 1,930 | 36.8 | 2,705 | 36.8 |
| Russia: stock sales | 0 | 0.0 | 775 | 10.5 |
| South Africa | 2,160 | 41.1 | 2,560 | 34.8 |
| North America | 990 | 18.9 | 900 | 12.2 |
| Zimbabwe | 0 | 0.0 | 265 | 3.6 |
| Others | 170 | 3.2 | 155 | 2.1 |
| Total | 5,250 | | 7,360 | |

## The palladium market

Palladium is traded on the New York Mercantile Exchange (NYMEX) and the London Platinum and Palladium Market. NYMEX also has palladium futures contracts and there is a palladium ETF trading on the London and New York stock exchanges. Palladium ETF holdings rose by 80% in 2010 reaching 64 tonnes, but fell by almost one-third in 2011, greatly increasing physical supply in that year. The outflow from ETFs at about 19m tonnes represented 20% of total supply in 2011.

## Price trends

At times, palladium has been more expensive than platinum – most recently in 2000 – but this relationship broke down during the 2000s as platinum prices made strong gains, largely because of increased investor demand. Platinum and palladium prices typically move in the same direction and more like those of industrial metals than the other precious metals, gold and silver. However, they moved in opposing directions during the early 2000s, with palladium prices falling from a peak of over $1,000 per troy oz in early 2001 to around $265/troy oz in April 2003. After this, palladium prices started to recover, rising in tandem with other industrial raw material and platinum prices. Palladium prices peaked at a monthly average of $590/troy oz in March 2008, before falling sharply again (see Figure 2.11). The subsequent recovery, which outstripped that in platinum prices, reflected palladium's use in petrol cars as well as an increasing awareness of its investment value.

Palladium prices were high in early 2011, which encouraged some selling from ETFs later in the year (though investors could also have been selling to cover losses elsewhere in their portfolios). There was also selling of palladium bars and coins in 2011. For much of 2012, palladium prices were weak before regaining some ground as the United States announced additional quantitative easing and the European Central Bank appeared to be taking a more proactive stance in sorting out the euro zone's woes. However, the annual average price still fell by 10.8% in 2012.

FIG 2.11 **Palladium and platinum prices**

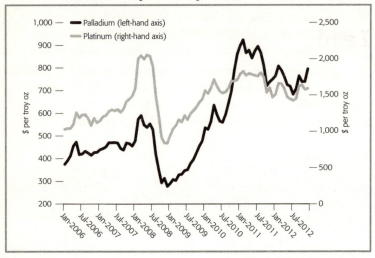

**Sources:** Haver Analytics; *Wall Street Journal*

## The future

- Russian stockpiles are now believed to be nearing depletion, which could mean that supply starts to weaken after 2012.
- In the EU, there is some substitution of platinum with palladium in lighter diesel vehicles.
- Stricter automobile-emission standards in China – which came into effect in mid-2011 – should support consumption in the medium term.

# Lead

**LEAD IS A BLUE-WHITE METAL** but discolours to grey on exposure to air. It is one of the scarcer non-ferrous metals in the Earth's crust. Lead has useful properties; in particular, it is highly resistant to corrosion and is malleable, melting and joining easily. Its high density makes it a valuable insulating material for electrical and radiation screening and soundproofing, and its electrochemical properties make it a useful component in storage batteries in motor vehicles and for some back-up power supplies.

However, an increasing awareness of the toxicity of lead has led to changes in the pattern of lead consumption. The first and most high-profile change took place in the 1980s, when lead was progressively removed from automotive fuels. For the same reason there has also been a decline in the use of lead in paints, solders and ammunition.

## Extraction, processes and reserves

Lead is usually found in ore form with silver, zinc and/or copper and is mined in conjunction with these metals. Only 5% of mined output is from lead-only mines. Mines are now geographically concentrated in China, Australia and the Americas but globally deposits are widespread, which explains why lead has been in use for thousands of years. It is easy to recover by reduction from sulphide or oxide ores. Today, much refined lead comes from secondary sources, particularly recycling.

Lead is plentiful compared with some other metals and hydrocarbons. The US Geological Survey (USGS) estimates known reserves at 85,000 tonnes (see Figure 2.12), but notes that, in recent

FIG 2.12 **Lead reserves, 2011**

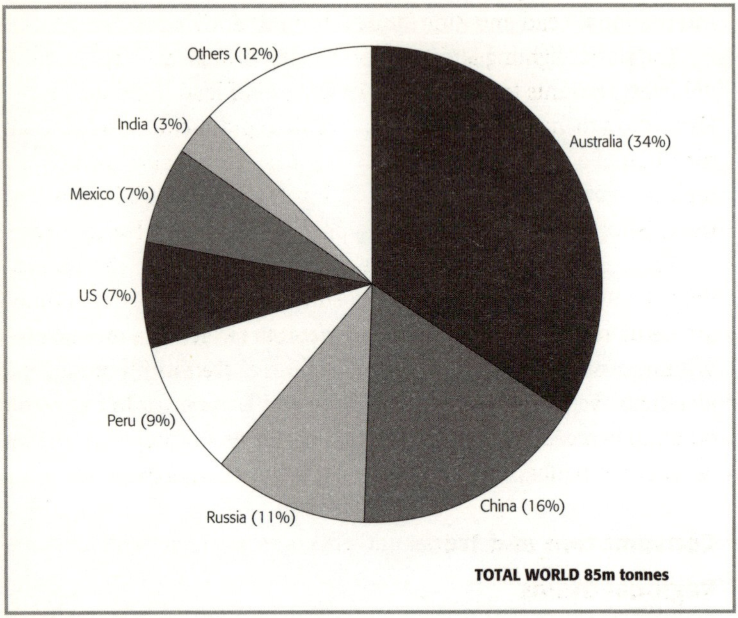

- Australia (34%)
- China (16%)
- Russia (11%)
- Peru (9%)
- US (7%)
- Mexico (7%)
- India (3%)
- Others (12%)

**TOTAL WORLD 85m tonnes**

**Source:** US Geological Survey

years, considerable deposits of lead have been found in association with silver, copper and zinc reserves. Identifiable reserves are estimated by the USGS at 1.5 billion tonnes.

## Products and uses

The metal has a broad range of industrial uses, especially in transport, construction and electrical goods. In applications such as cable sheathing, pipe and sheet it is used as unalloyed metal. It is also used in alloyed form (most importantly in lead battery grids) and in various lead-based chemical compounds such as lead oxide paste in batteries and pigments.

However, lead has faced competition from plastics and aluminium in applications such as cable sheathing, pipe and sheet. Substitution in these markets has been offset by the growth of the use of lead in battery manufacture, which now accounts for around 80% of total consumption compared with about 30% in the 1960s, according to the International Lead and Zinc Study Group (ILZSG).

The starter-lighting-ignition (SLI) battery, primarily for use in motor vehicles, accounts for about 80% of the use of lead in power storage. Here, growth has been driven by vehicle production and demand for original-equipment (OE) batteries. An even larger end-use is in replacement batteries. Here, demand will grow alongside growth in the existing stock of vehicles (as opposed to new-vehicle production).

There is still no technically or commercially viable alternative to the SLI battery for mass-produced vehicles, and ever greater demands are being made of batteries by the increase in electrical applications within cars and by hybrid vehicles. The increasing popularity of electric bicycles, particularly in China, has been a further source of demand in recent years. However, new battery technologies are likely to lengthen battery life, ultimately constraining lead demand.

## Consumption and trade
### Regional trends

There has been a shift eastwards in consumption of lead. The combined market share of the United States and the EU stood at just 30% in 2011 compared with 55% as recently as 2001 (see Table 2.18). Meanwhile, Asia's share of total consumption rose from 32% in 2001 to 61% in 2011.

China has dominated growth in lead consumption over the past ten years, fuelled by the growth in domestic vehicle production. It accounted for 44% of total consumption in 2011 compared with just 11% in 2001. Automotive production grew at an average annual rate of 24% between 2000 and 2010, and in 2009 (admittedly a year of depressed American economic growth) China displaced the United States as the world's largest vehicle producer. The other factor driving demand in China has been the relocation of battery manufacture to China from higher-cost countries.

In 2011 the Chinese government cracked down on heavily polluting battery-production plants, which could have significantly reduced lead consumption in that year. However, the permanent closures, which affected the smallest and oldest plants, merely freed up raw materials to allow unaffected plants (larger, modern facilities) to build up stocks or operate at higher capacity utilisation rates. Overall – despite the scale of the disruption – lead consumption still grew by 9.9% year on year in 2011. Consumption of lead remained strong in 2012, despite slower economic growth; preliminary data suggest that lead-acid battery production grew by over 25% in that year.

TABLE 2.18 **Leading lead-consuming[a] countries**

|  | 2001 | | 2011 | |
| --- | --- | --- | --- | --- |
|  | '000 tonnes | % of total | '000 tonnes | % of total |
| China | 700 | 10.8 | 4,632 | 44.1 |
| US | 1,695 | 26.1 | 1,601 | 15.3 |
| EU | 1,885 | 29.0 | 1,547 | 14.7 |
| India | 127 | 2.0 | 455 | 4.3 |
| South Korea | 314 | 4.8 | 409 | 3.9 |
| Japan | 284 | 4.4 | 234 | 2.2 |
| Mexico | 253 | 3.9 | 227 | 2.2 |
| Taiwan | 167 | 2.6 | 111 | 1.1 |
| Others | 1,070 | 16.5 | 1,278 | 12.2 |
| Total | 6,495 | | 10,494 | |

a Consumption of primary and secondary metal, excluding remelt.
**Sources:** International Lead and Zinc Study Group; World Bureau of Metal Statistics

## Trade

China's emergence as the leading source of mine supply as well as refined lead output has reduced the trade in lead concentrate, as has the large reduction in smelting capacity in Europe. Less than 20% (17% in 2011) of the refined lead produced is traded internationally – a smaller proportion than that of other major metals, largely because of the importance of the secondary lead industry, which tends to serve local markets. There is important intra-European trade in refined lead (and also in lead concentrate) and significant two-way trade in

North America. The most important trade flow is with China. Until recently China was the largest exporter of refined lead. However, the combination of low growth in production in 2007 and 2008 (owing to a shortage of lead concentrate) and strong domestic demand has led to a decline in Chinese refined exports to just 10,000 tonnes in 2011 compared with 538,000 tonnes in 2006. Australia is now the largest exporter (see Table 2.19).

TABLE 2.19 **Leading exporters and importers, 2011**

| | Exports | | | Imports | |
| --- | --- | --- | --- | --- | --- |
| | '000 tonnes | % of total | | '000 tonnes | % of total |
| Australia | 250.2 | 14.3 | US | 298.0 | 17.4 |
| Germany | 169.4 | 9.7 | South Korea | 140.2 | 8.2 |
| Kazakhstan | 138.4 | 7.9 | Germany | 112.6 | 6.6 |
| South Korea | 136.6 | 7.8 | Spain | 108.0 | 6.3 |
| Belgium | 130.6 | 7.5 | Italy | 97.9 | 5.7 |

**Source:** World Bureau of Metal Statistics

## Production and stocks

### Mine production

Mine production of lead is highly concentrated. In 2011 just five countries – China, Peru, Mexico, the United States and Australia – accounted for 80% of total output, with China alone accounting for 50% (see Table 2.20). Mine output has been rising over the past ten years but all the growth has been in China; in other parts of the world it has been falling. In 2010 and 2011 global mine output was up by 10% and 10.6% respectively, whereas in China output was up by 36% and 27% in the same two years. Among the second-tier lead mining countries, Mexico achieved growth of 14.3% in 2011 and India and Russia recorded strong gains, but output fell in the United States, Peru and Australia.

At the primary (mining) stage, lead and zinc are generally produced by the same companies, although new mines tend to have much higher zinc grades relative to those of lead. Many of the new zinc mines are based on copper-zinc rather than the traditional lead-zinc-silver deposits. The only large primary lead mine to be developed in the 2000s was the 100,000 tonnes per year (t/y) Magellan mine in Western Australia, but this has been beset by environmental concerns and was closed in 2011 pending a resolution of these issues.

TABLE 2.20 **Lead mine production**

|  | 1997 | | 2004 | | 2011 | |
| --- | --- | --- | --- | --- | --- | --- |
|  | '000 tonnes | % of total | '000 tonnes | % of total | '000 tonnes | % of total |
| China | 712 | 23.3 | 997 | 31.7 | 2,358 | 50.2 |
| Australia | 486 | 15.9 | 642 | 20.4 | 621 | 13.2 |
| Europe | 257 | 8.4 | 228 | 7.2 | 358 | 7.6 |
| US | 459 | 15.0 | 439 | 13.9 | 348 | 7.4 |
| Peru | 262 | 8.6 | 306 | 9.7 | 230 | 4.9 |
| Mexico | 174 | 5.7 | 118 | 3.7 | 209 | 4.5 |
| Canada | 186 | 6.1 | 77 | 2.4 | 59 | 1.3 |
| Others | 516 | 16.9 | 342 | 10.8 | 516 | 11.0 |
| Total | 3,051 | | 3,138 | | 4,700 | |

**Source:** International Lead and Zinc Study Group

Mining is widely integrated with smelting in the United States and Australia. However, there is a large custom smelting industry in Europe, Japan and South Korea, and more recently China, based mainly on imported lead concentrate (particularly from Australia, Canada and Latin America) or secondary production.

## Refined production and smelting capacity

Refined lead production has also been growing strongly in the past decade with the exception of 2009, when output stagnated. Production grew by 8% in 2011, led by a 10.7% increase in China's output (see Table 2.21). Based on ILZSG data, of the 780,000 t/y of new lead smelting capacity that was opened in 2011, 550,000 tonnes was located in China and included new operations in Inner Mongolia, Yunnan, Jiangxi, Guangdong, Heilongjiang and Hunan. Preliminary data suggest a further 380,000 tonnes of capacity was added in 2012. The only other notable additions to capacity in 2011 were in India and Mexico; and in 2012 the La Oroya primary smelting complex with capacity of 114,000 t/y reopened in Peru.

In recent years China has mounted a campaign to close and consolidate the lead refining industry, partly in an effort to reduce levels of pollution and increase efficiency. In general, new capacity in China, built to modern specifications and capable of operating at high environmental standards, is more than replacing outdated capacity that the government is targeting for closure.

Outside China, the top lead-producing companies are Xstrata (Switzerland), BHP Billiton (Australia), KGHM Polska Miedz (Poland), Teck Cominco (Canada) and Volcan Compañía Minera (Peru).

TABLE 2.21 **Leading refined lead-producing countries**[a]

|  | 2001 | | 2011 | |
| --- | --- | --- | --- | --- |
|  | '000 tonnes | % of total | '000 tonnes | % of total |
| China | 1,195 | 18.2 | 4,648 | 43.7 |
| EU | 1,682 | 25.6 | 1,628 | 15.3 |
| US | 1,376 | 20.9 | 1,317 | 12.4 |
| Japan | 302 | 4.6 | 249 | 2.3 |
| South Korea | 211 | 3.2 | 421 | 4.0 |
| Australia | 280 | 4.3 | 226 | 2.1 |
| Canada | 231 | 3.5 | 282 | 2.6 |
| Mexico | 234 | 3.6 | 348 | 3.3 |
| Others | 1,065 | 16.2 | 1,528 | 14.4 |
| Total | 6,576 | | 10,647 | |

a Primary and secondary refined output, excluding remelt.
**Source:** International Lead and Zinc Study Group

Recycling (primarily of vehicle batteries) now makes a big contribution to production, particularly in countries where no lead is mined; in 2011 secondary production accounted for just over 50% of total refined lead production. Another reason for the high level of secondary production in western Europe and the United States is the closure of primary smelting operations for economic and environmental reasons.

Outside the United States, secondary producers are more numerous, smaller and more geographically dispersed than primary producers; they serve local markets; and they are closer to end-users (the main source of scrap). Many recycling plants have a capacity of less than 25,000 t/y. Secondary production is increasing in China and the Commonwealth of Independent States but is still at a lower level (as a share of total refined output) than in Western economies. In 2011, China's secondary production accounted for 29% of total refined production, compared with 91% in the United States. The share of output accounted for by secondary production fell in China in 2012 owing to rapid growth in the country's mine supply.

## The lead market

Trade in lead concentrate is based on treatment charges, an arrangement for sharing the price of lead between miners and smelters. Concentrates are traded mainly on the basis of annual contracts, typically set in the first quarter of the year. The outcome of these negotiations reflects the balance between mine supply of concentrates and smelter demand, a low treatment charge favouring mining companies and a high charge benefiting smelters. The contracts are set on a basis price plus adjustments that take into account changes in London Metal Exchange (LME) lead prices.

As the only futures market for lead, the LME acts as the basis for prices for refined and intermediate products. There are LME warehouses for lead throughout Europe, in Singapore, Malaysia and the UAE, and at seven locations in the United States.

The LME contract specifies refined lead of minimum 99.97% purity for good delivery. However, LME quality specifications are out of line with industry requirements. Battery-makers, in particular, increasingly require metal of 99.985% purity or higher for the manufacture of high-quality alloy grids. Producer list prices at a substantial premium to the LME price in western Europe and Asia partly reflect this quality difference.

A North American producer price (NAPP, as published by *Metals Week*) is quoted for common-grade lead (99.97% purity), with premiums for better-quality material. The price is based on the average list prices of a number of American and Canadian producers, weighted by production in the previous year. Although the producer price is normally at a substantial premium to the LME price, the two markets often move in parallel, primarily because of the influence of secondary producers, many of which now base their quotations on the LME price.

## Price trends

Lead prices soared between 2003 and 2007, growing at an annual average rate of 45% a year. The reason was that mine supply was struggling (and failing) to keep pace with the emergence of China as a burgeoning new source of demand, with the result that global stocks were low. A lack of investment in capacity earlier in the decade created a shortage of lead concentrate. The tightness of the physical market reflected in prices was exacerbated by investors piling into futures markets in anticipation of further price rises. Global liquidity was high and the dollar was weak, enhancing the attractiveness of commodity investments.

Prices subsequently collapsed in late 2008 with the global economic slowdown when liquidity dried up immeasurably. The supply response was swift, with both mine output and refined output curtailed in 2009. This, coupled with a quick recovery in China's economic growth as a result of a massive government stimulus, led to a recovery in lead prices. Lead prices are also arguably more resilient during economic downturns because of the large share of consumption accounted for by replacement batteries. Even if auto production and sales slow sharply, consumers will still have to replace batteries in their vehicles.

Strong production growth in 2010 and 2011 restored stocks to

FIG 2.13 **Lead stocks and prices**

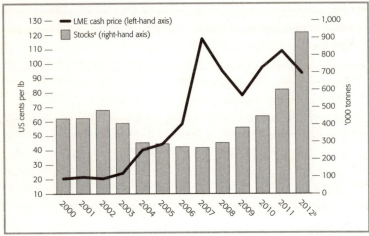

a Total reported commercial (LME, producer, consumer, merchant) stocks; end-period.
b EIU estimates.
**Sources:** London Metal Exchange; World Bureau of Metal Statistics

more than comfortable levels and in late 2011, in tandem with other base-metal markets, lead prices started to slip again (see Figure 2.13).

One feature of the lead market that is more powerful than in other metal markets is the ability of trends in the secondary market to influence prices. Lower lead prices tend to depress the supply of secondary lead (scrap), which in turn leads to reduced supply of total refined lead and thus leads to a renewed tightening of the market balance. The reverse is true when lead prices are high. In this way the secondary market acts as a kind of a pressure valve for the wider market.

## The future

- There is scope for significant increases in global vehicle numbers, as the vehicles per head figure is low in most emerging economies. China, for example, has around one car for every 150 citizens, compared with one for every 1.3 citizens in the United States and 1.8 citizens in the EU and Japan. However, it appears that lead-acid batteries perform poorly in hybrid and all-electric cars, with producers preferring to use other batteries, notably lithium. At the moment, these eco-friendly vehicles are too expensive to take a large market share, but prices could fall and the technology could improve in the medium term.

- Steps to reduce pollution and energy intensity in China could have negative consequences for the country's mining and smelting industries, at least in terms of increasing costs. Indeed, concerns about the negative impact of lead production more generally could be a constraint on supply in future years.
- Prices are likely to be more volatile, despite lead's recession-proof qualities. Automobile sales in developing countries (where all the growth in consumption will be) can be expected to fluctuate more markedly in tandem with the economic cycle, unlike sales in the more mature, largely saturated markets in the Western world.

# Nickel

NICKEL IS A SILVERY-WHITE METAL, which can be given a high polish and is the fifth most common element in the Earth's crust. It is tough but workable, and resistant to corrosion. These characteristics determine its predominant use as the main alloying metal with chrome in austenitic (iron-based) stainless steels and other special steels or superalloys.

## Extraction, processes and reserves

Nickel can be extracted from its ores by smelting (heating in a blast furnace), which produces ferronickel, which can be used directly by steelmakers. It can also be extracted with electrolysis (an electric current breaks down the ore into its constituents). A small proportion of nickel supply is derived from ores by acid leaching.

As nickel prices soared during 2006-07, Chinese producers of stainless steel developed a lower-cost input called nickel pig iron using low-grade (and cheaper) nickel ores. Iron-making blast furnaces were used to combine and smelt the low-grade nickel concentrates with iron and chrome ores. China's nickel pig iron capacity has expanded rapidly and stood at 250,000-300,000 tonnes/year (t/y) in 2011, and there are plans to expand capacity to 500,000 t/y. The raw materials are cheap, but this is not inherently a low-cost production route and the stainless steel is of low quality. As nickel prices fell, use of nickel pig iron also fell. China is now trying to move up the value-added chain in steel production and its new stainless steel capacity sometimes uses a higher-quality nickel pig iron when nickel prices are high.

Known reserves of nickel are plentiful and geographically

FIG 2.14 **Nickel reserves, 2011**

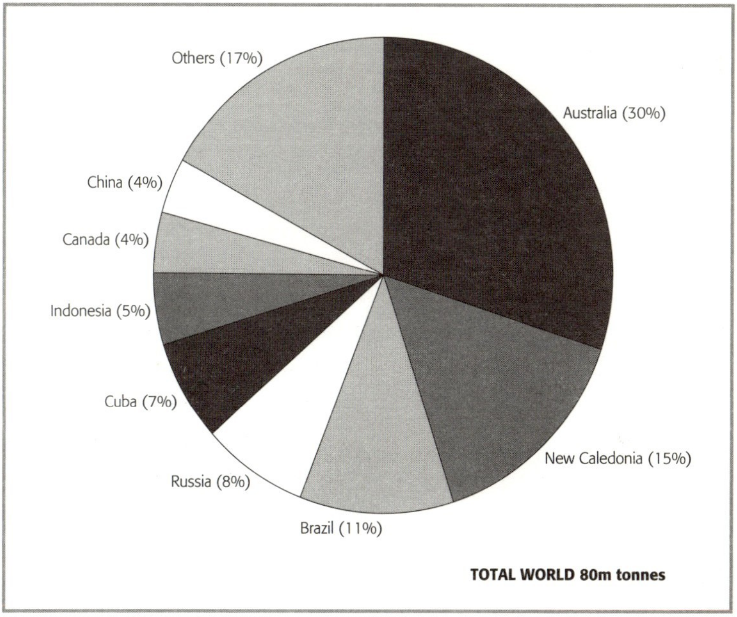

- Australia (30%)
- Others (17%)
- China (4%)
- Canada (4%)
- Indonesia (5%)
- Cuba (7%)
- Russia (8%)
- Brazil (11%)
- New Caledonia (15%)

**TOTAL WORLD 80m tonnes**

**Source:** US Geological Survey

well-dispersed, although Australia accounts for 30% (see Figure 2.14).

## Products and uses

The manufacture of austenitic stainless steel accounts for about two-thirds of total nickel consumption. Nickel can constitute 10% or more of austenitic steels, but the most common alloys contain 8% nickel and cheaper grades use as little as 6%. Nickel improves workability by counteracting the embrittling effect of chrome, while maintaining and enhancing corrosion resistance. Nickel is also used, in smaller quantities, to toughen tool steels and some high-strength steels that are not fully corrosion-resistant.

Nickel is also an important constituent of some special high-performance alloys, including superalloys (these are defined as quasi-steels containing less than 50% iron) and non-ferrous alloys such as cupro-nickel, examples of which are widely used in coinage. Nickel is occasionally used in pure or near-pure forms, most importantly in electroplating, providing a base for other coatings, particularly chrome, and sometimes directly as a final surface treatment. Many superalloys were originally developed for the aerospace and aero-engine industries. Nickel use in electroplating is more widespread; it has applications in many basic industrial products as well as those involving advanced technology. In the chemicals industry, nickel is used as a catalyst; and it is increasingly used in batteries for portable electronic equipment.

## Consumption and trade
### Regional trends

The most significant development of the past few years has been the rise in nickel consumption in China, owing to a rapid increase in stainless steel production capacity. The new capacity was ostensibly aimed at building the country's self-sufficiency in supplies for domestic industries, particularly manufacturers of household appliances such as washing machines and dishwashers. Many new production lines were effectively guaranteed a large share of Asian markets because they were set up in partnership with established international manufacturers, especially those based in Japan and South Korea. Rival producers in other countries, particularly the EU, have had to scale back production in the face of this China-based competition. China accounted for 43.1% of world consumption in 2011 (see Table 2.22).

The EU is the world's second largest nickel consumer, accounting for about 20% of total consumption in 2011. However, having peaked at 40% of total consumption as recently as 2002, EU consumption has been in decline, falling dramatically in the 2008–09 economic slowdown as significant amounts of steel capacity were taken offline. It has recovered since then, but moves to cut and consolidate EU steel-manufacturing capacity will limit further increases in consumption.

The United States accounted for about 8% of world consumption in 2011, but the market is interesting in that a high proportion of American nickel consumption, 10–15%, goes to producers of super-alloys and non-ferrous alloys. Only one-third of primary nickel consumed in North America (including Canada and Mexico) is by the steel industry.

TABLE 2.22 **Leading nickel-consuming countries**

|  | 1995 | | 2003 | | 2011 | |
| --- | --- | --- | --- | --- | --- | --- |
|  | '000 tonnes | % of total | '000 tonnes | % of total | '000 tonnes | % of total |
| China | 38 | 3.8 | 133 | 10.6 | 713 | 43.1 |
| EU | 374 | 37.5 | 445 | 35.7 | 335 | 20.3 |
| Japan | 196 | 19.6 | 188 | 15.1 | 174 | 10.5 |
| US | 125 | 12.5 | 117 | 9.4 | 134 | 8.1 |
| South Korea | 46 | 4.6 | 113 | 9.0 | 100 | 6.1 |
| Taiwan | 48 | 4.8 | 103 | 8.2 | 53 | 3.2 |
| Others | 170 | 17.0 | 151 | 12.1 | 145 | 8.7 |
| Total | 998 |  | 1,249 |  | 1,655 |  |

**Sources:** World Bureau of Metal Statistics; EIU

## Trade

Canada and Russia are the world's largest exporters of refined nickel (see Table 2.23). There is some refining capacity in Indonesia producing ferronickel but there are no exports of processed nickel from the Philippines. China overtook the United States in 2007 and is now the largest importer, with more than double the volume of American imports in 2011.

TABLE 2.23 **Leading exporters and importers, 2011**

|  | Exports ('000 tonnes) |  | Imports ('000 tonnes) |
| --- | --- | --- | --- |
| Russia | 304 | China | 212 |
| Canada | 128 | US | 117 |
| Norway | 93 | Germany | 68 |
| Finland | 40 | Japan | 41 |
| China | 32 | Italy | 38 |

**Source:** World Bureau of Metal Statistics

## Production and stocks
### Mine production

Russia has dominated mine production for decades, typically accounting for about 15–20% of global output. Russia's formerly state-owned Norilsk Nickel is the largest nickel producer in the world (see Table 2.24), originally because of its control of about 80% of Russian capacity, but since privatisation it has acquired capacity abroad and diversified into other metals. The main producing areas are on the Kola Peninsula (bordering Finland and northern Norway) and in Siberia; much of the capacity is north of the Arctic Circle. Annual output dropped during the chaotic conditions following the collapse of the Soviet Union but has since recovered, although it has still to reach the peaks of over 300,000 t/y reached before 1989.

The southern islands of the Philippine archipelago have substantial deposits of nickel ore and significant investment in recent years has raised output from just 29,400 tonnes in 2001 to an estimated 286,000 tonnes in 2011, catapulting the Philippines into the position of the world's largest producer in that year (see Table 2.25). However, a ban on new mining projects in 2012 coupled with the likelihood of higher royalty payments to the government have clouded prospects for further increases in output.

Indonesia is the world's third largest producer and, like the Philippines, an important exporter. Most of Indonesia's concentrate is exported, but ferronickel is produced locally by Aneka Tambang, a multi-metal producer set up originally by the government but now partly privatised. The government is actively encouraging domestic processing and, to this end, has announced a ban on nickel ore exports from 2014.

Canada is another important source of nickel minerals. It exports a high proportion of the nickel matte from its smelters and some of its mine concentrates for refining abroad, which reduces its share of refined nickel production. Production in Canada is dominated by Vale (Brazil) and Xstrata (Switzerland). Production almost halved in 2009 in the wake of the collapse in nickel prices, and although output has risen since then, labour disputes have acted as a constraint.

## TABLE 2.24 Leading nickel-producing companies, 2011

| Company | Country | Output, '000 tonnes |
|---|---|---|
| Norilsk Nickel | Russia | 286 |
| Vale SA | Brazil | 206 |
| Jinchuan Group | China | 127 |
| Xstrata | Switzerland | 106 |
| BHP Billiton | Australia | 83 |
| Sumitomo Metal Mining Co | Japan | 65 |
| Eramet | France | 54 |
| Anglo American | UK | 48 |
| Sherritt International Corp | Canada | 35 |
| Minara Resources | Australia | 30 |

Mine output in Australia expanded swiftly until it reached 200,000 tonnes in 2008, but late that year low prices forced the suspension of operations at some high-cost mines. As nickel prices recovered so did output, with a new all-time high of 212,000 tonnes

## TABLE 2.25 Nickel mine (or raw) production

|  | 1995 | | 2003 | | 2011 | |
|---|---|---|---|---|---|---|
|  | '000 tonnes | % of total | '000 tonnes | % of total | '000 tonnes | % of total |
| Philippines | 17 | 1.8 | 20 | 1.5 | 286 | 15.6 |
| Russia | 224 | 23.0 | 301 | 22.8 | 286 | 15.6 |
| Indonesia | 87 | 8.9 | 158 | 12.0 | 227 | 12.4 |
| Canada | 182 | 18.7 | 163 | 12.4 | 220 | 12.0 |
| Australia | 99 | 10.1 | 191 | 14.5 | 212 | 11.6 |
| New Caledonia | 120 | 12.3 | 112 | 8.5 | 131 | 7.1 |
| Others | 244 | 25.2 | 375 | 28.4 | 469 | 25.7 |
| Total | 973 |  | 1,320 |  | 1,831 |  |

**Sources:** International Nickel Study Group; World Bureau of Metal Statistics

recorded in 2011. BHP Billiton (Australia) is the dominant producer. New Caledonia (a department of France), to the east of Australia, had higher mine output than Australia until the 1990s. Production peaked in 1997 at 136,500 tonnes, but subsequently fell back. Since then, substantial investments, particularly by Vale at Goro and by Xstrata at Koniambo, are leading to higher output; production in 2011 was just short of the 1997 peak. During 2012, technical problems hampered output at Goro and there are concerns about the viability of the mines when nickel prices are low. Opposition from local groups delayed development of these projects and significantly raised the costs of production.

## Refining and secondary supply

China's nickel ore deposits are in geologically difficult areas but this has not deterred the country from increasing mine output and processing in a bid to reduce its stainless steelmakers' dependence on imported refined nickel. Production of nickel products (including an estimate of the nickel content of nickel-chrome pig iron) dipped sharply in 2008 but has since rebounded strongly, reaching a new all-time high of 480,000 tonnes in 2011 (or nearly 30% of global production – see Table 2.26).

Steelmakers meet a large proportion of their nickel requirements from scrap (secondary nickel), used alongside ferronickel, their preferred form of primary nickel feed. The scrap is mostly nickel-bearing steel, especially off-cuts of intermediate steel products and semi-manufactures ("new scrap").

As a substitute for primary nickel, scrap supply amplifies fluctuations in primary demand. The availability of new scrap depends on output at steelworks and throughput at fabricators in the recent past. When falling sales lead to reduced activity among fabricators, and, as a result, stainless steel output is reduced, new scrap supply (from an earlier period of high activity) is high relative to nickel demand. When, emerging from a recession, fabricating work increases and stainless steel output rises, scrap supply is low relative to demand.

The United States and the UK, which are net importers of stainless

TABLE 2.26 **Leading refined nickel-producing countries**

|  | 2001 | | 2011 | |
| --- | --- | --- | --- | --- |
|  | '000 tonnes | % of total | '000 tonnes | % of total |
| China | 50 | 4.3 | 480 | 28.9 |
| Russia | 248 | 21.5 | 260 | 15.7 |
| Japan | 151 | 13.1 | 157 | 9.4 |
| Canada | 141 | 12.2 | 142 | 8.6 |
| Australia | 128 | 11.1 | 117 | 7.1 |
| EU | 119 | 10.3 | 110 | 6.6 |
| Norway | 68 | 5.9 | 92 | 5.6 |
| Others | 250 | 21.6 | 301 | 18.1 |
| Total | 1,155 | | 1,661 | |

**Source:** World Bureau of Metal Statistics

steel semi-manufactures (such as hot-rolled coil, billet and bar), generate high tonnages of scrap, so can be expected to use a higher proportion in production. New steel producers – such as China – tend to be short of scrap. When they make large contributions to world output growth – as China has been doing – the proportion of primary nickel used in stainless steel production tends to rise.

## The nickel market

Before cash and 3-month contracts for nickel cathode were traded on the London Metal Exchange (LME) in late 1979, most nickel suppliers priced sales contracts with reference to public price quotations from Inco (a Canada-based mining company, now owned by Vale). Western nickel producers were hostile to nickel trading on the LME and initially tried to disregard LME prices in their contracts, but over time came to use it as a reference point of last resort.

Producers continue to quote prices for special types of products, and offer regular customers price formulas that smooth out the short-term price fluctuations on the LME. However, these formulas usually refer to the LME price, and the LME price has been incorporated into prices for scrap and ferronickel, neither of which is traded on the exchange. Although the price set in a particular contract may be settled without explicit reference to the LME price, there is widespread reliance on formulas linked to it to resolve price questions when parties are unable to reach agreement.

## Price trends

Nickel prices have been on a rollercoaster since 2004–05 (see Figure 2.15). The widespread use of scrap by the steel industry and the use of nickel pig iron in China (predominantly) complicate the supply/demand dynamics of the nickel market. Prices started to rise rapidly from early 2005 as consumption, led by China, surged. Speculators jumped on the strong demand bandwagon and exaggerated the price rise. It was this price bubble that inspired the adoption of nickel pig iron, which was a significant factor in the subsequent slump in price. Nickel prices were already falling before the collapse in financial markets more generally in the second half of 2008.

The financial crisis had a double impact on nickel prices. Tight liquidity constrained the operations of speculative funds and obliged some speculators to liquidate metal holdings, which drove down LME cash prices. Meanwhile the negative effect on the real economy reduced physical demand and generated a surplus that depressed prices further.

Nickel prices have recovered from the low recorded in the first quarter of 2009 and were particularly strong during 2010 owing to disruptions to supply. Labour disputes caused output to slump at Vale's Canadian operations and at BHP's Western Australian plants. Since then nickel prices have fallen back again and broadly followed sentiment in commodity markets more generally. In 2012, nickel prices were particularly weak compared with other base metals, partly because of rising stocks and the prospect of ample future supply.

## The future

- Weak prevailing prices in 2012, coupled with generally rising labour and energy costs, risk deterring future investment in

FIG 2.15 **Nickel stocks and prices**

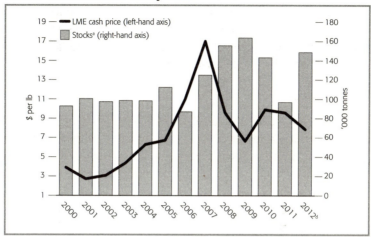

a Total reported commercial stocks; end-period. b EIU estimates.
**Sources:** London Metal Exchange; World Bureau of Metal Statistics

nickel mining. However, prices prevailing in mid-2012 were deemed to be in line with mine feasibility studies and a major collapse in investment and output is not expected unless prices fall further for a sustained period.

- Solid consumption growth is expected to be maintained despite cyclical lows and highs. Stainless steel plays an important role in urbanisation and industrialisation – trends that are expected to continue in the developing world.

- The Indonesian government has announced a ban on ore exports from 2014 and plans to develop domestic processing. This has significant implications for countries that import ore to refine locally (particularly China but also the EU). However, it is possible that the ban will not be fully implemented; Indonesia does not currently have sufficient smelter capacity to process all the ore it exports.

- The outlook for China's stainless steel industry is in the balance. Having gained a competitiveness advantage through the use of nickel pig iron (when nickel prices were high), China now faces the prospect of weak global (and lower domestic) demand growth and a loss of competitiveness, while capacity additions are still coming on stream.

# Tin

TIN IS ONE OF THE EARLIEST METALS known to man. During the Bronze Age, tin was added to copper to make bronze – the addition of tin makes the copper stronger and easier to cast. Tin has a low melting point, is malleable and resistant to corrosion, and alloys readily with other metals. It is also non-toxic and easy to recycle, attributes that have become increasingly important. Tin supply does, however, still rely on mining and the refining of tin-containing ores.

## Extraction, processes and reserves

Primary (hard rock) deposits account for about 30% of reserves and are mined by open-cast and underground methods, particularly in Peru, Brazil, Bolivia and Australia, before treatment in processing plants where it is crushed, ground and concentrated. Secondary or placer deposits, which derive originally from the weathering and erosion of primary deposits, account for about 70% of world tin reserves and occur mainly as alluvial material in river beds and valleys and on the sea floor close to shore. Most of the world's placer deposits are found in the so-called tin belt of East and South-East Asia, stretching from China through Thailand, Myanmar and Malaysia to Indonesia. The open-cast (easy access) nature of much of this mining means that there are many small-scale, often family-owned operations in South-East Asia, particularly Indonesia.

Today, tin is mined mainly in Asia and South America. Four countries – China, Indonesia, Peru and Bolivia – accounted for 85% of world output in 2011. Known reserves are concentrated in South-East Asia, South America, China and Russia (see Figure 2.16).

FIG 2.16 **Tin reserves, 2011**

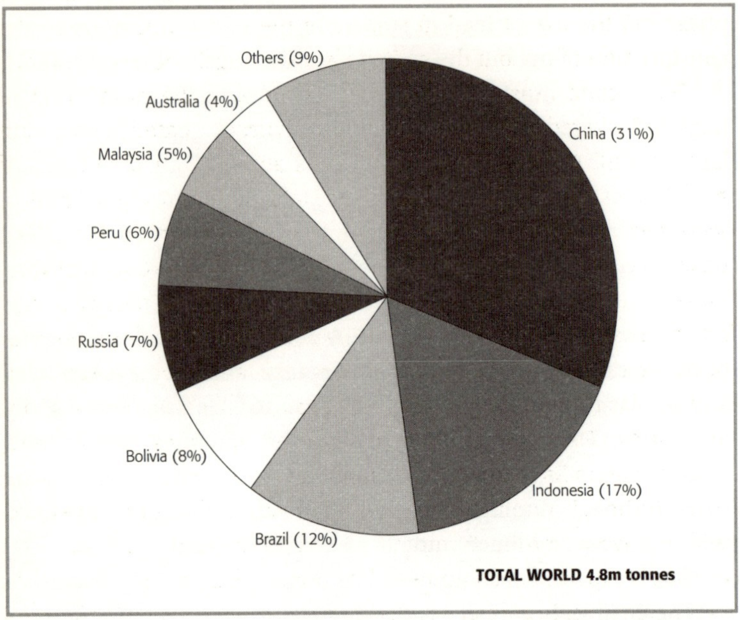

- Others (9%)
- Australia (4%)
- Malaysia (5%)
- Peru (6%)
- Russia (7%)
- Bolivia (8%)
- Brazil (12%)
- Indonesia (17%)
- China (31%)

**TOTAL WORLD 4.8m tonnes**

**Source:** US Geological Survey

To produce refined tin, tin concentrates are reduced to metal by heating to 1,250°C in a furnace. The molten tin is separated from waste products and cast into slabs. After smelting, the crude tin produced is refined to remove the remaining metallic impurities.

## Products and uses

The main use of tin is in solder alloys, which are widely used to attach components to circuit boards used in the manufacture of electronic equipment and electrical appliances, and for joining pipes in plumbing systems. The International Tin Research Institute (ITRI) estimates that solder production accounted for just under 52% of world tin consumption in 2011 (see Table 2.27); its use in the electronics industry means that solder accounts for a particularly high share of Asia's tin consumption. Solder's share of tin consumption has slipped recently perhaps because of slower growth in the electronics industry or the manufacture of goods that use less solder. A push from legislators to phase out the use of lead in solders in the mid-2000s boosted the consumption of tin, but the switch has now largely been achieved.

The second most important use of tin is in the production of tinplate (cold-reduced sheet steel electrolytically coated with a thin layer of tin). According to the ITRI, this accounts for about 16% of world tin use; a share which has been stable in recent years. Tinplate increased its share of total consumption in 2009 when the global downturn reduced demand from the electronics manufacturing industry. It is used primarily in food packaging, beverage cans and other containers, but it has been losing market share to aluminium for beverage canning, to glass for premium food and beverage products, and to plastics for a wide range of products including chilled foods and paint. Furthermore, where tinplate continues to be used, manufacturers have been experimenting with lighter gauges to cut costs. Although tinplate producers have responded to competition with innovative products and efforts to emphasise tin's recyclability, tinplate is expected to continue to lose market share to other materials.

The chemicals industry is the third most important consumer of tin and its market share has been increasing; it accounted for over 15% of total consumption in 2011. Tin is used in the manufacture of both organic and inorganic chemicals such as polyvinyl chloride (PVC), silicone resins (where it is used as a catalyst), polyurethane foam and ceramic pigments. However, some of these applications are at risk from legislation to phase out the use of heavy metals, including tin.

TABLE 2.27 **Tin end-uses, 2011**

|  | **Tonnes** | **% of total** |
| --- | --- | --- |
| Solder | 185,600 | 51.63 |
| Tinplate | 59,400 | 16.52 |
| Chemicals | 55,500 | 15.44 |
| Brass & bronze | 17,500 | 4.87 |
| Float glass | 7,200 | 2.00 |
| Others | 34,300 | 9.54 |
| Total | 359,500 | |

**Source:** International Tin Research Institute

Production of bronze ranks fourth among end-uses, accounting for around 5% of total consumption, followed by plate glass, accounting for about 2%. Potential new applications for tin include its use in rechargeable batteries, and a potentially significant application may be a nickel-tin-aluminium catalyst for the production of hydrogen for use in fuel cells, in competition with platinum.

## Consumption and trade

### Regional trends

Consumption of tin peaked at 373,000 tonnes in 2006, having grown from just 243,000 in 1997, as a result of the EU ban on lead in solder, the burgeoning growth of the predominantly Asia-based electronics industry and more general economic development in many populous developing countries, notably China. However, tin consumption started to fall in 2007 as the switch to lead-free solders slowed and high prices for tinplate led to substitution in packaging. Consumption continued to fall in 2008 and 2009 but bounced back in 2010, growing

TABLE 2.28 **Leading tin-consuming countries**

|  | 1997 | | 2005 | | 2011 | |
| --- | --- | --- | --- | --- | --- | --- |
|  | '000 tonnes | % of total | '000 tonnes | % of total | '000 tonnes | % of total |
| China | 38 | 15.7 | 116 | 33.5 | 154 | 42.8 |
| EU | 65 | 26.6 | 62 | 17.9 | 63 | 17.4 |
| US | 47 | 19.4 | 42 | 12.3 | 32 | 8.9 |
| Japan | 28 | 11.6 | 33 | 9.6 | 30 | 8.3 |
| South Korea | 12 | 4.8 | 18 | 5.2 | 14 | 4.0 |
| Taiwan | 10 | 4.0 | 14 | 3.9 | 8 | 2.3 |
| Brazil | 5 | 1.9 | 6 | 1.7 | 6 | 1.6 |
| Russia | 5 | 1.9 | 3 | 0.8 | 3 | 0.8 |
| Others | 35 | 14.2 | 52 | 15.1 | 51 | 14.0 |
| Total | 244 | | 345 | | 360 | |

**Source:** World Bureau of Metal Statistics

by 16.1% as consumers restocked and the global economy emerged from recession, but tin consumption has largely stagnated since then.

China overtook the EU as the world's largest consumer of tin in 2003 and in 2011 the country accounted for 43% of total consumption (see Table 2.28). Despite being the world's largest producer, China now needs to import as supply has failed to keep up with the growth in demand. Other Asian countries, particularly Japan, South Korea and Taiwan, are also large consumers of tin but consumption has been weakening in the past few years, perhaps reflecting companies moving operations out of their home countries to cheaper locations.

Tin consumption in Western industrialised countries is in long-term decline, owing mainly to the migration of electronics manufacturing and other tin-using industries to lower-cost countries. With the switch to lead-free solders, EU consumption rose to a peak in 2006–07 but has declined since then. Nevertheless, it remains the world's second-largest tin market, accounting for 17.4% of world consumption in 2011.

## Trade

Since overtaking China in 2002, Indonesia has been the world's leading exporter of tin metal, trading mainly through Singapore (see Table 2.29).

TABLE 2.29 **Leading exporters and importers**

|  | Exports, '000 tonnes | | | Imports, '000 tonnes | |
| --- | --- | --- | --- | --- | --- |
|  | 2001 | 2011 |  | 2001 | 2011 |
| Indonesia | 43.4 | 97.4 | US | 43.3 | 33.7 |
| Malaysia | 26.8 | 42.3 | Japan | 21.5 | 26.7 |
| Singapore | 38.9 | 37.0 | China | 2.8 | 22.2 |
| Bolivia | 11.1 | 14.6 | Germany | 24.0 | 21.1 |
| China | 45.8 | 1.2 | South Korea | 13.0 | 14.5 |
| Peru | 25.1 | 1.0 | France | 8.6 | 5.3 |

**Source:** World Bureau of Metal Statistics

Peru's exports of refined tin rose from zero in 1996 to a record of 39,400 tonnes in 2007, making it the world's second largest exporter with the United States the main market, but they have slipped every year since. After peaking at 62,400 tonnes in 2000, equal to 23% of world output that year, China's exports have steadily fallen and the country is now a net importer. The four largest import markets for refined tin are the United States, Japan, China and Germany, accounting for 36% of the total in 2011.

## Production and stocks

### Mine production

In 2011, China and Indonesia together accounted for 73% of total mine supply of tin, but output was declining in both countries, by 1.7% and 7.1% respectively, according to the WBMS (see Table 2.30). Outside Asia, the other important producing areas are in South America, particularly Peru and Bolivia and, to a lesser extent, Brazil. Tin is also mined in small quantities in Africa, principally the Democratic Republic of Congo but also Rwanda and Burundi. Until recently, much of the mining was illicit, and undertaken in often dangerous conditions. But there has been a campaign to legalise and improve oversight of the mining of so-called "conflict" minerals in Africa, and by the end of 2011 the authorities in many mining regions in eastern and central Africa had agreed to improve transparency. Australia is also a growing producer of tin with a large number of projects in the pipeline, and increasingly tin mines are being reopened or initiated in more developed countries, including the UK and Germany.

Tin mine output was growing strongly between 2003 and 2005 at an annual average rate of 11.7%, led by Indonesia, which roughly matched China's output in 2005. However, since then mine output has stagnated for a number of reasons. These include a government crackdown on unlicensed mining operations in Indonesia in 2006, an earthquake in Peru in 2007, strikes at mines in Bolivia (particularly in 2007) and labour disputes in Indonesia, where companies are also facing increasing difficulty in extracting ore and having to mine more deeply at a higher cost. Furthermore, in both Asia and South America, there are increasingly strong environmental lobbies making it more difficult to obtain licences to mine.

The business operating environment in many producing countries, including Indonesia, Peru and Bolivia, is highly uncertain for foreign mining companies, with governments often threatening to raise royalty payments, nationalise part or all of the operation or impose export taxes or quotas. Additional constraints on mining come from the labour market, such as a shortage of mining engineers and increasing union activity by mine workers.

TABLE 2.30 **Tin mine production**

|  | 1997 | | 2003 | | 2011 | |
| --- | --- | --- | --- | --- | --- | --- |
|  | '000 tonnes | % of total | '000 tonnes | % of total | '000 tonnes | % of total |
| China | 68 | 30.5 | 102 | 40.0 | 127 | 42.4 |
| Indonesia | 55 | 24.9 | 64 | 25.1 | 78 | 25.9 |
| Peru | 28 | 12.7 | 40 | 15.8 | 29 | 9.7 |
| Bolivia | 13 | 5.8 | 16 | 6.4 | 20 | 6.8 |
| Brazil | 19 | 8.6 | 12 | 4.8 | 10 | 3.2 |
| Others | 38 | 17.4 | 20 | 7.9 | 37 | 12.0 |
| Total | 221 | | 255 | | 301 | |

**Sources:** World Bureau of Metal Statistics; International Tin Research Institute

## Refining and secondary supply

As an industry, tin smelting is much more concentrated than mining. The world's four largest smelting groups, with outputs exceeding 30,000 tonnes per year (t/y), accounted for an estimated 47% of total production of refined metal in 2011. China is the world's leading producer of refined tin, accounting for 45.5% of world output in 2011 (see Table 2.31). Most of the smelters are based in the provinces of Hunan and Guangxi, where tin is mined, and many operate on a very small scale. Yunnan Tin, based in Hunan province, is China's (and the world's) largest producer with output of 56,174 tonnes in 2011 (see Table 2.32). The ITRI estimates that secondary tin accounted for 30%

of China's total refined tin production of 155,000 tonnes in 2010, with Guangdong by far the most important province for recycling.

Ranking second to China, Indonesia has more than doubled its refined tin production since the early 1990s. State-controlled PT Timah is the country's largest producer, with about 300 land-based gravel-pump mining units operated by private subcontractors and around 20 offshore dredges. PT Koba, a joint venture between Malaysia Smelting Corporation (MSC, 75%) and PT Timah (25%), was Indonesia's second largest producer until 2012 when operations halted largely because of falling profitability as tin prices fell. About 30 small-scale independent smelters have also set up operations in recent years, encouraged by higher tin prices and the availability of tin concentrates, with a combined capacity of about 60,000 t/y, much of it in the form of crude tin for further refining.

Malaysia and Thailand are important producers of refined tin, but with refining capacity far in excess of local mining capabilities, both MSC and Thaisarco depend on imported concentrates, primarily from Indonesia.

Peru ranks third as a producer of refined tin. Starting from less than 1,000 tonnes in 1996, Minsur, the country's sole producer, increased output to a record of 42,100 tonnes in 2005, but it has slipped since then, reflecting problems with mine output.

The ITRI estimates that the recycling input rate of tin is just under 32%.

## The tin market

The London Metal Exchange (LME) is the focal point for tin prices; trading of its tin futures contract represents a global reference price. Tin producers and their customers commonly agree business based on the LME price. Most (over 95%) of the LME's tin stocks are held in Singapore and Malaysia.

After peaking in 2009, as demand slumped, tin stocks fell throughout 2010–12 with the market in deficit and Indonesian output falling as prices dropped. Furthermore, stocks could potentially have been further drawn down were it not for problems in accessing them, owing to logistical delays at the warehouses.

TABLE 2.31 **Leading refined tin-producing countries**

|  | 1997 | | 2003 | | 2011 | |
| --- | --- | --- | --- | --- | --- | --- |
|  | '000 tonnes | % of total | '000 tonnes | % of total | '000 tonnes | % of total |
| China | 68 | 28.4 | 98 | 35.8 | 160 | 45.5 |
| Indonesia | 53 | 22.1 | 63 | 22.8 | 55 | 15.7 |
| South America[a] | 42 | 17.5 | 59 | 21.6 | 52 | 14.8 |
| Malaysia | 38 | 16.1 | 18 | 6.7 | 40 | 11.4 |
| Others | 38 | 15.8 | 36 | 13.2 | 44 | 12.5 |
| Total | 238 | | 274 | | 352 | |

a Bolivia, Brazil, Peru and Mexico.
**Source:** World Bureau of Metal Statistics

TABLE 2.32 **Leading tin-producing companies, 2011**

| Company | Country | Output, tonnes |
| --- | --- | --- |
| Yunnan Tin | China | 56,174 |
| Malaysia Smelting Corporation | Malaysia | 40,267 |
| PT Timah | Indonesia | 38,142 |
| Minsur | Peru | 30,205 |
| Thaisarco | Thailand | 23,864 |
| Yunnan Chengfeng | China | 15,430 |
| Guangxi China Tin | China | 15,375 |
| EM Vinto | Bolivia | 10,960 |
| Metallo-Chimique | Belgium | 10,007 |
| Gejiu ZiLi | China | 8,600 |

**Source:** CRU Group

The Kuala Lumpur Tin Market (KLTM) is an important trading forum and in early 2012 Indonesia launched its own tin reference price on the Indonesia stock exchange – but it is too early to say whether this will become an internationally recognised benchmark price.

FIG 2.17 **Tin stocks and prices**

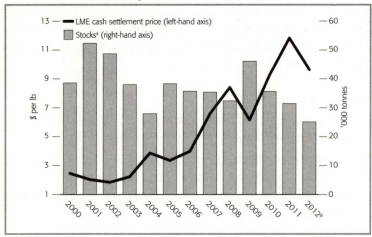

a Total reported commercial closing stocks.  b EIU estimates.
**Sources:** London Metal Exchange; World Bureau of Metal Statistics

## Price trends

The smallest (in volume terms) of the non-ferrous metals markets, the tin market is thinly traded, particularly when compared to the markets for copper and oil, and this adds to price volatility. In 1985, after a period of unsuccessful price management, the International Tin Agreement (a buffer-stock arrangement supported by export controls in producing countries) collapsed, resulting in the release of huge amounts of tin on the market and a consequent halving of the price. After a brief rally in the late 1980s, tin traded within a range of $5,200–6,200 per tonne ($2.36–2.81 per lb) throughout the 1990s. In the early 2000s, the price was constrained by increasing supply from Indonesia before embarking on a meteoric rise as a result of strong growth in demand, supply problems and the general bull run in commodity prices.

The global economic slowdown led to a rapid fall in prices, but they subsequently bounced back (see Figure 2.17). However, in August and September 2011 investors, anxious about the global economic outlook, sold commodities, and tin prices fell particularly sharply. In September 2011, 25 of Indonesia's registered tin exporters imposed an embargo on exports in response to the weakness in prices. However, the move had little impact on the market and exports resumed in December as producers faced insolvency. Prices were weak for much of 2012, with the annual average price falling by 19%, but the low stock position offered some support.

## The future

- Low stocks and the difficulties with mine supply suggest tin prices could rise strongly if consumption growth picks up.
- China's demand should rise strongly as its electronics industry is aiming to move up the value-added chain. Consumption of processed food is also rising strongly in China, requiring more tinplate packaging.
- The high concentration of tin mining makes the market vulnerable to supply shocks. It is likely that there will be some diversification of supply in the medium term, possibly in developed countries where investment risk is lower.
- The average cost of tin mining will rise (with implications for the price) as the easy-access alluvial-based mines become exhausted and companies have to dig deeper mines.

# Zinc

ZINC IS A BLUISH-GREY METAL that is present in the Earth's crust and is found in air, water and soil. Its properties include a resistance to corrosion and a low melting point, and it is a fairly good conductor of heat and electricity. Zinc is also an essential mineral in human well-being; it is found in high concentrations in red blood cells, which helps the functioning of the immune system.

## Extraction, processes and reserves

Zinc is usually mined in conjunction with a number of other metals, notably lead, silver, copper and, less frequently, gold. Approximately 80% of mines are underground operations, 10% open-pit and the remainder a combination of both. In terms of production, large open-pit mines account for as much as 15% of the total, with underground mines producing 65% and combined mines 20%. Known reserves are estimated by the US Geological Survey (USGS) at 250,000 tonnes and are particularly prevalent in Australia and China (see Figure 2.18). However, the USGS estimates identified resources globally much higher at 1.9 billion tonnes.

Typically, zinc ores contain 5–15% zinc and need to be concentrated to increase the zinc content to around 55%. A concentrate also contains 25–30% sulphur, which must be removed by roasting (sintering) before smelting. The hydrometallurgical process (HP) is by far the most important production process, accounting for nearly 90% of output. As part of HP, there is a leaching process in which zinc is separated from other materials. The zinc solution is electrolysed to produce zinc metal.

FIG 2.18 **Zinc reserves, 2011**

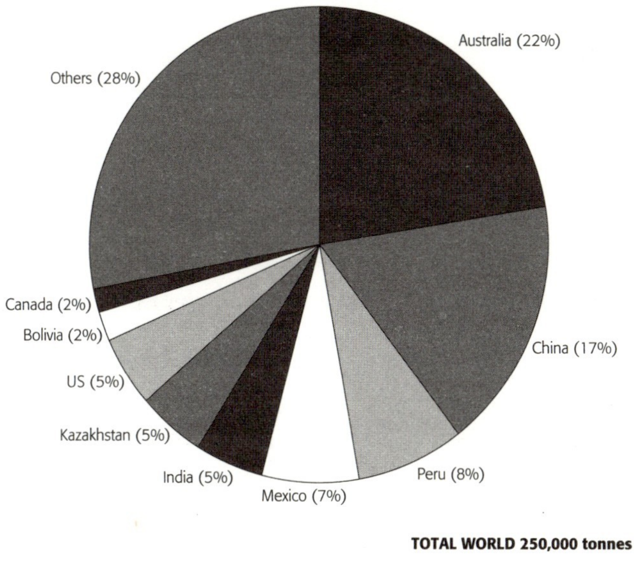

- Australia (22%)
- Others (28%)
- China (17%)
- Peru (8%)
- Mexico (7%)
- India (5%)
- Kazakhstan (5%)
- US (5%)
- Bolivia (2%)
- Canada (2%)

**TOTAL WORLD 250,000 tonnes**

**Source:** US Geological Survey

The imperial smelting process (ISP) is commonly used for treating concentrate with a high lead content. It is energy intensive, however, and high power costs combined with a lower output of high lead concentrates have led to the closure of many ISP operations. The zinc metal produced by ISP is of a lower grade compared with HP zinc.

## Products and uses

Zinc is used mainly in galvanising, die casting and brass (alloyed with copper), which together account for around 80% of its use. Galvanising is by far the largest market (about 50% of total zinc use, according to the International Lead and Zinc Study Group) and also the fastest-growing in volume terms. Zinc is also used to a lesser extent in batteries, chemicals and rubber.

In the galvanising process, steel is coated with a thin layer of zinc that corrodes sacrificially instead of the steel, significantly extending the steel's life. Normally, an almost pure zinc coating is applied. Galvanised steel sheet can also be painted for improved corrosion protection and aesthetics. Recent technical advances, which allow pre-painted galvanised sheet to be fabricated without surface distortion, have increased zinc's use in white goods such as fridges, freezers and washing machines.

Demand for more durable cars has increased the use of galvanised sheet for body parts in the automotive industry. Galvanised steel for car bodies was developed as a cost-effective way for vehicle manufacturers to meet consumer demand for extended corrosion protection.

Construction is the largest consumer of galvanised steel (45% of total zinc use), accounting for over half of the market. Transport accounts for approximately 25%, with consumer goods and electrical appliances at 23% and general engineering at about 7%.

Brass and die casting (for example, bathroom fixtures and office equipment) together account for about 30% of zinc consumption, but both are coming under pressure from substitution, particularly from lighter-weight (and sometimes cheaper) materials such as plastics and aluminium.

## Consumption and trade
### Regional trends

Between 2001 and 2011 zinc consumption grew at an average annual rate of 3.3%, rising from 8.9m tonnes in 2001 to 12.8m tonnes in 2011 (see Table 2.33). In the early part of the decade, China did not dominate the zinc market because galvanised steel production in developed economies was high, particularly in western Europe. In recent years, however, following the permanent closure of much steel capacity in the developed world as a result of the global financial crisis, China has increased its market share, with its consumption accounting for 43% of global consumption in 2011. The rapid growth in Chinese consumption has been underpinned by the use of zinc in the galvanising and battery industries.

Zinc consumption in the EU exceeded that of China until 2004; it still accounted for 17.3% of consumption in 2011 and Europe remains a net exporter of galvanised steel. The United States accounts for a small percentage of total consumption (7% in 2011) as its steel industry cannot meet domestic demand and the country is a net importer of galvanised steel.

TABLE 2.33 **Leading zinc-consuming countries**

|  | 2001 | | 2011 | |
| --- | --- | --- | --- | --- |
|  | '000 tonnes | % of total | '000 tonnes | % of total |
| China | 1,500 | 16.8 | 5,468 | 42.9 |
| EU | 2,466 | 27.6 | 2,205 | 17.3 |
| US | 1,179 | 13.2 | 923 | 7.2 |
| South Korea | 401 | 4.5 | 531 | 4.2 |
| India | 286 | 3.2 | 544 | 4.3 |
| Japan | 633 | 7.1 | 501 | 3.9 |
| Brazil | 198 | 2.2 | 237 | 1.9 |
| Taiwan | 276 | 3.1 | 221 | 1.7 |
| Others | 1,980 | 22.2 | 2,128 | 16.7 |
| Total | 8,919 | | 12,758 | |

**Sources:** International Lead and Zinc Study Group; World Bureau of Metal Statistics

## Trade

Because most refining takes place some way from where zinc is mined, there is a significant trade in zinc concentrate. Countries such as Japan and South Korea and parts of western Europe have to import nearly all the zinc concentrate needed by their smelters. China also has to import zinc concentrate despite being the world's largest zinc miner.

Most of the zinc concentrate is traded under long-term contracts, but with some degree of flexibility on quantity and price. This ensures a guaranteed outlet for a mine's production, and allows smelters to fine-tune their operations, by ensuring access to a particular blend of concentrates. Spot trading of concentrates nevertheless remains important for both miners and smelters. The rise in Chinese imports of concentrates since 2000 has increased the importance of the spot market.

Many of the major trade flows in refined zinc are intra-regional. The United States is by far the largest importer of zinc metal (see Table 2.34), but the bulk of its requirements are met by Canada, the world's biggest exporter. Similarly, a number of European countries are heavily reliant on imports, notably Germany, Italy and the Netherlands. The region also has a number of leading exporters, namely Belgium, Finland and Spain. Other significant exporters of refined zinc include South Korea, Kazakhstan, India and Peru.

TABLE 2.34 **Leading exporters and importers, 2011**

| Exports | Exports | | Imports | | |
|---|---|---|---|---|---|
| | '000 tonnes | % of total | | '000 tonnes | % of total |
| Canada | 482.5 | 11.1 | US | 672.7 | 15.6 |
| Peru | 386.5 | 8.9 | Germany | 394.0 | 9.1 |
| South Korea | 375.7 | 8.7 | China | 347.8 | 8.1 |
| Spain | 351.4 | 8.1 | Netherlands | 273.4 | 6.3 |
| Kazakhstan | 344.4 | 7.9 | Italy | 244.6 | 5.7 |

**Source:** World Bureau of Metal Statistics

## Production and stocks
### Mine production

Although a handful of countries dominate zinc mine output, there are many small producers in more countries than is the case for many base metals. This is partly because it is often mined as part of a copper-mining operation or there may be combined lead and zinc mines. In 2011 four of the largest producing countries – Australia, China, Peru and the United States – accounted for 62% of total mine output, compared with just over 50% in 1997 (see Table 2.35). The increase is accounted for by the 156% surge in China's production over the 15-year period, coupled with 44.7% and 56% increases in the output of Peru and Australia respectively. These gains more than offset the 9% fall in American production during the period.

Mine output is expected to increase, despite some high-profile closures such as Xstrata's (Switzerland) Brunswick and Perseverance mines in Canada and the UK-based Vedanta's Lisheen mine in Ireland. Dugald River and Lady Loretta in Australia and Dairi in Indonesia are some of the major new mines expected to start operation, and there are smaller mines at Perkoa (Burkina Faso), Neves Corvo (Portugal), Lalor Lake (Canada), Kyzyl Tashtygskoe (Russia) and Altintopkan (Tajikistan). Additional capacity is also expected to come on stream at existing mines, including Peñasquito (Mexico), Tennessee Mines (United States), Rampura-Agucha (India) and Khandiza (Uzbekistan). The leading zinc-mining companies are Glencore (Switzerland), Hindustan Zinc (India), Xstrata, Minmetals Australia and Teck Resources (Canada).

TABLE 2.35 **Zinc mine production**

|  | 1997 | | 2004 | | 2011 | |
| --- | --- | --- | --- | --- | --- | --- |
|  | '000 tonnes | % of total | '000 tonnes | % of total | '000 tonnes | % of total |
| China | 1,210 | 16.5 | 2,391 | 24.6 | 4,308 | 33.8 |
| Peru | 972 | 13.2 | 1,298 | 13.3 | 1,516 | 11.9 |
| Australia | 868 | 11.8 | 1,209 | 12.4 | 1,256 | 9.8 |
| Europe | 595 | 8.1 | 1,006 | 10.3 | 1,117 | 8.8 |
| India | 137 | 1.9 | 340 | 3.5 | 830 | 6.5 |
| US | 632 | 8.6 | 739 | 7.6 | 771 | 6.0 |
| Canada | 1,077 | 14.7 | 791 | 8.1 | 612 | 4.8 |
| Mexico | 379 | 5.2 | 426 | 4.4 | 603 | 4.7 |
| Others | 1,467 | 20.0 | 1,532 | 15.7 | 1,748 | 13.7 |
| Total | 7,337 |  | 9,732 |  | 12,762 |  |

## Refining and secondary supply

Smelting is usually located close to the market rather than a mine, and it is even less concentrated than mining. China is the only exception to this rule with its ten largest smelters accounting for 50% of domestic production. However, even in China, numerous medium-sized or small-scale smelters account for the remaining 50% of output.

China is the largest producer of refined zinc, accounting for 40% of total output in 2011; the next single largest producer, South Korea, accounted for just 6.3% (see Table 2.36). Significant smelting capacity is located in Europe, with Spain being the largest producer.

One recent development has been the growth in India's refined zinc production, led by the expansion of Hindustan Zinc (owned by UK-based Vedanta Resources). India was the world's third largest producer in 2011, with output having risen from just 231m tonnes in 2002 to 790m tonnes in 2011. Asia as a whole produced 61% of total output in 2011 compared with 44% in 2002.

The leading refined zinc-producing companies are Nyrstar (Belgium), Korea Zinc Group (South Korea), Hindustan Zinc (India), Votorantim (Brazil) and Boliden (Sweden).

Unlike the lead industry, secondary (using scrap) production of refined zinc is on a much smaller scale, although data on production outside Western countries is scarce. Rough estimates suggest secondary zinc output accounts for between 10–15% of total refined output.

TABLE 2.36 **Leading refined zinc-producing countries**

|  | 2001 | | 2011 | |
| --- | --- | --- | --- | --- |
|  | '000 tonnes | % of total | '000 tonnes | % of total |
| China | 2,038 | 22.1 | 5,222 | 39.9 |
| EU | 2,278 | 24.7 | 2,041 | 15.6 |
| South Korea | 508 | 7.2 | 828 | 6.3 |
| India | 184 | 2.0 | 790 | 6.0 |
| Canada | 661 | 5.5 | 662 | 5.1 |
| Japan | 644 | 7.0 | 545 | 4.2 |
| Australia | 556 | 6.0 | 517 | 3.9 |
| US | 329 | 3.6 | 252 | 1.9 |
| Others | 2,209 | 24.0 | 3,028 | 23.1 |
| **Total** | **9,223** |  | **13,095** |  |

**Sources:** International Lead and Zinc Study Group; World Bureau of Metal Statistics

## The zinc market

The London Metal Exchange (LME) is the main futures market for zinc. The metal is also traded on the Shanghai Futures Exchange and on exchanges in the Netherlands, the United States and Singapore. Pricing on the LME provides the benchmark for sales of refined metal and concentrates throughout much of the world. There are LME warehouses for zinc throughout Europe, in Singapore, in Dubai and in various places in the United States. The LME special high grade (SHG) zinc contract specifies a minimum zinc content of 99.995%. Futures trading is possible up to 27 months forward, and traded options are available.

Contract treatment charges for zinc concentrates are negotiated between miners and smelters annually in the first quarter of the year. The treatment charges paid by a miner for the processing of concentrates are largely determined by supply and demand in the concentrate market. Contract treatment charges are linked to an agreed reference or basis price, with the actual fee automatically adjusted in response to changes in LME prices.

## Price trends

Zinc prices were the first of the LME metals prices to peak in the bull market in late 2006, with the cash price reaching $4,620 per tonne. The turnaround in the market was caused by the expectation of increased zinc supply as producers reacted to the exceptionally high price. This took the market out of a structural deficit in 2004–06, initially to a near-balanced position in 2007 and eventually to a sizeable surplus. Towards the end of 2008, the main feature of the market was a collapse in demand, which came about despite only a modest increase in reported inventories.

Since 2007 the zinc market has been in surplus, with stocks building steadily. Indeed, one of the factors supporting the zinc price has been China building strategic zinc reserves. After bouncing back strongly in 2010 as the global economy emerged from recession, zinc prices have since struggled to rise, weighed down by the comfortable stock position.

FIG 2.19 **Zinc stocks and prices**

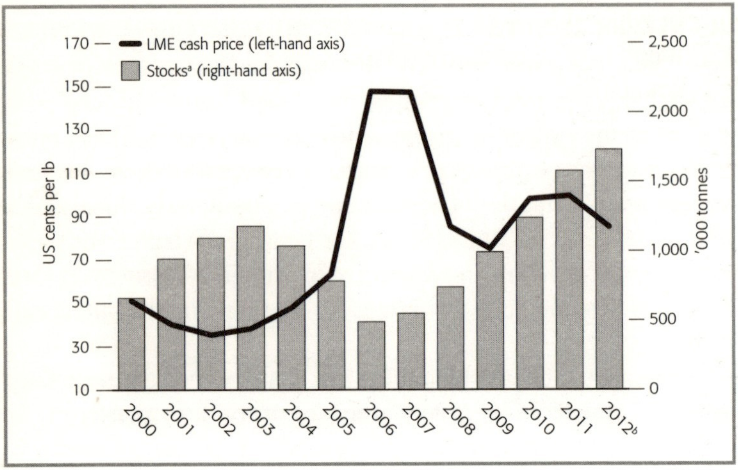

*a Total reported commercial (LME, producer, consumer, merchant) stocks; end-period.*
*b EIU estimates.*
**Sources:** London Metal Exchange; World Bureau of Metal Statistics

## The future

- Zinc's heavy use in the construction industry meant that consumption was severely affected by the 2008-09 recession in the developed world. Indeed, the collapse in property demand in the United States, which preceded the 2008-09 financial crisis, explains why zinc prices started falling as early as 2007. The subsequent collapse in many southern European property markets and slower growth in those of such former hotspots as Dubai and, more recently, China have contributed to price weakness. In 2012 there were tentative signs of recovery in the American housing market; this and China's policy on property and infrastructure are important areas to watch.

- Another important industry to watch is automobiles. There has been some switching away from galvanised steel in vehicles to aluminium, which is lighter in weight and thus more fuel-efficient.

- Supply has improved but low prevailing prices and the risks associated with future demand (see above) could lead to lower investment in the zinc industry in future. Small-scale projects, of which there are many in the zinc industry, often owned by junior mining companies that can struggle to obtain financing, could be particularly vulnerable.

# PART 3

# Energy

# Coal

COAL IS A FOSSIL FUEL or hydrocarbon. Similar to oil, it has been formed over millions of years by the geological effects of temperature and pressure on prehistoric vegetation, but it is much more plentiful and accessible than oil. Coal has been used as a source of energy for thousands of years, with evidence of use in Ancient Greece, Imperial China and the Roman Empire. However, both production and consumption soared during the industrial revolutions of the 18th and 19th centuries in Europe and the United States as it was used to power the steam engine and in the manufacture of iron. At this time, it also started to be utilised to warm buildings while oil and gas made from coal were employed in lighting. Coal dominated as the leading global energy source until around the 1950s when it started to be superseded by environmentally cleaner oil and, more recently, natural gas.

## Reserves and types, extraction and uses

Global coal reserves were estimated at 861 billion tonnes in 2011 in the *BP Statistical Review of World Energy 2012* (see Figure 3.1) and at over 1 trillion tonnes by the International Energy Agency (IEA), and they are geographically widespread. Based on current production, the world's reserves of coal will last another 118 years, according to the World Coal Association. The United States has the world's largest reserves, followed by Russia and China. Other countries with large reserves include Australia, India, Kazakhstan, Germany and Ukraine.

The "oldest" coals generally have the highest carbon content and therefore the highest energy content. There are four main types of coal: anthracite (about 1% of total reserves, with the highest carbon

FIG 3.1 **Coal reserves, 2011**

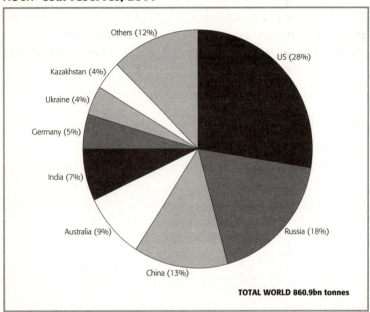

**Source:** *BP Statistical Review of World Energy 2012*

content), bituminous (about 50% of reserves), sub-bituminous (about 30% of reserves) and lignite (about 19% of reserves), with the lowest carbon content).

The two main types of coal that are used and traded are thermal or steam coal, used primarily in power generation, and metallurgical or coking coal (much rarer), used by the steel industry. Coal also plays an important role in the manufacture of many other goods including cement, pharmaceuticals, chemicals and man-made fibres.

Coal mines are open-pit or surface (40%) and underground (60%). Once mined, coal is cleaned or washed to remove any impurities or dirt; the complexity of the washing process is determined by its intended use. Coal is transported by road or conveyor for short distances, and by train or barge for longer distances. As a bulk commodity, the economic way of transporting it is by ship. In some cases, coal can be mixed with water and sent through pipelines.

Coal is predominantly used in power generation. According to the IEA, it generated 34.2% of electricity in OECD countries in 2011 and 46.2% of electricity in non-OECD countries in 2010. However, coal is versatile and can be processed into liquid fuel, chemicals or gas. This is becoming increasingly important given the finite nature and lower reserves of other fossil fuels.

## Consumption and trade
### Regional trends

Coal consumption has been growing strongly, at an annual average rate of 5.2% in 2002-11. However, there have been divergent trends across the world: consumption in the EU and the United States has been declining, whereas in the developing world it has been growing strongly. Easy accessibility and low prices (compared with other energy fuels) mean that coal has been the fuel of choice in the rural electrification plans of many countries, including India and Indonesia. It is also cheaper to build and run coal-fired electricity plants. However, freight costs are an important consideration if coal has to be imported.

China is by far the largest consumer of coal, accounting for 48% of total consumption in 2011 (see Table 3.1), with growth of 9.7% in that year. Coal accounts for more than 80% of the country's power generation. Despite also being the world's largest coal producer, China became a net importer of thermal coal in 2007 and the world's largest importer in 2011. Growth in coal consumption had slowed to just 2.8% year on year in the first three quarters of 2012 and was estimated to have been just over 3% in the year as a whole, reflecting slower economic growth and higher hydroelectric output.

In the United States, the world's second largest consumer, coal consumption has been in decline, partly because of the boom in shale gas drilling and production and the subsequent sharp fall in natural gas prices in 2011-12. The share of coal in electricity generation in April 2012, at 32%, was the same as that of gas for the first time since records began around 40 years ago, although coal use started to pick up later in the year. Consumption is also being constrained by federal efforts to curtail carbon emissions, increased electricity output from nuclear and renewable sources such as wind, and slow economic growth since 2008. Against this backdrop, American coal exports soared, rising by 31% year on year in 2011, compared with average annual growth of 11.9% in 2005-10.

In contrast, in 2012, coal consumption in the EU was encouraged by high European gas prices, coal being a cheaper alternative. The EU has ambitious plans to reduce carbon emissions, but certainly for much of 2012 carbon prices were low, enhancing the appeal of coal to European utility companies.

India is another large consumer, accounting for 9.3% of global consumption in 2011. It is also a big importer of coal, having struggled in recent years to raise domestic output to meet strong growth in demand. In the 2011/12 fiscal year, India had to import 160m tonnes to fill the shortfall. Consumption would probably be higher if domestic supplies were more plentiful.

TABLE 3.1 **Leading coal-consuming countries**

|  | 1992 | | 2000 | | 2011 | |
| --- | --- | --- | --- | --- | --- | --- |
|  | m tonnes | % of total | m tonnes | % of total | m tonnes | % of total |
| China | 1,088 | 24.4 | 1,124 | 24.6 | 3,678 | 47.8 |
| US | 823 | 18.5 | 983 | 21.5 | 906 | 11.8 |
| EU | 1,029 | 23.1 | 821 | 17.9 | 767 | 10.0 |
| India | 256 | 5.7 | 366 | 8.0 | 715 | 9.3 |
| Russia | 296 | 6.6 | 229 | 5.0 | 237 | 3.1 |
| South Africa | 134 | 3.0 | 159 | 3.5 | 190 | 2.5 |
| Japan | 114 | 2.6 | 153 | 3.3 | 183 | 2.4 |
| Australia | 101 | 2.3 | 128 | 2.8 | 129 | 1.7 |
| South Korea | 39 | 0.9 | 64 | 1.4 | 119 | 1.5 |
| Turkey | 60 | 1.3 | 81 | 1.8 | 104 | 1.4 |
| Others | 514 | 11.5 | 465 | 10.2 | 665 | 8.6 |
| Total | 4,453 | | 4,574 | | 7,694 | |

**Sources:** Energy Information Administration; International Energy Agency

## Trade

According to the World Coal Association, trade in coal reached 1,142m tonnes in 2011, with steam coal accounting for the majority, 75%, coking coal 24% and lignite 0.4%. Trade has increased significantly – it was just 921m tonnes in 2009 – largely because of the sharp rise in imports in China and India. China is by far the largest importer, followed by other Asian countries, particularly Japan, South Korea and India. Europe is also a net importer of coal, led by Germany and the UK.

Indonesia was the largest exporting country in 2011, with thermal-coal exports of 309m tonnes, but Australia was a close second with 284m tonnes (see Table 3.2). Russia and the United States are also important exporters and, of the smaller producers, South Africa and Colombia.

TABLE 3.2 **Leading exporters and importers, 2011**

|  | Exports | | | Imports | |
| --- | --- | --- | --- | --- | --- |
|  | m tonnes | % share |  | m tonnes | % share |
| Indonesia | 309 | 27.1 | China | 190 | 16.6 |
| Australia | 284 | 24.9 | Japan | 175 | 15.3 |
| Russia | 124 | 10.9 | South Korea | 129 | 11.3 |
| US | 97 | 8.5 | India | 105 | 9.2 |
| Colombia | 75 | 6.6 | Taiwan | 66 | 5.8 |
| South Africa | 72 | 6.3 | Germany | 41 | 3.6 |

**Source:** World Coal Association

## Production and stocks

Coal production grew at an average annual rate of 5.1% in 2002–11, keeping pace with demand. Again, there were divergent trends. China's annual growth in output averaged an astonishing 10.2% between 2002 and 2011, compared with India's 5.2%, Russia's 3.8% and Colombia's 7.8%. Meanwhile, in the developed world, the United States and Germany's production contracted at an annual average rate of 0.2% and 1.2% respectively during the same period. Regional production trends may appear to have been tracking consumption trends, but there were a few exceptions. Australia's output grew by nearly 3% a year in 2000–10, with the bulk of it exported to markets in Asia. Similarly, Colombia's drive to increase production was primarily for the export market. Meanwhile, a number of other exporting countries, especially South Africa and Indonesia, are finding that strong domestic consumption growth is starting to eat into the volume of coal available for export (typically more profitable than supplying the domestic market).

The three largest coal-mining regions in China are Inner Mongolia, Shanxi and Shaanxi in the north of the country; they typically account for about two-thirds of national output. In response to falling prices in 2012, growth in China's coal output appeared to be faltering. Many of the country's coal-mining operations are high cost, with the result that production can fall in times of low global prices when imports are competitive. Labour costs have been rising sharply, as have safety costs (following government efforts to raise safety standards) and regional taxes. Furthermore, much of the coal is transported by road, which is expensive.

Nevertheless, substantial new capacity is coming on stream. According to the authorities, which appear keen to accelerate restructuring (consolidation) in the industry, 95m tonnes of coal production capacity with advanced mining technology were added in 2011, while 407 mines with a total capacity of 25m tonnes/year (t/y) were shut down. China has also invested heavily in development of the rail and port infrastructure in order to overcome constraints.

In India coal production has struggled since 2009 as a result of government efforts to protect the environment, problems with land acquisition and poor rail infrastructure. In draft proposals for the country's 12th five-year plan (2012/13–2016/17), the government forecasts coal output of 795m tonnes by 2016/17, compared with 539m tonnes in 2011/12, suggesting an increase of nearly 50% over the period. Even with this growth there would be a rising import requirement, as coal demand is forecast to increase to 980m t/y by 2017. Such output growth plans seem ambitious in the light of recent trends and the institutional and bureaucratic obstacles, but the government appears to be taking a more proactive approach to encouraging the sector.

Indonesia's coal output has expanded the most rapidly in the past decade, with annual average growth of 15.3% between 2000 and 2011. Operating costs are low and the country is an important supplier to the global market. However, the operating environment is uncertain. The government is building thermal power stations in rural areas and wants to ensure that domestic coal is preserved for national use. There has been talk of a ban on unprocessed coal from 2014, export taxes, production quotas and constraints on foreign ownership. As yet no formal coal policy has been announced, but it seems likely that there will be restrictions on the volume of exports in an effort to meet strong growth in domestic consumption.

In Russia, the government's energy policies will support consumption over the medium to long term. The energy strategy to 2030 envisages substituting coal for gas in thermal power stations and increasing coal's share in electricity generation to 34–36% by 2030,

TABLE 3.3 **Leading coal-producing countries**

|  | 1992 | | 2000 | | 2011 | |
| --- | --- | --- | --- | --- | --- | --- |
|  | m tonnes | % of total | m tonnes | % of total | m tonnes | % of total |
| China | 1,115 | 24.8 | 1,154 | 26.0 | 3,474 | 45.3 |
| US | 905 | 20.1 | 974 | 21.9 | 992.7 | 12.9 |
| India | 254 | 5.6 | 336 | 7.6 | 578 | 7.5 |
| Indonesia | 22 | 0.5 | 77 | 1.7 | 397 | 5.2 |
| Australia | 228 | 5.1 | 307 | 6.9 | 395 | 5.2 |
| Russia | 316 | 7.0 | 240 | 5.4 | 337 | 4.4 |
| South Africa | 183 | 4.1 | 226 | 5.1 | 255 | 3.3 |
| Germany | 314 | 7.0 | 205 | 4.6 | 189 | 2.5 |
| Kazakhstan | 127 | 2.8 | 77 | 1.7 | 116 | 1.5 |
| Colombia | 22 | 0.5 | 38 | 0.9 | 86 | 1.1 |
| Others | 1,007 | 22.4 | 805 | 18.1 | 845 | 11.0 |
| Total | 4,491 | | 4,439 | | 7,666 | |

**Sources:** Energy Information Administration; International Energy Agency

compared with 26% in 2008. On the export front, there will be a diversification away from traditional Western export markets towards the faster-growing Asia-Pacific region. However, significant upgrades in infrastructure would be needed for large-scale exports to Asia.

South Africa's coal industry has faced many problems, including infrastructure deficiencies, labour issues and regulatory obstacles that have constrained output. The capacity of the Richards Bay Coal Terminal, the world's largest coal export terminal, has been expanded to 91m t/y and the rail infrastructure is being improved, but there are questions about whether coal output can keep pace with transport capacity additions. Production costs are generally low, enabling South Africa to be a competitive exporter; but increasing domestic needs mean that the future of exports is in doubt.

Australia has ambitious plans to develop its already large coal reserves, but recent low prices and sharp rises in operational costs (particularly wages and taxes) are raising concerns about profitability. Coal output in Colombia, the world's fourth largest coal exporter, grew by 15.4% year on year in 2011. With rising Asian demand and the expansion of the Panama Canal opening up Asian markets to Colombian exports, foreign companies have been investing heavily in Colombia.

## The coal market

The wide geographical spread of coal reserves meant that trade was limited until recently. It started to become significant during the 1960s with the rapid economic development of Japan, which lacked natural resources, particularly hydrocarbons. Japan's import demand (and later demand in the industrialising countries of South Korea and Taiwan) was met by Australia, Indonesia and even western Canada. However, the purchasers held all the power and prices were set in an annual bargaining round between Japanese Steel Mills (JSM) and supplier countries. The other steel mills in the region would then pay the prices (based on the higher-value coking coal) agreed with JSM. In later years, China's steel mills joined the bargaining round. For the coal producers, this arrangement led to weaker prices.

It is not clear why this relationship broke down in the 2000s and producers were able to command higher prices. For most of this time, China was not a major importer of coal so it could not have had a significant influence. It is more likely that because of the low prices, only a few large companies could afford to exploit coking-coal resources. With a large part of the coking-coal market in the hands of just a few multinationals, the producers were able to dictate terms.

Although these developments directly affected coking coal, the thermal-coal market has followed a similar trend, moving away from long-term contracts towards pricing based on a number of spot markets. Nevertheless, in Japan annual contracts in the thermal-coal market are still signed in March, effective in April, often after talks between the large miners and Japan's utility companies.

Spot markets have evolved around the main export hubs. These include the Newcastle spot index for Australian exports and the Richards Bay index for South African exports. The Northwest Europe (ARA) price is the benchmark for imports into Europe. Many countries have their own coal indices, for example NYMEX spot and futures prices in the United States. The Bohai Rim price in China tracks power-station coal prices at six ports. However, the physical trading of coal has faced a few challenges, particularly liquidity problems and difficulty in matching buyers' needs with supply. There are significant variations in the types of coal on offer (with regard to energy per volume and impurities) and the quality of coal demanded (because of environmental requirements or the technical specifications of power plants).

## Price trends

Thermal coal prices rose strongly during the 2000s in response to strong demand. Years of underinvestment as a result of low prevailing prices meant that the market struggled to meet the rise in consumption, particularly when China entered the market for the first time in 2007. However, since the collapse in commodity prices in 2008–09, prices have struggled to make ground. Coal was more resilient during the global downturn than many of the industrial raw materials, but supply has now increased significantly, removing any tightness in the market. Meanwhile, weak global economic growth and the increase

FIG 3.2 **Coal prices**

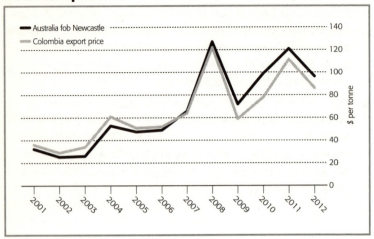

Source: World Bank

in American gas production have constrained consumption. Prices fell for much of 2012, and annual average prices were typically 20% lower.

## The future

- In the medium term efforts to curtail emissions are likely to constrain coal consumption, or at least the growth in consumption. Although it will not be easy for China to wean itself from its dependence on coal, the 12th five-year plan (2011–15) sets climate-change targets for the first time and envisages, as well as an improvement in overall energy efficiency, an increase in the use of gas, nuclear and renewables in electricity production, thus reducing coal's share. The United States, meanwhile, is closing down significant amounts of coal-fired generation capacity. However, coal's relative price competitiveness (without carbon pricing) and abundance suggest that it has an important role to play in raising the standard of living in poorer parts of the world.

- Carbon capture and storage (CCS, whereby the carbon emissions from coal-fired power generation are captured and stored so that they do not enter the atmosphere) could be adopted on a much greater scale. However, technological advances are probably needed to reduce its current high cost and to allay concerns about possible leakages from storage.
- The nuclear disaster in Japan in March 2011 as a result of damage caused by a massive earthquake has raised questions about the future of nuclear power. It appears unlikely that nuclear power will be abandoned, as it is cheap to run and is a domestic source of energy. However, if many countries eschew nuclear power, coal will be a beneficiary.

# Natural gas

NATURAL GAS IS A FOSSIL FUEL or hydrocarbon gas. It is found in underground rock beds or with other hydrocarbons (oil and coal deposits). Historically, gas was not considered commercially viable and the gas produced by oil drilling was just burnt off or flared. By the 1970s, it was recognised that gas was a viable commodity in its own right, and "associated" (with oil) gas is now transported from oil wells by pipeline (some is reinjected into the oil well as a means of improving extraction rates). Non-associated gas is derived from pure natural gas fields, and coal bed methane is extracted from coal-bearing rock formations.

## Reserves and types, extraction and processes

Reserves were estimated at 208.4 trillion cubic metres in 2011 in the *BP Statistical Review of World Energy 2012* and are geographically fairly concentrated (see Figure 3.3). According to the International Energy Agency (IEA), known gas reserves will last for 59 years based on its estimates of future consumption, but this largely excludes sources of unconventional gas. Russia has the world's largest reserves, followed by Iran, Qatar and Turkmenistan. Other countries with large reserves include oil-producing countries in the Middle East and Africa (Saudi Arabia, Iraq, the United Arab Emirates, Algeria and Nigeria) and Australia. However, if unconventional reserves were included, total reserves could double (estimates vary, so this is a tentative figure) – and they would be less geographically concentrated.

As the technology has become available, gas has started to be extracted from less accessible rock formations. These "unconventional"

FIG 3.3 **Gas reserves, 2011**

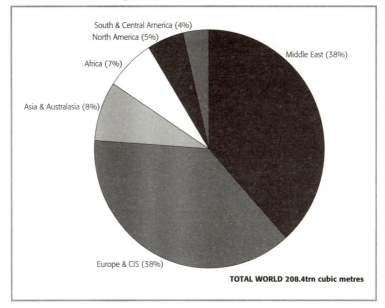

**Source:** *BP Statistical Review of World Energy 2012*

gases include tight gas, which is extracted from low-permeability rock formations, and shale gas, which is extracted from shale formations. Unconventional gas accounted for 16% of global gas output in 2011. These gases cost more to extract because of the advanced technology used and the amount of energy involved. Sour gas, or gas containing large amounts of hydrogen sulphide, has also become commercially viable. The hydrogen sulphide has to be removed before gas can be used.

Gas must be processed following extraction to remove impurities. The by-products of the extraction process – ethane, propane and butane – are then viable for commercial sale in their own right.

Liquefied natural gas (LNG) is a clear liquid that is created when natural gas is cooled to around –160°C. The volume shrinks hugely, making the gas easy to store and transport. It is usually treated at source, transported in LNG trains (ships) and then regasified in plants at its destination. LNG, production of which started in 1960s and has since significantly increased, has created flexibility in the natural gas market, which previously relied on pipelines to transport gas. Floating liquefied natural gas (FLNG) is now being developed – the liquefaction process will take place at sea where there are offshore gas fields.

The carbon emissions associated with the combustion of gas are lower than for coal or oil, so gas is perceived to play a major role in efforts to control (and reduce) such emissions globally. Typically, carbon emissions from gas are about 50% lower than those associated with coal and about 25% lower than those associated with oil.

## Consumption and uses

The electricity-generating industry is by far the largest consumer of gas, followed by buildings (where gas is used to power boilers generating hot water and space heating, primarily in the OECD) and industry (metal refining, petrochemicals, iron and steel). There is growing consumption in the transport industry, but this accounts for only a tiny proportion of total consumption. The use of gas in the utility sector grew rapidly in Europe during the 1970s and 1980s as a result of the 1970s oil-price shocks. Gas now accounts for just over 20% of the feedstock for power generation globally.

Gas consumption grew steadily at an annual average rate of 2.4% in 2001–11, but trends in individual consumers were much more marked. China's consumption grew at an annual average rate of 16.2% in 2001–11, albeit from a low base, while western Europe's grew by just 0.8%. In the United States, consumption fell by an average of 1.2% a year for the first five years of the 2000s before picking up and growing at an annual average rate of 4.5% in 2007–11, despite the 2008–09 recession and subsequent weak economic growth. Consumption growth in the United States was a result of strong growth in domestic production and falling domestic prices, particularly relative to coal. This is in sharp contrast to Europe, where gas prices during the same period were much higher, thus encouraging energy conservation. European gas demand was also constrained by the weak regional economy, the relative cost advantage of coal and strong growth in renewable energy production.

Unlike most commodity markets, where in the past ten years it has come to dominate consumption, China accounted for a small share of

TABLE 3.4 **Regional gas consumption**

|  | 1993 | | 2011 | |
| --- | --- | --- | --- | --- |
|  | bn cu metres | % of total | bn cu metres | % of total |
| **North America** | 692.5 | 32.7 | 852.3 | 26.5 |
| US | 588.7 | 27.8 | 689.9 | 21.4 |
| Canada | 76.2 | 3.6 | 103.3 | 3.2 |
| **Eastern Europe & the CIS** | 603.3 | 28.5 | 557.5 | 17.3 |
| Russia | 403.6 | 19.0 | 424.6 | 13.2 |
| **Western Europe** | 396.3 | 18.7 | 528.9 | 16.4 |
| UK | 68.3 | 3.2 | 82.2 | 2.6 |
| Germany | 66.4 | 3.1 | 72.5 | 2.3 |
| Italy | 46.8 | 2.2 | 71.3 | 2.2 |
| France | 32.3 | 1.5 | 40.3 | 1.3 |
| **Asia & Australasia** | 197.8 | 9.3 | 615.4 | 19.1 |
| Japan | 53.2 | 2.5 | 105.5 | 3.3 |
| China | 15.3 | 0.7 | 130.7 | 4.1 |
| India | 15.1 | 0.7 | 61.1 | 1.9 |
| South Korea | 5.8 | 0.3 | 46.6 | 1.4 |
| **Middle East** | 121.0 | 5.7 | 401.2 | 12.5 |
| Iran | 26.6 | 1.3 | 152.3 | 4.7 |
| Saudi Arabia | 35.9 | 1.7 | 99.2 | 3.1 |
| **Central & South America** | 65.1 | 3.1 | 154.5 | 4.8 |
| **Africa** | 43.7 | 2.1 | 109.8 | 3.4 |
| **Total** | 2,119.9 | | 3,219.6 | |

**Sources:** US Energy Information Administration; International Energy Agency; BP

global gas consumption at 4% in 2011 (see Table 3.4). In comparison, the largest consumer, the United States, accounted for 21% of global consumption and Russia for 13%. However, China is still an important player in the gas market, as it needs to import significant (and growing) amounts of gas. These imports are in the form of pipeline gas (from central Asia, particularly Turkmenistan) and LNG. LNG imports have grown rapidly, increasing by 31% in volume terms year on year in 2011 and by 29% in the first half of 2012. The Chinese government has made a strategic commitment to gas, aiming to increase the contribution of natural gas to total primary energy consumption to 8.3% in 2015, compared with 4.8% in 2011, as part of a wider effort to reduce carbon emissions and combat pollution.

Gas demand in India doubled between 2003 and 2010 and was met by higher domestic production and by rising imports. Natural gas accounts for just over 10% of India's total primary energy consumption. Although the country is a sizeable gas producer, it also has to import LNG.

Russia is a large consumer of gas, which accounts for over half of energy consumption (56% in 2011, compared with 28% in the United States). This means there is little scope for further increases in consumption, particularly as the government is pushing for further increases in domestic gas tariffs and energy efficiency, as well as increased consumption of the country's plentiful coal supplies.

In the Middle East, Saudi Arabia, the United Arab Emirates (UAE) and Kuwait have faced shortages of natural gas in recent years, as demand for power and water (gas is used in desalination plants) has soared because of the high growth rates of their economies and populations. In 2011, the Middle East (excluding North Africa) accounted for 12.5% of total consumption. The potential shortage of gas has encouraged the Gulf states (apart from Qatar) to invest more in domestic gas extraction, which should enable gas consumption to continue to grow strongly.

## Production

A few large producers dominate gas production. In 2011, Russia and the United States together accounted for 39% of total gas production; other large producers include Qatar, Iran, Canada, China and Norway (see Table 3.5).

Russian gas production is growing modestly. The main west Siberian fields of Gazprom, the state gas monopoly, are maturing, and progress has been slow in developing its two main strategic projects, the Yamal Peninsula and Shtokman. Indeed, in August 2012 Gazprom

TABLE 3.5 **Regional gas production**

|  | 1993 | | 2011 | |
| --- | --- | --- | --- | --- |
|  | bn cu metres | % of total | bn cu metres | % of total |
| North America | 678.3 | 32.9 | 864.2 | 26.4 |
| Eastern Europe & the CIS | 657.3 | 31.9 | 776.1 | 23.7 |
| Western Europe | 267.8 | 13.0 | 277.0 | 8.4 |
| Asia & Australasia | 189.7 | 9.2 | 479.1 | 14.6 |
| Middle East | 125.5 | 6.1 | 526.1 | 16.0 |
| Africa | 79.4 | 3.9 | 202.7 | 6.2 |
| Central & South America | 65.1 | 3.2 | 153.2 | 4.7 |
| Total | 2,063.1 |  | 3,278.4 |  |

announced that the Shtokman gas field would be put on hold because of its high cost relative to prevailing prices. This could also be a response to the development of shale gas in the United States (much of the Shtokman output had been earmarked for the American market) and the discovery of easy to extract (and thus cheaper) gas off East Africa and in the Mediterranean. About half of Russia's gas exports go to markets in western Europe. Russia is keen to expand its exports to Asia, but this will require considerable investment in infrastructure.

Gas production in the United States grew by 7.9% year on year in 2011, boosted by increased output of shale gas (unconventional gas already accounts for over 50% of American gas production). Shale gas has transformed the outlook for gas production, which had appeared to be on a declining trend. However, the extraction techniques used in shale gas extraction – hydraulic fracturing and horizontal drilling – have proved controversial. Vast amounts of water mixed with chemicals are used which could, it is feared, contaminate underground aquifers and deplete water resources. A lot of energy is also used. The government has supported the industry, as long as it is environmentally responsible, and has increased environmental scrutiny. The outlook remains uncertain, however, partly because of exceptionally low domestic gas prices in 2011–12 which threatened profitability. Some companies are focusing their efforts on potentially more rewarding oil shale activities, but as the extraction process is new and untested, the depletion rates of the wells are not known. As of the end of 2012, permission had been granted to one company to start exports of LNG (probably in 2015) and approximately 20 other companies have applied for licences. If exports of LNG are permitted on a significant scale, this would probably lead to higher domestic gas prices.

The long-term stagnation in western European production of natural gas is likely to continue, with particularly marked declines in the UK's North Sea output. There is growing interest in developing unconventional gas resources in Europe to offset the decline in conventional gas production. The extent of Poland's reserves is uncertain, but the country has already granted a large number of unconventional gas exploration licences. It depends heavily on coal-fired power generation and imported Russian gas, so it is keen to develop alternatives. The UK, Spain and France also have the potential to develop shale gas production, but this is constrained by environmental concerns, particularly regarding the extraction technology, and the high cost. A number of European countries, including France, have already banned the "fracking" extraction process.

LNG production expanded strongly in 2010 and 2011, with the largest producer, Qatar, responsible for the bulk of new supply. Qatar's gas production doubled between 2008 and 2012 as it pursued its target of an LNG export capacity of 77m tonnes per year, which was reached in 2011. It has no plans to increase this capacity, and its additional gas production is devoted to the domestic market, including processing into petrochemicals and use in gas-to-liquids (GTL) plants.

Australia was a relatively small gas producer in 2011, accounting for just 1.4% of global supply. However, projects are well under way to significantly increase output of LNG, to 85m tonnes per year (t/y) compared with 28m t/y currently, by liquefying both natural gas and coal bed methane. As a result, Australia would overtake Qatar as the world's largest LNG producer by 2017.

There have been various attempts, led by Russia and Iran, to create an OPEC-style gas organisation, and Qatar, Venezuela, Nigeria, Libya, Indonesia, Egypt and Algeria have taken part in periodic discussions with them about the gas market. However, an organisation that can influence prices by co-ordinated changes in output does not seem feasible with the dislocation in global gas markets (see below).

## The gas market

Gas is one of the few commodities for which there is no global benchmark price forming the basis of most international trade. This is partly because of the difficulty in transporting gas. Traditionally, long-term sales contracts would be signed between producer and consumer countries, and a pipeline would then be constructed to fulfil these obligations. The price would be indexed through a formula (typically involving a time lag) based on international oil prices.

However, developments in the past decade or so have led to a partial breakdown of this arrangement: robust demand growth in Asia that could not be met by local supplies; and a massive increase in Qatar's production of LNG. LNG is not a new technology, but the huge increase in supply in recent years has added a much more flexible and international dimension to gas supplies.

By 2012, three distinct and very different market hubs for gas had developed: the high-priced Asian spot market for imported LNG; the European market mixture of pipeline gas and LNG imports; and the American domestic market, priced using the Henry Hub benchmark. However, despite the emergence of spot gas markets, long-term contracts for pipeline gas and LNG are still being signed, often with some form of indexation to the international oil price. In 2012, it was reported that European utility companies had managed to secure more flexible contract terms with Russia, so that regional gas prices would not be purely indexed to oil prices but would also reflect the regional spot-market prices. By the end of 2012 there were also reports that Japan had managed to sign long-term LNG supply contracts based in part on (at the time, much lower) American Henry Hub prices.

## Price trends

It is not possible to generalise about gas prices in the way that is possible for many commodities. This is because of the differences in regional markets.

FIG 3.4 **Regional gas prices**

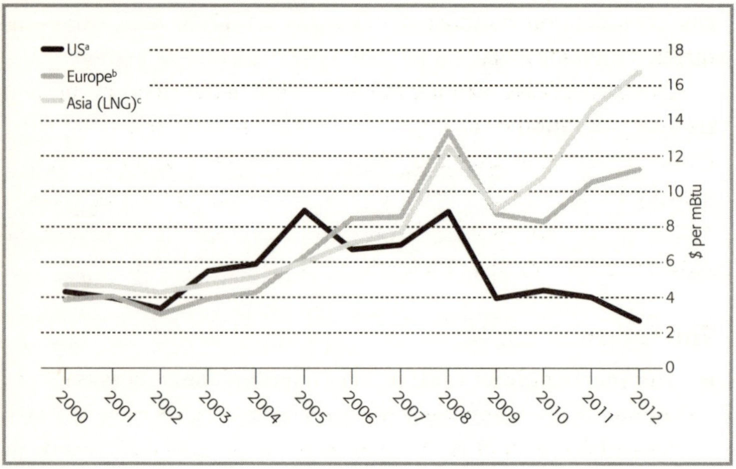

- US[a]
- Europe[b]
- Asia (LNG)[c]

a Henry Hub.  b Average price paid for European imports.  c Based on Japanese prices.
**Source:** World Bank

In the United States, the strong (and somewhat unexpected) increase in domestic production has reversed what had been an upward trend in prices around 2000–01. Between 2003 and 2008, American gas prices (Henry Hub) averaged $7.14 per million British thermal units (mBtu) and peaked on a quarterly basis at $11.35/mBtu in the second quarter of 2008. After falling sharply in response to the 2008–09 recession, prices stabilised at around $4/mBtu in 2010 and 2011 before plummeting in early 2012 (see Figure 3.4). At one point in the first half of 2012, prices fell below $2/mBtu, reflecting strong growth in domestic production, coupled with weak domestic demand growth. They subsequently rallied to over $3.5/mBtu in late 2012, partly because of lower than expected nuclear-power generation as well as lower drilling activity.

The average import prices of gas in Europe have broadly followed the trajectory of international oil prices over the past decade, unsurprisingly since most imports were on contracts indexed to oil prices. Spot markets for gas in Europe have grown in recent years but continue to suffer from a lack of liquidity, perhaps with the exception of the UK-based National Balancing Point (NBP). LNG is an increasingly important source of supply, but in 2011-12, as Europe's gas consumption contracted, the trade in LNG was increasingly directed towards Asia.

The price of LNG exports to Asia soared between 2003 and 2008, rising at an annual average rate of almost 21%, reflecting robust demand growth in Asia and Europe and limited supplies. Prices fell sharply in 2009 in the wake of the global recession but started to recover thereafter, growing by 21% and 35% respectively in 2010 and 2011. They rose again in 2012, averaging around $17/mBtu.

## The future

- The energy policies of large economies will determine the future for gas. It remains to be seen whether governments take measures to reduce carbon emissions which would favour gas relative to other hydrocarbons. The promotion of renewable energy would also benefit gas, as it is perceived to be the best alternative fuel to act as a back-up power source in periods of low generation by renewables.
- China has already stated its intention to increase the share of gas in its energy mix. There is huge scope for China to increase consumption. At present only 10% of households have access to natural gas, compared with a global average of 40%, according to the IEA.
- Prevailing low prices could deter investment in gas production in the United States in the near term.
- By 2015, there will be large increases in the supply of LNG, particularly from Australia but also from smaller producers in Africa and Papua New Guinea. The United States and Canada could also start to export on a significant scale at that time. This could depress prices and deter future investment in gas resources.
- Although there is no shortage of untapped gas reserves, many of these reserves – such as Arctic field development – will be expensive to tap, given the increasing complexity of extraction. This has implications for long-term supply and prices.

- Unconventional gas production is expected to continue to increase its share of global production. This will take the form of shale gas (North America, Poland, China), coal bed methane (Australia, China) and tight gas (Middle East, Latin America, Africa).

# Crude oil

CRUDE OIL IS A HYDROCARBON, composed mostly of hydrogen and carbon, formed in a fossilising process over millions of years. It is typically found in underground or undersea reservoirs. It is extracted by a number of methods, using either the natural pressure in the reservoir or pumps. As the oil becomes more difficult to extract, recovery-enhancing techniques such as injecting water or gas can be used. The extraction of less conventional crude from oil sands or oil shale requires more of a mining-style approach.

There are numerous varieties of crude oil, ranging from light or sweet to heavy or sour depending on its API (American Petroleum Institute) gravity. The gravity measure compares how light or heavy the oil is relative to water. Historically, lighter oil has commanded a price premium as it is more suited to the production of petroleum in the refinery.

## Processes and products

Crude oil is refined into various products such as petrol, middle distillates and fuel oil. Petrol consists of aviation and motor petrol, and light distillate feedstock (LDF). Middle distillates consist of jet and heating kerosene, and gas and diesel oils. Fuel oil includes marine fuels (bunkers or oil used in maritime transport) and crude oil used directly as fuel. Other products are liquefied petroleum gas (LPG), solvents, petroleum coke, lubricants and bitumen. Of the total consumption of refined products, middle distillates accounted for 36.5% in 2011, light distillates for 32.1% and fuel oil for 9.8%.

The market for crude consists primarily of refiners, many of which are integrated downstream into the distribution and sale of petroleum products, or upstream into exploration or production, or both. Historically, crude oil refining took place in consuming countries, as crude oil is cheaper to transport than its products. Although more refining is now taking place in producing countries, the United States still accounted for 19% of total refining capacity in 2011.

Refining has generally been less profitable than other parts of the oil business, with margins being squeezed by the costs of meeting tougher environmental standards. Since the 2008–09 global economic slowdown, some refining capacity has been closed in both the United States and Europe. A growing problem is a mismatch between the nature of refining capacity and the sort of crude oil available. Much of the refining capacity in the United States and Europe has been designed to treat lighter crudes, but it is the heavier, sourer crudes that have been growing in volume in recent years. The demise of refinery capacity in Western countries is, however, being offset by rapid growth in capacity in other parts of the world. Japan, Singapore, China and India have considerable refining capacity, with much of the remainder located in producing countries such as Russia, Venezuela and the Middle East. China accounted for nearly 12% of global refining capacity in 2011, with about 10% of its capacity composed of so-called teapot refineries (small, independent refineries).

## Reserves

World oil reserves were estimated at 1.65 trillion barrels in 2011 (see Figure 3.5), according to the *BP Statistical Review of World Energy 2012*, with the largest in Venezuela (the Orinoco Belt, extra-heavy crude) and Canada (including the oil sands). Excluding the less conventional forms of crude oil, the largest reserves are in Russia, Saudi Arabia, Iraq and Iran. At current production rates, the International Energy Agency estimates that there are 46 years of supply left; BP's estimate, which includes more unconventional reserves, is somewhat higher at 54 years. In fact, the level of global reserves has risen and technology is opening up reserves that were previously deemed inaccessible.

At current output rates, Middle East oil reserves are believed to be good for another 79 years. In all other regions of the world – excluding

FIG 3.5 **Crude oil reserves, 2011**

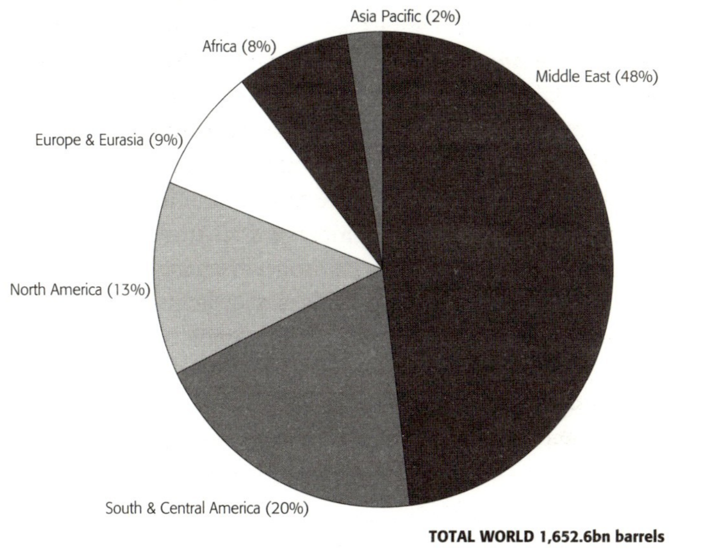

- Asia Pacific (2%)
- Africa (8%)
- Middle East (48%)
- Europe & Eurasia (9%)
- North America (13%)
- South & Central America (20%)

**TOTAL WORLD 1,652.6bn barrels**

**Source:** BP Statistical Review of World Energy 2012

Venezuela and Canada – the reserves to production (R/P) ratio is less than 45. However, the latest data do not include estimates of unconventional oil such as tight or shale oil. Oil shale appears to have the potential to significantly extend the life of the world's oil supply, although it is too early to assess this accurately.

## Consumption and trade

### Uses

Oil still dominates as a source of commercial energy, accounting for 30–35% of demand (although this share has fallen from 50% in the early 1970s), despite the fact that its consumption by the electricity sector has fallen sharply. Within the global primary energy mix, oil's share was the largest at 33% in 2011 (but this represents a significant low), followed by coal at 28.8% (compared with 24% in 2006) and natural gas at 23.2%, according to the *BP Statistical Review of World*

*Energy* 2012. Energy accounts for the bulk of crude oil consumption, of which transport and power generation are the largest. Non-energy uses of oil, mainly feedstock for plastics, synthetic fibres and rubber, account for less than 10% of demand.

Transport accounts for around half of the oil consumed globally, with industry (including manufacturing, agriculture, mining and construction) accounting for approximately one-third. Household and commercial uses account for the remainder. Despite the rise in consumption of biofuels and compressed natural gas, petroleum products remain dominant in the transport industry.

Oil's share of energy supply has declined hugely since the first oil-price shocks back in the 1970s, and recent high prices have further deterred utility companies from using oil in power generation. Other reasons for the decline are that gas-fired power stations are cheaper to build than oil-fired ones and are environmentally friendlier (lower carbon emissions. Meanwhile, coal is typically cheaper than both oil and gas and has been the fuel of choice in many developing countries, particularly those with large domestic reserves such as India and Indonesia). However, burning coal produces more emissions than burning oil.

## Regional trends

Typically, oil consumption follows the path of GDP growth. However, since 1976 demand has grown less rapidly than GDP, implying a fall in oil intensity (the amount of oil needed for every additional unit of GDP or national output). The decline is expected to continue, especially in more mature economies. OECD countries' share of total oil consumption declined from 70% in 1975 to 51% in 2011 (of which North America accounted for 26.4%, Europe 16% and the Pacific region about 9% – see Table 3.6). High oil prices, concerns about global warming and general energy conservation efforts, as well as weak economic growth (particularly since 2008), have contributed to this decline. Since the 2008–09 global economic slowdown, North American consumption has also been in decline (apart from a modest rebound in 2010), suggesting that the region could be joining Europe and Japan in a long-term trend of declining consumption.

TABLE 3.6 **Oil consumption**

|  | 1997 | | 2011 | |
| --- | --- | --- | --- | --- |
|  | m barrels/day | % of total | m barrels/day | % of total |
| North America | 22.7 | 31.0 | 23.5 | 26.4 |
| Europe | 15.0 | 20.5 | 14.3 | 16.0 |
| Pacific | 9.0 | 12.2 | 7.9 | 8.9 |
| Total OECD | 46.7 | 63.7 | 45.7 | 51.3 |
| China | 4.2 | 5.7 | 9.5 | 10.7 |
| Other Asia | 6.8 | 9.2 | 10.7 | 12.0 |
| Middle East | 4.0 | 5.4 | 8.0 | 9.0 |
| Latin America | 4.8 | 6.6 | 6.5 | 7.3 |
| CIS | 3.8 | 5.2 | 4.7 | 5.3 |
| Africa[a] | 3.1 | 4.2 | 3.1 | 3.4 |
| Total non-OECD | 26.6 | 36.3 | 42.4 | 48.7 |
| Overall total | 73.3 |  | 88.2 |  |

a Includes other non-OECD Europe.
**Sources:** International Energy Agency; EIU

By contrast, the share of non-OECD countries in total consumption has increased, with annual average growth of nearly 4% a year since 2002. It continued to grow during the 2008–09 economic downturn, albeit at a lower rate. Consumption has been rising fastest in Asia, at an annual rate of around 5.5% between 1995 and 2007. The region accounted for 23% of total consumption in 2011, compared with less than 16% in 2000. China's booming industrial and economic growth has been responsible for much of the increase. Coal currently meets much of China's power needs, but demand for oil in the transport sector is growing rapidly.

Elsewhere, Latin America's 6–7% share of consumption has been fairly static, although growth has picked up in the past five years. The Middle East's share has grown more rapidly, from 5.2% in 1995 to 9% in 2011; extensive retail price subsidies across the region partly account for the brisk rates of growth. Most governments are reluctant to eliminate these subsidies, despite the high fiscal cost in non-producing countries, for fear of causing social and political unrest. Africa's share has been fairly constant in recent years at about 3.8%, compared with around 3% in 1996–2006.

## Trade

There is more international trade in oil than in any other commodity, in both volume and value, and oil exports account for around 60% of production. Crude oil still predominates, but trade in products is rising. Most oil is transported by sea (via tankers) or overland through pipelines. Tankers, which are low cost, efficient and flexible, have made intercontinental transport of oil possible. A large amount of oil is traded on short-term and spot-market contracts against the major crude benchmarks, underpinning futures trading on exchanges, interregional movements and arbitrage of physical tanker cargoes.

The United States is the world's largest single crude oil importer, accounting for 14% of trade in 2011, and in recent years imports met more than half of its needs. However, strong growth in domestic production of shale oil will reduce American imports. Japan and Germany are more than 90% import-dependent. Exports are dominated by the Middle East and Russia, accounting for 46% and 17% respectively of the world total in 2011 (see Table 3.7).

### TABLE 3.7 **Leading exporters and importers, 2011**

| | Exports | | | Imports | |
|---|---|---|---|---|---|
| | '000 barrels/day | % share | | '000 barrels/day | % share |
| Middle East | 17,660 | 46.4 | Europe | 9,322 | 24.1 |
| Russia | 6,413 | 16.9 | US | 8,937 | 14.1 |
| West Africa | 4,501 | 11.8 | China | 5,080 | 13.0 |
| Latin America[a] | 4,147 | 10.9 | Japan | 3,560 | 5.8 |
| Canada | 2,243 | 5.9 | India | 3,407 | 4.5 |

a Includes Mexico.
**Source:** BP Statistical Review of World Energy 2012

## Production and reserves
### Countries and companies

Over the past 30 years or so the structure of the oil industry has changed, mainly through mergers and acquisitions, of which the most notable have been the Chevron-Texaco, ExxonMobil and BP-Amoco deals. Until the 1970s the industry was dominated by a small group of large, vertically integrated international oil companies known as the Seven Sisters (Exxon, Shell, BP, Mobil, Gulf, Texaco and Chevron). Now the Seven Sisters (now five, Exxon having merged with Mobil and Chevron with Texaco) account for less than 20% of total crude production.

Ownership and control of crude resources and production have to a large extent passed from private oil companies to national governments or state-owned companies. In terms of capital value, the oil majors are still massive; but in terms of resource ownership, they are dwarfed by national oil companies (NOCs). Saudi Aramco, Venezuela's PDVSA, the National Iranian Oil Company and the Iraq National Oil Company are the biggest holders of oil reserves (see Table 3.8). The development goals of the NOCs are not always aligned with commercial objectives.

Meanwhile, the oil majors are finding it difficult to augment or even maintain their oil reserves. Access to new reserves is proving increasingly difficult as established oil provinces are either in decline or belong to NOCs. Other reserves are physically difficult or expensive to access (deepwater fields, oil and tar sands, the Arctic, among others). NOCs are for the most part cash rich thanks to recent high prices, while the international oil companies are typically rich in technology, capital and expertise. In some cases, successful partnerships are formed. International oil companies have also expanded their range, becoming involved in shale gas projects in the United States and even in renewable energies.

The Organisation of Petroleum Exporting Countries (OPEC) was set up in Baghdad, Iraq, in September 1960 to co-ordinate opposition to cuts in posted prices by the multinational oil companies. It has since expanded its role in an effort to manage the oil market. OPEC seeks to maintain prices within a target range by balancing global supply of

TABLE 3.8 **Leading holders of oil reserves[a], 2012**

| Company[b] | Country | bn barrels |
|---|---|---|
| Saudi Arabian Oil Company (Aramco) | Saudi Arabia | 267.02 |
| Petróleos de Venezuela SA (PDVSA) | Venezuela | 211.17 |
| National Iranian Oil Company (NIOC) | Iran | 151.17 |
| Iraq National Oil Company | Iraq | 143.1 |
| Kuwait Petroleum Corporation | Kuwait | 104.0 |
| Abu Dhabi National Oil Company (ADNOC) | UAE | 97.8 |
| National Oil Corporation | Libya | 47.1 |
| Nigerian National Petroleum Corporation | Nigeria | 37.2 |
| ExxonMobil | US | 24.9 |
| Rosneft | Russia | 22.8 |

a Oil equivalent (includes some gas).
b All state owned except ExxonMobil and Rosneft, in which the government has a 75.16% stake.
**Sources:** Energy Information Agency; Platts

oil with demand in order to achieve a target price. Production quotas – shares in collectively agreed production ceilings, adjusted from time to time – are allocated among its members, which in 2012 were Algeria, Angola, Ecuador, Iran, Iraq, Kuwait, Libya, Nigeria, Qatar, the United Arab Emirates, Saudi Arabia and Venezuela. (Asia's sole member, Indonesia, left the cartel in early 2008, a few years after it had become a net oil importer.)

OPEC members produced about 40% of the world's oil in 2011 (see Table 3.9) and accounted for 72.4% of proven reserves. OPEC has had more success than most cartels. Much of this has been attributable to Saudi Arabia's ability – and willingness – to forgo oil production and revenue and act as OPEC's main swing producer, even though this has sometimes been exploited by other cartel members.

For OPEC members, and their state oil companies, holding or cutting supply leaves more oil in the ground for the future, whereas for multinational companies short-term profitability is more important.

TABLE 3.9 **Oil production**

|  | 1997 | | 2011 | |
| --- | --- | --- | --- | --- |
|  | m barrels/day | % of total | m barrels/day | % of total |
| Total OPEC | 30.5 | 40.6 | 35.7 | 40.4 |
| Total non-OPEC | 43.0 | 57.3 | 50.6 | 57.2 |
|   OECD | 22.0 | 29.3 | 18.9 | 21.3 |
|   Latin America | 3.2 | 4.2 | 4.2 | 4.8 |
|   Asia | 5.4 | 7.2 | 7.7 | 8.7 |
|   Others | 12.4 | 16.5 | 19.8 | 22.4 |
| Processing gains | 1.6 | 2.1 | 2.1 | 2.4 |
| Overall total | 75.0 |  | 88.4 |  |

**Sources:** International Energy Agency; EIU

## Trends, issues and developments

Annual oil production growth averaged barely 1% in 2006–11, largely because of disruptions to supply in producing countries. OPEC action to limit supply in response to the 2008–09 global economic slowdown was also a factor. Unforeseen disruptions to supply in recent years include adverse weather (the hurricane season in the United States), civil unrest (Libya, Yemen, Sudan and Syria), labour unrest (Norway), politically motivated sanctions (Iran), accidents (the Macondo oil spill in the Gulf of Mexico) and unanticipated maintenance (the North Sea).

However, oil supply grew strongly in 2012, by as much as 3.5%, as a result of higher OPEC output and increases in North American production. OPEC production was boosted in 2012 by the restarting of production in Libya and increases in output in Iraq, Saudi Arabia, Nigeria and the Gulf states. This more than offset weakening Iranian production as the country struggled with ageing fields, a lack of investment and difficulty in finding markets because of stringent sanctions. On the non-OPEC front, unconventional North American production – the oil sands in Canada and shale oil in the United States – grew strongly in 2012, offsetting particularly weak North Sea production.

Before the development of oil shale, US oil production appeared to be in terminal decline, falling from 8.53m barrels per day (b/d) in 1996 to a low of 6.92m b/d in 2008. Production stood at 8.13m b/d in 2011, according to the IEA. However, production from oil shale fields alone added at least 700,000 b/d to US output in 2012 – more than the production of a small OPEC producer such as Ecuador (500,000 b/d). Oil shale projects have a much shorter lead time (1–2 years) than conventional oil projects (at least 4–5 years), so they may represent a more flexible form of supply. As yet, it is unclear what the decline rate in oil shale projects and the potential for production will be. However, the consequences could be far-reaching, as oil shale reserves are believed to be widespread across the world; apparently China has already located large reserves.

Saudi Arabia reports that it has existing capacity to produce 12.5m b/d and its output averaged around 10m b/d for much of 2012. There are a number of new developments in the pipeline, including the 900,000 b/d (at full capacity) Manifa field, but much of this new output will replace production from declining wells and be destined for the home market because of strong growth in domestic consumption. However, with reserves estimated at 267bn barrels in 2012, the country will remain among the largest producers and exporters for some time.

The Iraqi government has an ambitious long-term target to raise oil production to 12m b/d, compared with around 3m b/d in 2012, largely through a series of development contracts awarded to international oil companies. Iraq overtook Iran as OPEC's second largest producer in 2012, but constraints on production, such as security risks and infrastructure bottlenecks, remain. International investor interest is also uncertain because of the difficult operating environment in Iraq and lack of clarity over contract terms.

Russia and Saudi Arabia currently vie for the position of top global oil producer, but Russia's proven reserves are lower at around 88 billion barrels. In recent years, Russia's oil industry has had to cope with new taxes and an uncertain business climate coupled with resource nationalism, with Gazprom clawing back some of the assets of foreign companies. However, the tax regime has improved, particularly for brownfield development (enhancement of existing oil sites), and new fields, mainly in eastern Siberia, are coming on stream.

Natural-gas-to-liquid (NGL) production also has been rising strongly.

Brazil will continue to increase output, but there are reports that its mature oilfields are declining more rapidly than envisaged. However, it has embarked on a programme of deep drilling off the coast (below layers of salt – until recently, it was not possible to do seismic surveys below this layer of the Earth's crust), which will lead to more marked increases in output from 2014–15 – assuming the economics of this high-cost development remain attractive.

Output from the North Sea (primarily UK and Norwegian fields) appears to be in terminal decline as new fields coming on stream are not sufficient to offset rapidly declining output in mature fields.

In recent years, production of NGLs has been rising, particularly in OPEC countries. OPEC production grew at an average annual rate of over 4% in 2005–11 (and an annual average of 9% in 2010–11) and stood at 5.8m tonnes in 2011. In 2012, there were particularly strong increases in NGL production in Qatar and the UAE; Libya, Angola, Nigeria and Algeria have also been adding to production. NGL is a useful source of non-oil liquid fuel, but it is not a perfect substitute for crude oil and reportedly cannot substitute for middle distillates.

## The oil market

Spot and futures markets exist in the principal crudes traded internationally. Because oil comes in a changing variety of types, no single crude can be taken as fully representative of the market price. The nearest to this is the series maintained by the IEA in Paris, which calculates a weighted average of the cif (cost, insurance and freight) cost of all crude oils imported by OECD countries. The dominant benchmarks for crudes are Brent Blend (North Sea crudes, seaborne oil) and the land-based West Texas Intermediate (WTI) for North America. Brent is currently used as the basis for the pricing of nearly 70% of the global trade in oil. Other important benchmarks include Russian Urals (Russia-focused), Dubai/Oman (Omani crude oil sold on the Dubai Mercantile Exchange), Mexican Maya and Nigerian Forcados, and there are many more based on either the source of the oil or its characteristics.

WTI and Brent are both traded in New York on NYMEX and in London on ICE Futures Europe. Traditionally, WTI traded at a small premium to Brent, but in 2009 this relationship reversed, and at times in 2012 Brent was trading as much as $20 above WTI. This reflects strong growth in production of North American crudes (WTI is based in land-locked Cushing in Oklahoma); the Brent benchmark, however, reflects problems with North Sea production and tightness in the oil market resulting from weak Iranian oil exports. The unusual situation developing at Cushing, with exceptionally high stocks, suggests that WTI is losing its attractiveness as a global benchmark.

Seasonal demand swings influence the supply/demand balance and the price of oil. Normally, prices increase in the fourth quarter when demand is boosted by stock-building for the northern hemisphere winter months, and decrease in the spring months when space-heating demand falls. However, this is slowly changing as emerging-world consumption increases.

Speculative activity in the oil market is often blamed for price volatility and price spikes. In the run-up to the global financial crisis in 2008, such activity largely took the form of funds investing in customised or structured derivatives (futures or options), investment vehicles designed for exposure to the oil market. These were usually traded in the over-the-counter (OTC) market. As they did not involve physical buying of oil there was no hoarding, but futures prices do influence both the spot price and physical markets.

The crack spread is the differential between the price of crude oil and the petroleum products that are derived from it – essentially the refinery's profit margin. This spread can be traded in futures markets through a spread trade: simultaneous buying and selling contracts in crude oil and a petroleum product, usually gasoline or heating oil. Oil refineries can trade the crack spread as a hedge against the price risk of their operations.

## Price trends

Since 1973, when dominance of the market passed from the international oil companies to OPEC, oil prices have been volatile. The oil shocks of 1973 (the Arab oil embargo) and 1979 (the Iran-Iraq war) were followed by five years of relative calm. In 1986 Saudi Arabia, in an assertion of its authority over OPEC, returned to full

FIG 3.6 **Oil prices**

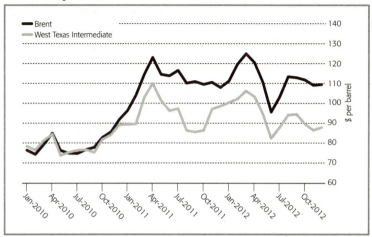

**Source:** Energy Information Administration

production and prices collapsed, falling from an average of $28 per barrel in 1985 to $14/b in 1986. Prices remained weak until 1991 and the first Gulf war, when Iraq invaded Kuwait, but then fell to a low of $12/b in 1998 during the financial crisis in South-East Asia.

Prices started to rise in the early 2000s when the American-led war in Iraq began. Rising demand from emerging markets (coupled with strong economic growth in OECD markets) met with a sluggish response from world oil producers and a real shortage arose. From $25/b in 2002, annual average oil prices (Brent) reached $65/b in 2006 and $73/b in 2007. In the first half of 2008 oil prices soared, reaching a peak in mid-July of nearly $150/b, fuelled by persistent geopolitical risk in oil-producing regions, concerns about long-term supply (particularly in non-OPEC producers), the rising price of other energy sources (principally gas and coal), the weakness of the dollar and speculation in futures markets. Prices subsequently collapsed as investors withdrew from the oil market and the global economy showed clear signs of entering a deep recession. By December 2008, prices were hovering above $30/b, but they recovered quickly and in 2011 the average annual price (Brent) was over $100/b (see Figure 3.6).

In 2012 prices started the year strongly, reflecting a ratcheting up of tensions between Iran and the West over the former's nuclear programme. However, in the second quarter, amid signs of weakening economic indicators in Europe (largely expected) and, more surprisingly, the United States and China, oil prices started to slip. Indeed, futures prices fell to their lowest levels since the third quarter of 2010. Prices started to rally later in the year, buoyed by central bank action in Europe and the United States and the announcement of stimulus in China. For the year as a whole, average prices were slightly higher in 2012 at $111.7/b, compared with $111.4/b in 2011.

## The future

- An increased emphasis on conservation and fuel efficiency will help to contain consumption growth, as will the use of biofuels and some demand rationing (if the price stays high), as well as some substitution of oil by cheaper hydrocarbons. However, outside the OECD consumption is expected to grow steadily, albeit from a low base, as per head incomes and car ownership increase (notwithstanding cyclical downturns in growth). This will ensure a steady expansion in global consumption in the medium term.
- The global economic slowdown could delay or deter investment in refining capacity, as well as lead to some capacity closures. If demand for products recovers strongly, refining bottlenecks could re-emerge.
- Geopolitical risks to supply are numerous: a renewed deterioration in the security situation in Iraq; the possibility of a military strike against Iran to disrupt its nuclear programme; civil disturbance in Nigeria's delta region; nationalism in Venezuela and Russia; and terrorist threats to oil facilities.
- Oil projects are becoming increasingly complex and are subject to delay. Costs are also much higher and some projects face environmental obstacles or technological constraints.
- Transport needs will determine long-term demand, as there are substitutes for oil in almost all its other uses. If a cost-effective, easily accessible alternative to running cars on oil is found, global oil prices would collapse.

# PART 4

# Agriculture

# Cocoa

COCOA IS GROWN mainly in tropical parts of the world, close to the equator and predominantly on smallholdings. Cocoa trees need plenty of rain and sun and protection from strong winds. The main producing countries have two crops a year: a main one and a subsidiary crop, usually called the mid-crop. Disease is often a problem, particularly fungal diseases that are encouraged when conditions are too wet, such as witch's broom, which has caused extensive damage in Brazil, black pod (prevalent everywhere, but especially in Africa) and Vascular-Streak Dieback (VSD). Pests, such as the cocoa-pod borer in South-East Asia, can also be destructive.

Most of the world's cocoa is derived from the Forastero variety of the cocoa plant but two other varieties, Criollo and Trinitario (a hybrid of Criollo and Forastero), are cultivated for their individual taste. Once trees reach maturity, which takes 3–4 years, yields increase for some years and then reach a plateau, which can be maintained for up to 30 years, before going into decline.

Cocoa farmers typically sell their beans to a local co-operative or buyer, which then sells the beans on to grinders. These can be either local companies or foreign buyers, which then ship the beans abroad – or, increasingly, foreign-owned companies operating in the cocoa-growing countries. Some of the large grinders are trading companies and are not involved in the final stage of making the chocolate or confectionery.

## Processes and products

Cocoa beans are cleaned, roasted and ground to produce cocoa liquor. The liquor is then processed to give two intermediate products: cocoa butter and cocoa powder. More than 98% of cocoa ends up in chocolate, other confectionery, bakery products and drinks, with the pharmaceutical and cosmetic industries taking the rest. Cocoa butter, liquor and powder are combined to make chocolate, along with other inputs – mainly milk and sugar.

Historically, cocoa-producing countries exported most of their cocoa beans for processing in their end markets, particularly in Europe and the United States. However, in recent years there has been an

TABLE 4.1 **Leading cocoa-bean-processing countries**[a]

|  | 2005/06 | | 2010/11 | |
| --- | --- | --- | --- | --- |
|  | '000 tonnes | % of total | '000 tonnes | % of total |
| **Importing countries** | 2,230 | 63.6 | 2,329 | 59.3 |
| EU | 1,328 | 37.8 | 1,481 | 37.7 |
|     Netherlands | 465 | 13.3 | 540 | 13.8 |
|     Germany | 307 | 8.7 | 439 | 11.2 |
|     France | 155 | 4.4 | 150 | 3.8 |
|     UK | 138 | 3.9 | 87 | 2.2 |
| US | 432 | 12.3 | 401 | 10.2 |
| Others | 470 | 13.4 | 447 | 11.4 |
| **Exporting countries** | 1,278 | 36.4 | 1598 | 40.7 |
| Côte d'Ivoire | 336 | 9.6 | 361 | 9.2 |
| Malaysia | 265 | 7.5 | 305 | 7.8 |
| Brazil | 223 | 6.3 | 239 | 6.1 |
| Ghana | 85 | 2.4 | 230 | 5.9 |
| Indonesia | 130 | 3.7 | 190 | 4.8 |
| Others | 239 | 6.8 | 273 | 7.0 |
| **Overall total** | 3,508 |  | 3,927 |  |

a Crop year October–September.
**Source:** International Cocoa Organisation

expansion in cocoa-bean grindings in producing countries as they try to move up the value chain. (Nevertheless, beans are sometimes easier to sell than semi-processed cocoa; those who make cocoa-based products generally use a mixture of different beans.)

Grindings in producing countries stood at 41% of total grindings in 2010/11 (the cocoa year is October–September) compared with around 37% in 2005/06 (see Table 4.1). To encourage the move towards domestic processing of cocoa beans and confectionery companies to invest, in 2010 Indonesia started to levy export tax on unprocessed cocoa beans. Lower labour costs in producing countries have been an incentive for foreign companies to invest in local processing.

Mergers and acquisitions among processing companies have led to increased efficiency, but the grinding process is now dominated by a number of large multinationals including Archer Daniels Midland (United States), Barry Callebaut (Belgium), Blommer (United States), Petra Foods (Singapore) and Cargill (United States).

## Consumption and trade

### Regional trends

Cocoa is one of the few agricultural commodities to suffer in an economic downturn, reflecting its status as a luxury item rather than an essential food. Grindings fell sharply in 2008/09, according to the International Cocoa Organization (ICCO). After a strong rebound in the following two seasons, grindings slowed again in 2011/12 in line with weaker economic growth, particularly in western Europe, the main market for cocoa. The growth in cocoa demand in emerging countries is proving more robust, but this is from a low base. Rising cocoa consumption in developing markets is, however, influencing the balance of demand between cocoa butter and cocoa powder, leading to a shift in demand from butter, which is used in richer products like chocolate confectionery, to cocoa powder, which is used in products like chocolate biscuits, cakes and drinks.

The ICCO estimates that the EU and the United States together accounted for 59.6% of final consumption of cocoa in 2010/11, compared with 65.7% in 2002/03. (However, final consumption is difficult to assess because of changes in stocks and variations in the way countries measure the cocoa content of products.) Consumption in Asia (including Japan) rose from 10.7% of total consumption to 13.3% during the same period.

Global consumption of cocoa per head was an estimated average of 0.61kg in 2010/11, compared with 0.56kg in 2002/03. Consumption per head is highest in western Europe, although some northern markets may be close to saturation and growth has slowed. In the Commonwealth of Independent States, consumption per head doubled between 2002/03 and 2010/11 but still stood at just over 1kg per head a year in 2010/11, compared with 2.9kg per head in Europe. Asia's consumption was just 0.15kg per head, while Africa's was just 0.2kg per head.

Demand for more expensive dark chocolate with its high cocoa content, often made with single-origin, organic or "Fair Trade" beans, has been an important market development over the past decade, owing to the perception (supported to some extent by medical research) that dark chocolate is "healthier". However, because of its higher cost, the market for dark and premium chocolate is more vulnerable to the economic cycle. Dark chocolate accounts for about 10% of the chocolate market.

## Trade

Over 85% of world cocoa output is exported, either as raw beans or as processed products, as most producing countries are small final

TABLE 4.2 **Leading exporters and importers, 2010/11[a]**

|  | Exporters | | | Importers | |
| --- | --- | --- | --- | --- | --- |
|  | '000 tonnes | % share |  | '000 tonnes | % share |
| Côte d'Ivoire | 1,079 | 36.1 | Netherlands | 806 | 24.1 |
| Ghana | 697 | 23.3 | US | 472 | 14.1 |
| Indonesia | 275 | 9.2 | Germany | 434 | 13.0 |
| Nigeria | 219 | 7.3 | Belgium | 194 | 5.8 |
| Cameroon | 204 | 6.8 | France | 149 | 4.5 |

a Crop year October–September.
**Source:** International Cocoa Organisation

consumers of the commodity. Exceptions include Brazil, which in some years is a net importer, Mexico and Colombia. The leading exporters –Côte d'Ivoire, Ghana, Indonesia, Nigeria and Cameroon – accounted for 83% of all cocoa-bean exports in 2010/11 (see Table 4.2). In the five seasons to 2010/11, Africa had a 77.4% share of the world export market, with shares of 37% and 22% for Côte d'Ivoire and Ghana respectively. In the same period, Asia's share was 16.4% and Latin America's 6.2%.

In 2010/11, Europe (mainly the EU) accounted for 57% of world imports and the United States 14%. Asia, including Japan, accounted for 13.4%, compared with 8.4% in 2002/03.

## Production and stocks

Cocoa production is highly concentrated in certain parts of the world, principally West Africa, Indonesia and Brazil. Côte d'Ivoire is the world's largest producer, accounting for 35% of the crop in 2010/11 (see Figure 4.1), but production growth has been held back in recent years by civil unrest, which has starved the sector of investment. Other West African countries, particularly Ghana and Cameroon, have been increasing output; Ghana's production increased at an average annual rate of 12.9% between 2002/03 and 2010/11. Accurate assessment of crops in individual West African countries can be skewed, however, by cross-border smuggling, as farmers look for the best price for their beans. Together, the four largest producers in West Africa accounted for 70% of global production in 2010/11. Indonesia is the world's third largest producer of cocoa.

In 2010/11 cocoa production grew by a provisional 18.6% to a new record of 4.3m tonnes, following bumper crops in West African producers and Brazil, another important producer. This was underpinned by La Niña, a global weather phenomenon that can favour West African cocoa production, and attractive prices for beans that encouraged better farm maintenance. However, weather conditions in West Africa were less favourable in the 2011/12 season and the global crop fell to 4m tonnes.

Cocoa production tends to be inelastic in response to price as it takes several years to establish a commercially productive plantation.

FIG 4.1 **Cocoa production,**[a] **2011/12**

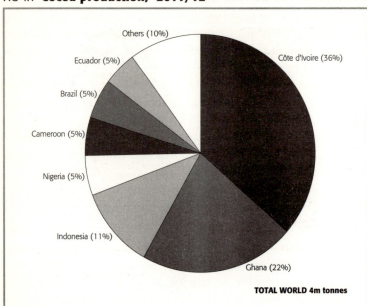

a Gross production; October–September.
**Source:** International Cocoa Organization

However, yields can be improved through increased use of fertilisers and pesticides.

The 1990s were characterised by oversupply and the 2000s by undersupply, at least until the slump in demand in 2008–09. Stocks, however, have remained comfortable. Traditionally, the bulk of stocks were held in importing countries, particularly western Europe's main entry ports, but this has changed in recent years with the growth in processing in producing countries. In 2010/11, a bumper crop and weak consumption growth boosted stocks, and this was one of the factors that led to falling prices during 2011–12.

## The cocoa market

Cocoa futures are traded on the London (Euronext-LIFFE) and New York (NYBOT) stock exchanges, and these provide a reference point for

FIG 4.2 **Cocoa stocks and prices**

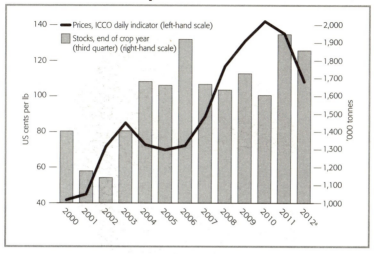

a EIU estimates.
**Source:** International Cocoa Organization

the physical trade in cocoa. Having benchmarks set in London or New York makes it harder for producers or buyers to manipulate prices in local markets. Usually the local markets are free and competitive – apart from Ghana where the Cocoa Marketing Board (Cocobod) is a monopsony buyer. Cocobod exports either directly or through major exporters. In 2012 Côte d'Ivoire launched a number of reforms designed to end years of poor management, dwindling yields and the steady exodus of farmers to other crops. As part of these reforms, a minimum price to be paid to farmers (equivalent to 50–60% of the international price) and forward auctions to ensure farmers a market for their cocoa have been established. Other African producers are likely to adopt similar pricing mechanisms. Fair Trade organisations set prices independently of the market.

The activity of investment funds on futures markets has in recent years played a big role in short-term price movements. They were an important contributing factor in the 50% rise in price from mid-2007 to mid-2008 and the subsequent sharp fall during the global economic slowdown.

## Price trends

In the past couple of decades, cocoa prices have been hugely volatile. This is partly because supply is concentrated in only a few producers, so adverse weather or civil unrest (which disrupts output or trade) in any of the large producers leads to market shortages. Financial investors in the cocoa market have also contributed to price volatility.

Average annual prices rose by 23% and 32% in 2007 and 2008 respectively (see Figure 4.2) before slipping back as investors fled commodity markets, consumption slumped and crops flourished in West Africa. A bumper crop in 2010/11, high stocks and weak global growth depressed prices in 2012, notwithstanding the poorer outlook for supply in West Africa.

## The future

- The outlook for cocoa supply is positive (barring unforeseen shocks such as adverse weather), constraining the potential for sharply higher prices in the medium term. There are ambitious production targets (and, in some cases, investment) in the large producers and also many of the smaller ones, particularly Peru, Papua New Guinea, the Dominican Republic, Colombia, Mexico, Central America, Bolivia, Vietnam, India and Tanzania.
- The impact of El Niño, a global weather phenomenon, is an ever-present short-term supply issue. When severe, El Niño can bring damaging dry weather to cocoa plantations in Indonesia – and possibly in West Africa too, although the link is far from being proved – and heavy rainfall to Ecuador and Brazil.
- Slow global growth in recent years and price-conscious consumers have led to some switching by confectionery-makers from cocoa butter to cheaper vegetable-oil substitutes (for example, palm kernel oil).

# Coffee

COFFEE BEANS ARE NOT ACTUALLY BEANS but are the seeds within a fruit (or cherry) of a tropical tree grown in a large number of countries across Asia, Africa and Latin America. Two principal varieties of coffee are traded internationally: arabica and robusta. Arabica trees grow at high altitudes, often on volcanic soils, and because they are more difficult and costly to grow, the beans trade at a premium. Robusta trees grow at lower altitudes and the beans, while stronger, are considered to have less flavour. Many countries produce both varieties. There are a lot of smallholders growing coffee as well as large farms and estates, particularly in Latin America and Kenya.

As with cocoa, farmers typically sell their beans (or green beans, as they are called before they are roasted) to local co-operatives or buyers, who sell them on to exporters for roasting or processing in the consuming country. Roasters then sell directly to retailers. Coffee roasting is a concentrated activity; nearly 40% of the world's coffee is traded by four companies and 45% is processed by three coffee-roasting firms.

## Processes and processors

There are two primary processing methods: a "dry" method used for most robusta and some arabica coffees (both of which are mainly used in blends and for soluble coffee); and a "wet" process used for most arabica and some robusta coffees. Wet-processed or mild coffees are ideal for making filter coffee and are produced mainly in Colombia, Central America, Mexico, Kenya and Tanzania. Dry-processed coffee is more bitter, ideal for espresso coffees, and is produced largely in Brazil and Ethiopia. Often, the two varieties are mixed or blended.

Most processing takes place in end-user countries and they still dominate. However, all growth in processing is now occurring in producing countries, though they remain only small processors compared with Europe and the United States.

## Consumption and trade
### Regional trends

Between 2006/07 and 2010/11 (September–October), world coffee consumption grew at an annual average of 2.3%. The growth was driven by increasing consumption in coffee-exporting countries and in countries without a tradition of coffee drinking but where incomes were rising, particularly in Asia and Russia. However, consumption suffered in the wake of the global recession in 2008–09, falling by nearly 1% in 2009 (despite a sharp drop in price), because in many of the newer markets coffee is perceived as a luxury good. Indeed, consumption has also fallen in the European market where consumption could have been expected to be more inelastic.

In recent years, the spread of branded coffee shops has contributed to consumption growth in developed markets, particularly in the United States, as well as in newer consuming countries. Speciality coffees, such as Fair Trade, organic, eco-friendly and single origin, have also taken an increasing market share, particularly in developed markets. Furthermore, as global economic growth has slowed, there has been an expansion in household coffee-making equipment, which enables consumers to recreate at home the brews available in coffee shops.

At 19.1m bags in 2010/11 Brazil is the world's second largest coffee consumer after the United States (see Table 4.3). Consumption growth has been strong, at around 4% in recent years, but considering the abundance of supply, coffee consumption levels are still modest (around one-third of the level in most European countries), owing to a lack of a coffee-drinking culture. Consumption has also been rising strongly in other exporting countries, including Ethiopia, Mexico and Vietnam. Increasing urbanisation in these emerging markets, the gradual development of a café culture and firm growth in private consumption are underpinning growth in coffee demand. At just 600,000 bags, annual consumption in China is extremely low for a country its size.

TABLE 4.3 **Leading coffee-consuming countries**[a]

|  | 2006/07 | | 2010/11 | |
| --- | --- | --- | --- | --- |
|  | m 60kg bags | % of total | m 60kg bags | % of total |
| Importing countries[b] | 93.1 | 72.7 | 95.5 | 70.1 |
| EU | 41.2 | 32.1 | 41.0 | 30.1 |
| US | 21.2 | 16.5 | 21.8 | 16.0 |
| Japan | 7.3 | 5.7 | 7.1 | 5.2 |
| Others | 23.5 | 18.3 | 25.6 | 18.8 |
| **Exporting countries** | 35.0 | 27.3 | 40.7 | 29.9 |
| Brazil | 16.3 | 12.7 | 19.1 | 14.0 |
| Ethiopia | 2.7 | 2.1 | 3.4 | 2.5 |
| Indonesia | 2.8 | 2.2 | 3.3 | 2.4 |
| Mexico | 2.0 | 1.6 | 2.4 | 1.7 |
| Others | 11.1 | 8.7 | 12.5 | 9.2 |
| **Total consumption** | 128.1 | | 136.2 | |

a Crop year September–October. b Defined as net disappearance.
**Source:** International Coffee Organisation

## Trade

Brazil is by far the largest coffee exporter, accounting for around one-third of global exports in 2010/11, followed by Vietnam and Colombia, with nearly 19% and 7% of the market respectively (see Table 4.4) according to the International Coffee Organization (ICO).

The United States was the largest single importing country in 2011, accounting for 24.2% of total imports. Germany is the second largest import market, while the EU as a whole accounted for 65% of global imports. Japan is another important source of import demand.

Historically, coffee was shipped in its raw form, but there are moves towards more processing being undertaken in the producing countries. However, processed coffee can result in higher shipping

TABLE 4.4 **Leading exporters and importers**

|  | Exports, 2010/11 | | | Imports, 2011 | |
| --- | --- | --- | --- | --- | --- |
|  | '000 bags | % of total |  | '000 bags | % of total |
| Brazil | 31,880 | 30.6 | US | 26,088 | 24.2 |
| Vietnam | 19,575 | 18.8 | Germany | 20,926 | 19.4 |
| Colombia | 7,017 | 6.7 | Italy | 8,362 | 7.8 |
| Indonesia | 6,185 | 5.9 | France | 7,544 | 7.0 |
| India | 5,939 | 5.7 | Belgium | 5,828 | 5.4 |

**Source:** International Coffee Organisation

charges or import duties, and consumers often seek to have more control over the roasting process. Nevertheless, exports of soluble coffee (green bean equivalent) by coffee-growing countries have been rising and now account for about 8–10% of total exports, compared with 5.3% in 2000. Brazil is by far the biggest soluble exporter. The dominance of a few multinationals in the coffee business – in particular Nestlé (Switzerland), Sara Lee/Douwe Egberts (United States) and Kraft (United States) – has reduced the power of coffee farmers to influence prices or the market more generally.

## Production and stocks

Global coffee production grew at an average annual rate of 3.2% between 2006/07 and 2011/12, but this marks a slowdown from annual growth of nearly 4% during the 1990s. This reflects a lack of investment (particularly in Brazil) as well as a series of weather-related disruptions to supply. Brazil is by far the largest producer (see Figure 4.3), accounting for 32% of production in 2011/12 (a biennial down year). Historically, changes in Brazilian output could make the difference between a seasonal global shortage or a surplus, but in recent years, strong growth in other suppliers, especially Vietnam, has meant that the market is no longer so sensitive to performance in Brazil. The potential dangers to the Brazilian harvest are frosts from early June to August in the south, and drought from September to December in the north, by far the more important producing region.

FIG 4.3 **Coffee production, 2011/12**

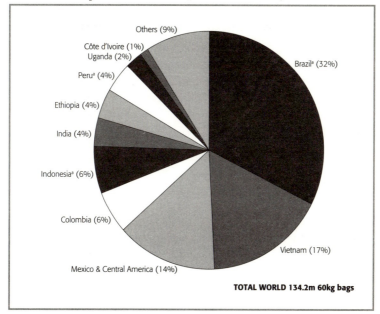

a Crop year April–March, all others October–September.
**Sources:** International Coffee Organization; US Department of Agriculture; EIU

The biennial cycle of the country's arabica trees also affects the size of the harvest. (Brazil is the only significant producer with marked "on" and "off" seasons for yields.) Colombia, Peru, Ecuador, Mexico and Central America are all important coffee-growing regions, but Colombia's output has fallen in recent years, partly because of adverse weather and partly because of a rejuvenation programme, the rewards of which will come later.

Asia (primarily India, Indonesia and Vietnam) accounts for about 25% of global production. Despite stagnation in the traditional supplier, Indonesia, growth in production in Vietnam, in particular, and India has been strong. Coffee (robusta) production in Vietnam continues to benefit from an expansion in coffee plantations and better farm maintenance. It is now the world's largest coffee exporter (reflecting very low domestic consumption) and second largest producer, with a harvest of 22.5m bags in 2011/12.

Africa, where coffee farming has been starved of investment and at times hit by civil disturbance, now accounts for little more than 12% of exportable supply. However, many countries in the region, including Uganda, Tanzania (which is extending credit provision to farmers) and Cameroon, have ambitious expansion plans. Coffee production in Côte d'Ivoire is also expected to pick up following the disruption to supply caused by civil unrest.

## The coffee market

The main international futures markets for coffee are in New York (arabicas) and London (robustas); a screen-based robusta contract was opened in New York in late 2007. Sizeable futures markets also exist in São Paulo and Tokyo. Physical trading of green coffee takes place in New York and in Europe at Le Havre, Marseilles, Hamburg and Bremen. Internet auctions for premium arabica coffees are also becoming established.

## Price trends

For decades (between the 1960s and 1980s), coffee prices were controlled by International Coffee Agreements (ICAs), which sought to manage exports in a bid to maintain prices at a level acceptable to both consumers and producers. Intervention ended in July 1989, and prices were subsequently hit by large increases in coffee production in Brazil and Vietnam. Coffee prices were particularly low in 2001–03, averaging just 63 cents per lb (arabica) before a series of poor crops led to lower stocks at a time of robust demand to send prices soaring (see Figure 4.4). Prices were averaging nearly 140 cents/lb by 2008, boosted by speculation in the run-up to the 2008–09 global financial crisis.

Coffee prices proved surprisingly resilient during the subsequent global economic downturn, largely because of disappointing crops which meant that the market was in deficit for five years between 2007/08 and 2011/12. Prices reached an annual average of 271 cents/lb in 2011. However, improving supply and negligible consumption growth at this time (perhaps partly because of the high price) led to a subsequent sharp fall in prices in 2012: arabica prices fell by 31% and robusta prices by 6%.

## FIG 4.4 Coffee stocks and prices

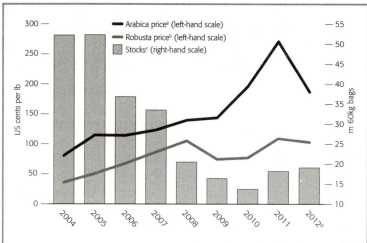

a ICO Other Milds indicator. b ICO Robusta indicator.
c Gross stocks in exporting countries and estimated inventories in importing countries on September 30th.
d EIU estimates.
**Source:** International Coffee Organization

## The future

- Global stocks of coffee were still low in 2012 and will only reach a more comfortable level after a few years in which production exceeds demand by a significant amount. Any severe disruption to supply from a large producer could cause prices to spiral higher.

- Supply should continue to grow as many countries have rehabilitation schemes in place or on the drawing board aimed at boosting yields and cutting costs. Furthermore, the legacy of several years of historically high prices has allowed farmers to invest in better crop maintenance and expand planted area.

- The outlook for global coffee consumption is for sluggish growth, with lower growth in most OECD countries (Europe in particular) than in non-traditional markets (mainly in the developing world) for some time.

# Fibres

## COTTON

Cotton is a soft fibre that grows on a variety of plants of the *gossypium* species, which is a member of the mallow family. Four main types of cotton plant are cultivated: *gossypium hirsutum*, which originated in Central America and accounts for 90% of world production; one native to Peru; one native to the Middle East and Africa; and a tree variety that originated in South Asia. Cotton grows around the seeds of the plant in a protective pod or boll and is almost pure cellulose, which means that is soft, breathable and absorbs moisture easily.

Cotton used to be picked manually in what was an arduous process, but now most picking is mechanised. Once harvested, the cotton is combed to remove the seeds. This was also a manual job before the invention of the cotton gin, which is now used to prepare the cotton for spinning. Cotton is typically spun to make a yarn or thread. The intermediate processing stages are many: spinning, weaving, knitting, dyeing, finishing, the manufacture of clothing, and so on.

## Consumption and trade
### Regional trade

While cotton competes with other natural fibres such as wool, flax, jute and bamboo, more serious competition has come from synthetic (petroleum-based) and artificial (cellulose-based) fibres. Today, the use of cotton in products such as net draperies, sportswear, hosiery and technical textiles is small. In many other products – woven shirts, for example – cotton is often blended, usually with polyester. Cotton

TABLE 4.5 **Leading cotton-consuming countries**[a]

|            | 1992/93  |            | 2001/02  |            | 2011/12  |            |
|------------|----------|------------|----------|------------|----------|------------|
|            | m tonnes | % of total | m tonnes | % of total | m tonnes | % of total |
| China      | 4.59     | 26.1       | 5.70     | 29.1       | 8.64     | 37.8       |
| India      | 2.10     | 12.0       | 2.91     | 14.9       | 4.42     | 19.4       |
| Pakistan   | 1.51     | 8.6        | 1.86     | 9.5        | 2.16     | 9.5        |
| Turkey     | 0.68     | 3.8        | 1.30     | 6.6        | 1.30     | 5.7        |
| Brazil     | 0.80     | 4.5        | 0.83     | 4.2        | 0.89     | 3.9        |
| US         | 0.11     | 0.6        | 0.24     | 1.2        | 0.72     | 3.2        |
| Bangladesh | 2.23     | 12.7       | 1.68     | 8.6        | 0.70     | 3.1        |
| EU         | 0.45     | 2.5        | 1.08     | 5.5        | 0.18     | 0.8        |
| Others     | 5.12     | 29.1       | 3.97     | 20.3       | 3.82     | 16.7       |
| Total      | 17.57    |            | 19.57    |            | 22.83    |            |

a Years ending July 31st.
**Source:** International Cotton Advisory Committee

accounted for an estimated one-third of world fibre consumption in 2010, compared with almost half in 1990.

Approximately 60% of cotton consumption is in the manufacture of clothing, notably jeans, shirts and t-shirts. A significant proportion is used to make household textiles: towels, table linen, bedding, curtains and upholstery fabrics. Other uses are in non-woven products such as cotton wool and bandages and in more industrial products such as thread and tarpaulins.

Cotton consumption has been in long-term decline in Europe, Japan and the United States as textile manufacturing has moved to lower-cost parts of the world, particularly in Asia. The 1994 North American Free Trade Agreement (NAFTA) boosted the use of cotton by the textile industries of Mexico and the Caribbean, mainly for export as apparel to the United States. Since 2005, however, these countries have lost market share as a result of competition from lower-priced imports, mainly from China.

Accession to the World Trade Organisation (WTO) in December

2001 boosted China's textile and apparel industries. The expiry of the Agreement on Textiles and Clothing (ATC) on January 1st 2005 has had an even bigger impact; exports by China and the Indian subcontinent have boomed.

China is now the largest consumer of cotton, accounting for an estimated 38% of total consumption in 2011/12 (August-July); India is the second largest consumer, accounting for 19.4% of the market in the same year (see Table 4.5). However, the recent spikes in prices coupled with the need to import raw cotton have led to Chinese spinners switching from cotton either to pure man-made fibres or to blends of cotton and man-made fibres.

## Trade

Exports accounted for 36% of world cotton production in 2011/12, according to the International Cotton Advisory Committee (ICAC). The United States is typically the largest exporter of raw cotton, accounting for 2.5m tonnes or 25% of world exports in the same year (see Table 4.6). Second to the United States was India, followed by Australia, with shares of 24% and 10% respectively. Although small producers individually, the African franc zone countries are becoming increasingly important exporters, accounting for 5.5% of global exports in 2011/12. India, in particular, sometimes restricts exports of cotton in

TABLE 4.6 **Leading exporters and importers, 2011/12[a]**

| | Exports | | | Imports | |
|---|---|---|---|---|---|
| | '000 tonnes | % of total | | '000 tonnes | % of total |
| US | 2,526 | 25.9 | China | 5,342 | 55.0 |
| India | 2,410 | 24.3 | Bangladesh | 680 | 7.0 |
| Australia | 1,043 | 10.5 | Turkey | 519 | 5.3 |
| Uzbekistan | 585 | 5.9 | Indonesia | 440 | 4.5 |
| African franc zone[b] | 550 | 5.5 | Thailand | 275 | 2.8 |

a Years ending July 31st. b Benin, Burkina Faso, Cameroon, Central African Republic, Chad, Côte d'Ivoire, Madagascar, Mali, Niger, Senegal, Togo.
**Source:** International Cotton Advisory Committee

a bid to protect its large textile sector; this can distort the market and be a powerful determinant of prices.

China is the largest importing country, accounting for 55% of global imports in 2011/12. Other East and South-East Asian countries – Indonesia, South Korea, Taiwan, Thailand and Japan – are also large importers. Total Asian imports accounted for 75% of global trade in 2011/12. In September 2011, the Chinese government initiated a massive reserve buying programme, which led to increased imports in the following year, notwithstanding markedly slower growth in textile production and exports.

## Production

The United States was displaced by China as the world's largest producer of cotton in 2002/03, and in 2006/07 it was pushed into third place by India. China was the world's largest producer of cotton in 2011/12, accounting for nearly 27.4% of global output, but India was not far behind with a 21.5% market share (see Table 4.7).

The American government subsidises cotton producers and exporters; in recent years this has proved controversial, with Brazil and African countries challenging the subsidies. EU countries, particularly Spain and Greece, also offer subsidies, but output is small and thus this has not been the subject of debate. China offers incentives to producers, but as it is a net importer of cotton this is not deemed to be a market-distorting activity. India and many African producers offer minimum support prices to farmers, but the level of subsidy is generally low.

Genetically modified (GM) crops have become widespread, particularly in India where they account for 90–95% of production, and have led to a significant increase in cotton output in recent years. However, because of a fall in prices, India's cotton farmers are considering other crops such as soybeans which are less labour intensive, need fewer pesticides and have a shorter crop cycle (so they can have a second crop in one calendar year).

Production in eastern Europe and central Asia declined after the break-up of the Soviet Union, but it has since recovered in Uzbekistan, Turkmenistan, Tajikistan and Kazakhstan and is typically price competitive. In the African franc zone, production has been hit by low prices (initially) and irregular seasonal rains. However, efforts to invest in the sector are now leading to larger harvests.

Cotton is liable to infestation, so herbicides and pesticides are used extensively. In the past decade, growers have started to produce considerably more expensive 'ethical' organic cotton, grown without the use of pesticides and harvested in ways that do not involve human exploitation.

TABLE 4.7 **Leading cotton-producing countries**[a]

|  | 1992/93 | | 2001/02 | | 2011/12 | |
| --- | --- | --- | --- | --- | --- | --- |
|  | m tonnes | % of total | m tonnes | % of total | m tonnes | % of total |
| China | 4.51 | 25.1 | 5.32 | 24.8 | 7.40 | 27.1 |
| India | 2.38 | 13.2 | 2.69 | 12.5 | 6.00 | 22.0 |
| US | 3.53 | 19.6 | 4.42 | 20.6 | 3.39 | 12.4 |
| Pakistan | 1.54 | 8.6 | 1.78 | 8.3 | 2.29 | 8.4 |
| Brazil | 0.42 | 2.3 | 0.77 | 3.6 | 1.88 | 6.9 |
| Uzbekistan | 1.31 | 7.3 | 1.06 | 4.9 | 0.88 | 3.2 |
| Others | 4.31 | 23.9 | 5.44 | 25.3 | 5.43 | 19.9 |
| Total | 18.00 | | 21.48 | | 27.27 | |

a Years ending July 31st.
**Source:** International Cotton Advisory Committee

## The cotton market

The Cotlook A index is the internationally recognised benchmark price for spot cotton trading. It is calculated based on the five cheapest cottons available in the Asian market. Futures and options are traded on the ICE Futures exchange in New York. There are around 20 cotton exchanges around the world, in both producing and consuming countries, where raw cotton is traded.

Cotton is graded by country of origin, staple length, fineness and maturity. Objective grading criteria have been introduced, of which the micronaire ranking of fibre quality is the most significant.

## FIG 4.5 **Cotton stocks and prices**

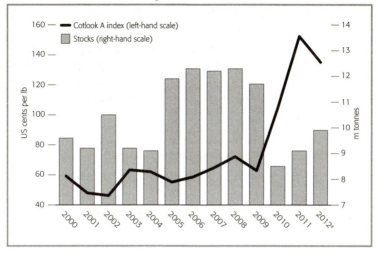

a EIU estimates.
**Source:** International Cotton Advisory Committee

## Price trends

Cotton prices are affected by trends in other industrial raw material prices, by the prices of possible substitutes (wool and man-made fibres), developments in the textile sector, the value of the dollar, and the demand and supply fundamentals associated with cotton. As a result, prices have been extremely volatile in recent years.

During the strong global growth years of 2003–08, cotton prices rose at an annual average rate of 8.6% boosted by strong demand from China's textile export sector. Supply responded and the market was generally in surplus during this period, with a steady build-up of stocks. Like the prices of all industrial raw materials, cotton prices fell in 2009, by nearly 13%, in response to weaker demand. A poor crop in 2009/10 sent the market into deficit and there was a surge in cotton prices; annual average prices rose by nearly 67% in 2010 and 45% in 2011 in response to the tighter supply outlook (see Figure 4.5). However, demand growth was weak (partly because of the rise in prices), and in the second half of 2011 prices started to tumble and continued to fall during 2012. Another bumper crop in 2011/12, encouraged by the earlier high prices, further undermined prices. Buying by China to replenish state reserves was one of the few factors offering support to the price.

## The future

- In 2012 domestic prices in China were significantly higher than international prices, so spinners started using man-made fibres or imported yarn made from cheaper cotton. The government also imposes quotas on fibre imports. Such interventionist policies could undermine cotton consumption.
- The sharp fall in cotton prices in 2012 should encourage cotton consumption, although man-made fibres are still cheaper.
- Cotton is a sustainable fibre (in that it comes from a crop that can be grown again, whereas most man-made fibres are based on petroleum, a finite resource), which should boost its attractiveness in the medium term.

## WOOL

Sheep are reared for their wool or their meat, or both. With incomes rising and meat consumption growing in the developing world, sheep farmers are increasingly focusing on the production of meat rather than wool.

### Consumption and uses

Around two-thirds of the world's wool is used to make clothes, with the remainder (usually coarser wools) used in the manufacture of carpets and furniture upholstery. Wool was traditionally used to make heavy woollen fabrics for overcoats and suits, but in recent years demand has fallen and now wool is used increasingly to make lightweight woollen fabrics. Efforts have also been made to ensure that wool is more user friendly with the development of machine-washable wools. Of the synthetic fibres, acrylic and increasingly polyester compete most successfully with wool in knitwear and blankets.

Consumption of wool has been affected in a similar way to cotton, as the textile industry has moved to lower-cost parts of the world. Scourers and manufacturers of wool tops for spinning account for most of wool's immediate market.

During the 1980s the EU, the United States and the former Soviet Union were the largest consumers of wool, but these markets have been in decline over the past couple of decades. The break-up of the Soviet Union led to a fall in regional demand for wool, military clothing having been a significant end-use. The EU remains an important, although declining, market accounting for 16% of consumption in 2010/11. Italy and Turkey are still large clothing manufacturers, and Belgium is a significant manufacturer of carpets. Although wool consumption in the EU appears to be in structural decline, the trend has been exacerbated by the global economic slowdown. There are clear signs of a switch by price-conscious consumers away from garments made of pure wool to those made of cheaper wool mixed with man-made fibres or pure man-made fibres. There is also a more general move away from wool floor coverings in favour of wooden floors, which is reducing consumption of the coarser wools. However, the decline in consumption might have been greater without the UK-led "Campaign for Wool", which has encouraged the use of wool in designer wear and promoted the environmental benefits of wool vis-à-vis man-made fibres.

China is now the world's largest consumer, accounting for an estimated 38% of the market in 2010/11 (see Table 4.8). In machinery to process wool, it also accounts for 25% of global installed long staple spindles and 20% of wool looms. Moreover, China's wool-processing industry has continued to invest and upgrade machinery. However, weak demand in destination markets, particularly Europe, has led to lower growth in China's wool consumption. The second largest consumer is India, accounting for 8% of the market.

TABLE 4.8 **Leading wool-consuming countries, 2010/11**[a]

|  | '000 tonnes | % of total |
|---|---|---|
| China | 402 | 37.8 |
| EU | 170 | 16.0 |
| India | 82 | 7.7 |
| Turkey | 46 | 4.3 |
| Russia | 16 | 1.5 |
| Uzbekistan | 16 | 1.5 |
| Japan | 11 | 1.0 |
| US | 7 | 0.7 |
| Others | 315 | 29.6 |
| Total | 1,065 |  |

a Years ending June 30th.
**Sources:** International Wool Trade Organisation; EIU estimates

## Production

Supply is dominated by Australia (see Figure 4.6), where wool has traditionally been sold at auction in greasy (unwashed) form. Merchants mediate between producers and processors (mainly located in the northern hemisphere, particularly China and Europe),

FIG 4.6 **Wool production,**[a] **2010/11**

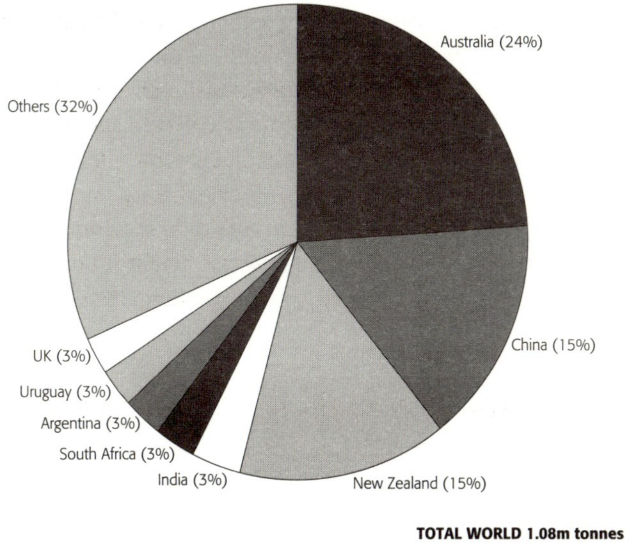

- Australia (24%)
- Others (32%)
- UK (3%)
- Uruguay (3%)
- Argentina (3%)
- South Africa (3%)
- India (3%)
- New Zealand (15%)
- China (15%)

**TOTAL WORLD 1.08m tonnes**

a Years ending June 30th; clean equivalent.
**Sources:** International Wool Trade Organisation; EIU

matching supplies of the various grades with the needs of the textile trade. An increasing proportion of Australian sheep are crossbreeds, which produce coarser wools and are primarily bred for meat production, rather than merinos, which produce the finer wools.

In China, increasing demand for sheepmeat has led to a fall in the sheep population in recent years, after strong growth in the 1990s. The production of wool has also been falling. However, the 12th five-year plan (2011–15) places great emphasis on the wool textile industry with respect to eco-sustainability, improved pollution control, and advanced spinning and dyeing technologies; and provincial governments are now providing financial incentives to domestic wool producers. This is unlikely to be totally successful, however, because high prices and high demand mean that sheepmeat will still be more profitable. Furthermore, in some regions agricultural land, which contains natural resources such as coal, gas and oil, is being redeveloped, with the result that wool is no longer the main income for farmers.

New Zealand, also an important source of supply of coarser wools (generally the by-product of sheep farming for meat), is the world's third largest wool producer. However, as the sheep population has fallen, so has wool production. This is largely because land has been used for different purposes, particularly dairy; and despite high wool prices, farmers have not been discouraged from increasing sheep slaughterings to meet the growing demand for sheepmeat.

Australia is the dominant producer of fine apparel-type wools, whereas China, New Zealand and the former Soviet Union are the dominant producers of coarser carpet-type wools. Argentina, Uruguay and South Africa are also important wool producers, mainly of apparel-type wools.

## The wool market

The grading of wool recognises sheep breed (merino, crossbred, and so on), condition (greasy or clean), fibre quality and degree of contamination. In general, the longer and finer the staple, the higher the grade. Objective grading techniques are usually employed.

The Australian Wool Exchange (AWEX) compiles data on auction prices and the AWEX Eastern Market Indicator (EMI) is considered the benchmark wool price (it is priced in Australian cents per kg). The AWEX indicators are also used as the basis for any wool derivatives trading. Most Australian wool is still sold in open outcry auctions, which run for approximately 46 weeks in the year and take place in Sydney, Melbourne, Fremantle and Newcastle. New Zealand Wool Services compiles data on wool sales in New Zealand; these prices are considered the benchmark for coarser carpet wools.

## Price trends

Wool prices were historically stable and were largely unaffected by the commodity price boom in 2003–08, with apparel wools falling at an annual average of 1% and coarser wools rising by an annual average of just 2.3%. A general trend of falling wool production since then has been positive for prices, which started to soar in 2010 and rose

FIG 4.7 **Wool stocks and prices**

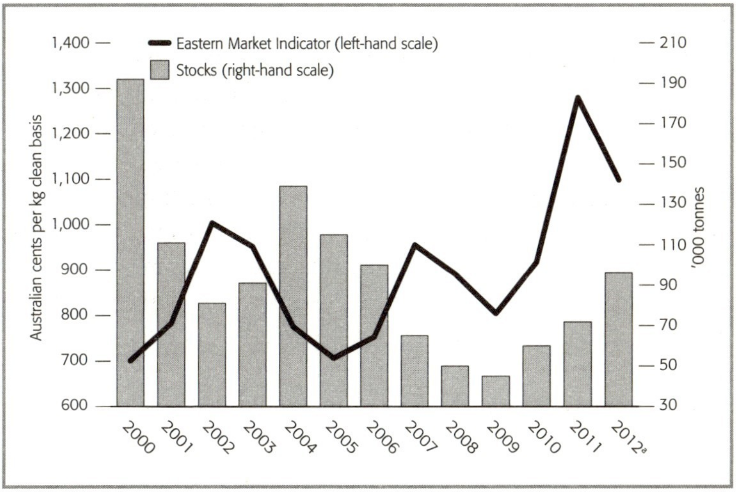

- Eastern Market Indicator (left-hand scale)
- Stocks (right-hand scale)

Australian cents per kg clean basis / '000 tonnes

a EIU estimates.
**Source:** International Wool Trade Organisation

by nearly 40% in 2011 (see Figure 4.7). Stocks had also fallen to a low in 2008/09, requiring some stock-building, which supported prices. Part of the increase in price was no doubt also a result of the rally in cotton prices, for which wool can be a substitute. Prices subsequently weakened in 2012 owing to weak demand and the strength of the Australian and New Zealand currencies, which increases the cost to importers. (Wool is one of the few commodities that does not have a benchmark US dollar price.)

## The future

- Although prices have fallen, wool is expected to remain expensive compared with synthetic fibres and even cotton, which will deter consumption, at least until global growth picks up.
- In the medium term, as incomes rise in the developing world, there should be higher uptake of more expensive woollen garments, although this may depend on fashion.

- The wool textile industry in China is starting to face structural problems including overcapacity, rising labour and energy costs, and difficulty in obtaining financing (perhaps because of the other three issues). However, moving up the value chain to make more expensive woollen clothing means China's wool consumption may continue to grow.
- Like cotton, wool is a sustainable fibre compared with most man-made fibres, which could add to its attractiveness in the medium term.
- Wool production will continue to suffer from the rising demand for sheepmeat and a move away from breeding sheep just for shearing.

# Maize

MAIZE IS A CEREAL GRAIN native to North and Central America. It grows best in warmer climates and needs sun and well-drained soil to thrive, although it can grow in less ideal conditions.

## Uses

In 2011/12 global consumption reached 853m tonnes, 41% more than in 2000/01. About 60% of the total is used for animal feed, with human consumption typically accounting for about 11%. The remainder is used by industry, mainly for ethanol and starch. The huge American feed industry absorbs about 15% of global supply. There is substantial consumption in other regions where maize is a major crop, including China, southern and eastern Europe, Brazil and Mexico, as well as in some non-producing countries such as Japan with large livestock numbers. Maize is particularly well-suited for pig and poultry feeds, but may be partly displaced by wheat, sorghum, soybeans or industrial co-products such as distillers' grains when they are cheaper.

Increasing demand for meat is one of two forces driving the global maize economy. The establishment of large-scale poultry and pig farming, which has made meat affordable even in lower-income developing countries, has greatly stimulated demand for maize. Since the late 1990s, outbreaks of pig and poultry diseases, especially in East and South-East Asia, have undermined consumer confidence and disrupted the meat trade, leading in turn to fluctuations in maize feeding and imports. However, recovery from these reversals has generally been rapid.

The other main determinant of demand is biofuel production. Maize-based ethanol is made mainly in the United States, where tax concessions have led to massive growth in manufacturing capacity and demand for feedstock. The impact on feed and food prices as demand for maize soars has raised questions, both within the United States and worldwide, about the wisdom of the policy. China is the second largest producer of maize-based ethanol, followed by the EU and Canada.

## Consumption and trade
### Regional trends

Consumption of maize in the United States, the world's largest consumer, passed 200m tonnes for the first time in 2001/02 and stood at 279m tonnes in 2011/12 (see Table 4.9), with consumption dominated by stockfeed and the ethanol sector, which has been consuming about 110m tonnes of maize a year. Feed demand is influenced by cyclical changes in livestock numbers, which in turn are linked to wider trends in the United States and global economies, and by the maize price, since substitutes exist. American ethanol consumption is underpinned by a Renewable Fuels Standard (RFS), which mandates minimum inclusion of renewables in automotive fuel. However, maize use for ethanol fell for the first time in 2011, probably in response to high maize prices in that year as well as a fall in total petrol consumption. The starch industry's consumption has been slipping in recent years as the economic downturn lowered demand for construction materials and paper products; and consumption of maize-based sweeteners, including high-fructose corn syrup (HFCS), is also falling.

China is the second largest maize-consuming country, using around 181m tonnes in 2011/12, of which feed use accounted for around two-thirds. The government has limited the use of food and feedgrains to make ethanol, and some plants have switched to imported cassava chips. China has been a net importer of maize since 2009/10 and the government operates a policy of buffer stocks to try to stabilise retail prices.

In Brazil, feedgrain requirements have increased as a result of growing poultry and pigmeat exports, as well as rising domestic

TABLE 4.9 **Leading maize-consuming countries**[a]

|  | 2001/02 | | 2011/12 | |
| --- | --- | --- | --- | --- |
|  | m tonnes | % of total | m tonnes | % of total |
| US | 200.9 | 32.4 | 278.9 | 32.7 |
| China | 123.1 | 19.9 | 181.0 | 21.2 |
| Other East Asia | 64.2 | 10.4 | 84.7 | 9.9 |
| Brazil | 35.0 | 5.6 | 51.1 | 6.0 |
| Mexico | 25.5 | 4.1 | 29.8 | 3.5 |
| Other Latin America | 24.1 | 3.9 | 32.9 | 3.9 |
| EU | 50.4 | 8.1 | 68.4 | 8.0 |
| Sub-Saharan Africa | 35.9 | 5.8 | 55.6 | 6.5 |
| North Africa | 15.6 | 2.5 | 18.0 | 2.1 |
| Others | 45.3 | 7.3 | 52.8 | 6.2 |
| Total | 620 |  | 853.0 |  |

a Local marketing years.
**Sources:** International Grains Council; US Department of Agriculture

meat consumption. The government's "zero hunger" subsidised food distribution programme, although mainly based on rice, has stimulated the use of maize for food, mostly in north-east Brazil. In Mexico, home-grown white maize is a food more than a feedgrain. Although consumers have diversified their diets in recent years, the enduring popularity of white tortillas and continued population growth are increasing the food use of maize. Feed use of yellow maize (most of which is imported from the United States) in Mexico is primarily for the poultry industry.

In the EU, maize is primarily used for animal feed, and quantities vary with the price and availability of alternatives. Since the EU's grain surpluses were run down in the early 2000s domestic supply has fluctuated, and large imports are sometimes needed. The EU continues to have a zero-tolerance policy on unapproved varieties of GM maize.

Having grown steadily for the past ten years at an annual average rate of 3.5%, annual consumption of maize is expected to fall in 2012/13 for the first time since 1995/96, following a severe drought in the United States in 2012, which limited availability and in turn consumption. High prices will lead to some demand rationing.

## Trade

Growth in world maize trade has been underpinned by increasing demand for animal feed. Total trade in 2010/11 and 2011/12 averaged 96m tonnes or about 11% of total output. The import needs of several middle-income developing countries with growing livestock industries have risen, although in many parts of East Asia lower-cost meat imports are putting pressure on the domestic livestock industry and imports of feed are slowly decreasing. China is now a net importer of maize, with imports reaching an estimated 5.3m tonnes in 2011/12. Mexico is also a significant buyer (11.2m tonnes in 2011/12), its imports sourced exclusively from the United States.

In general, EU countries obtain most of their maize from France, except when the crop is poor, but newer member states source their maize imports more widely.

Most countries in Sub-Saharan Africa are self-sufficient in maize in good crop years, but they may buy (or receive as food aid) significant amounts during a drought. Non-GM white maize, preferred for food use, is usually available from South Africa. Some countries are prepared to import GM maize if it can be milled at the port of entry without risk of contaminating the domestic crop.

The United States is by far the biggest maize exporter, with exports of 38.5m tonnes in 2011/12 (see Table 4.10). It has not used export subsidies in recent years, but competitors claim that indirect support has the same effect. Shipments that (inadvertently) included unapproved types of GM maize have occasionally caused problems between the United States and its trading partners.

Argentina is traditionally the second largest maize exporter, with exports of 16.7m tonnes in 2011/12. Shipments are normally concentrated in the few months after harvest, peaking in April and encountering little competition during the northern hemisphere winter. Unlike its main competitors, Argentina's maize exports are taxed. In recent years the authorities, alarmed by the effect of exports on domestic prices and tightening availability, have also sometimes closed the export registries, adding to the uncertainties facing exporters and producers. Brazil's booming production has made it an important player in export markets and it has increased its share of the European market, where the non-GM status of its maize is an added advantage.

TABLE 4.10 **Leading exporters and importers, 2011/12**

| | Exports | | | Imports | |
|---|---|---|---|---|---|
| | m tonnes | % of total | | m tonnes | % of total |
| US | 38.5 | 37.5 | Japan | 15.0 | 14.6 |
| Argentina | 16.7 | 16.3 | Mexico | 11.2 | 10.9 |
| Ukraine | 15.0 | 14.6 | South Korea | 7.5 | 7.3 |
| Brazil | 12.7 | 12.4 | Egypt | 7.1 | 6.9 |
| India | 4.4 | 4.3 | EU | 6.3 | 6.1 |

**Source:** US Department of Agriculture

## Production and stocks

World maize output has risen strongly in recent years and again reached 858m tonnes in 2011 (see Table 4.11). The United States is by far the biggest producer, accounting for 37% of the world total. Most is grown in the Midwest, where Illinois and Iowa together account for almost 33% of production. Output is vulnerable to local weather conditions, especially drought during the short period in midsummer when the crop is pollinated, as happened in 2012. There is considerable switching between maize and soybeans, depending on their relative price, by American farmers.

Maize yields in the United States continue to rise faster than those of other grains. GM maize, incorporating insect or herbicide resistance, is now planted on more than three-quarters of the maize area, compared with one-quarter in 2001. Farmers like GM maize because of its greater reliability and lower input costs. The American feed industry, unlike its counterparts in Europe and East Asia, is relaxed about using GM grain, but inclusion of unapproved varieties of GM maize in shipments to less tolerant countries means that better ways must be found to segregate varieties.

Since 2001, economic difficulties have forced Argentina's government to introduce taxes in the agricultural industry. However, strong export demand has generally encouraged production, and investment in water management and farm machinery continues. Marginal land is also being brought into use, sometimes growing GM maize. Maize increasingly competes with soybeans, the latter crop being cheaper to grow as it needs less fertiliser.

Brazil is also an important maize producer. Output, which has been growing rapidly in recent years because of favourable prices and increasing export opportunities, reached nearly 73m tonnes in 2011 (compared with 35m tonnes in 2001). Cultivation has been moving north and west, but transport to the main centres of demand is expensive. Some varieties of GM maize have now been approved for commercial production. Although Brazil's non-GM produce has won valuable export markets, particularly in the EU, farmers appear keen to embrace the new technology and GM plantings are likely to increase in future.

China's government continues to support grain production, and the country is the world's second largest maize producer – but it still needs to import to meet demand. Although China appears to have few problems with biotechnology, its maize varieties remain GM-free. In recent years, high domestic prices and good profitability have resulted in annual increases in plantings, partly at the expense of cotton and soybeans. The exact level of maize production in China remains unclear, and there are doubts about the accuracy of government data, which consistently show year-on-year increases in output, despite the recent rise in prices and surging imports.

EU maize production varies because of the crop's susceptibility to drought, especially in central and eastern European member states. Output was around 66m tonnes in 2011. Sowings in France, the biggest producing country, have been falling as the availability of water for irrigation declines. For farmers in the newer member states, much of the benefit of a wider market is offset by higher transport costs. Some GM maize is grown in Spain, but public opinion in much of the

EU remains hostile to GM production or use. Helped by favourable returns and solid export demand, farmers in Ukraine have become enthusiastic growers and exporters of maize in recent years.

TABLE 4.11 **Leading maize-producing countries**[a]

|  | 2001 | | 2011 | |
| --- | --- | --- | --- | --- |
|  | m tonnes | % of total | m tonnes | % of total |
| US | 241.4 | 40.5 | 313.9 | 36.6 |
| China | 114.1 | 19.1 | 177.0 | 20.6 |
| Other East Asia | 30.1 | 5.0 | 56.0 | 6.5 |
| Brazil | 35.3 | 5.9 | 72.8 | 8.5 |
| Argentina | 14.7 | 2.5 | 21.0 | 2.4 |
| Mexico | 20.4 | 3.4 | 19.0 | 2.2 |
| Other Latin America | 9.9 | 1.7 | 14.3 | 1.7 |
| EU | 50.1 | 8.4 | 66.0 | 7.7 |
| Sub-Saharan Africa | 43.4 | 7.3 | 59.9 | 7.0 |
| Others | 36.8 | 6.2 | 59.4 | 6.9 |
| Total | 596.2 |  | 858.2 |  |

a Mainly harvested July–December (in the southern hemisphere early the following year).
**Sources:** International Grains Council; US Department of Agriculture

Most of the world's maize stocks are held in two countries: China and the United States. The exact amounts in China are unknown, as there is a tradition of on-farm storage and of keeping assets out of sight of the authorities, as well as secrecy surrounding the strategic reserve and national stocks. At an estimated 50m tonnes, around 45% of global stocks are thought to be stored in China.

American stocks are of greater significance to the market as they are available for export. Markets become nervous, and prices volatile, when the American carryover falls, or is predicted to fall, to what seems an unsafe level. Maize stocks were low in the main exporting countries at the end of 2011/12 at just 35m tonnes.

FIG 4.8 **Maize stocks and prices**

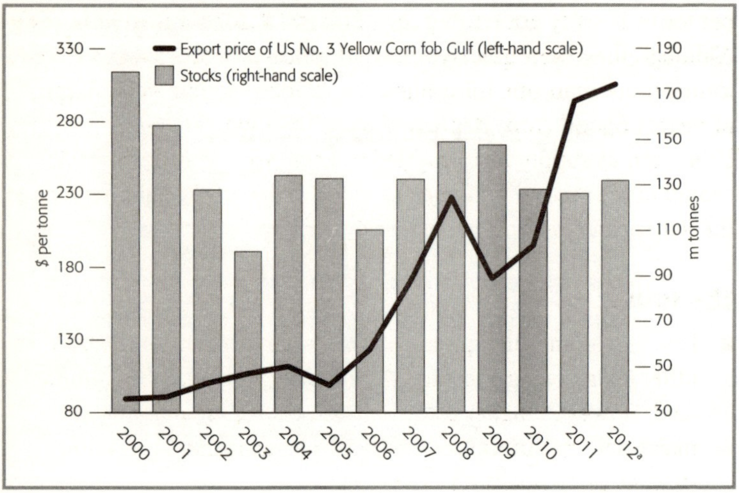

*Source:* International Grains Council
a EIU estimates.

## The maize market

Maize prices are chiefly determined by the balance between American supply and demand (domestic and overseas), but they are also influenced by availability in Argentina and China. They have reflected changes in the prices of other grains, but in recent years maize has been a significant determinant of grains prices as a result of poor crops and low stocks.

Maize prices and futures traded on the Chicago Board of Trade come nearest to representing a global benchmark, but there are many other regional and national exchanges, in China and Latin America in particular. Maize futures are also traded on the London-based Euronext-LIFFE.

## Price trends

Rising American demand for ethanol production and growing competition between the industry, domestic stockfeed producers and exporters, were the reasons for the surge in maize prices between the end of 2007 and the middle of 2008 (see Figure 4.8). Prices (basis US

No. 3 Yellow Corn fob Gulf Ports) subsequently rose from around $100 per tonne in early 2006 to a peak of almost $320/tonne in June 2008. Although they then quickly retreated, prices in 2008 averaged $228/tonne, more than one-third higher than the previous year. A couple of years of good crops depressed prices in 2009, but since then they have risen as supply has struggled to keep pace with demand. Prices soared in the second half of 2012 as the extent of drought damage to the American crop became evident.

## The future

- Low stocks and high prices will constrain consumption, with other grains being substituted for maize, particularly in animal feed. However, higher prices will encourage the planting of maize and consumption growth can be expected to resume strongly once stocks start to be rebuilt.
- Maize needs more fuel and fertiliser than other crops and, as input costs rise or credit facilities disappear, farmers in many countries, especially in South America, may turn to soybeans.
- As more exporters grow GM grains, importing countries, especially the EU, may need to reconsider their objections.
- Although much will depend on official policy and the underlying price relationship between maize, ethanol and oil prices, there may be some pullback in demand for ethanol blending.
- Low-grade wheat and industrial co-products will continue to displace maize in livestock feed in North America and parts of Asia, particularly if prices stay high.

# Rice

**A MEMBER OF THE GRASS FAMILY,** rice produces seeds that are used for human consumption. It thrives in areas with heavy rainfall; the traditional method of cultivation involves flooding the fields with water (paddies), which helps to repel weeds and pests. It is usually an annual crop, but in some countries (India, for example) a winter and a summer crop can be sown.

There are many varieties of rice, but almost all are grown for human consumption, which accounts for about 90% of (milled) production. Some lower-quality rice and surpluses that cannot be marketed may be sold for animal feed. Rice is used also to make spirits or starch, but it is a highly differentiated market. The multitude of types – including long-grain, medium-grain and short-grain, fragrant, parboiled, broken and brown forms – each serve different markets, mostly functioning independently of each other.

## Consumption and trade

### Regional trends

Rice is culturally important in South and East Asia, and food habits are slow to change, especially in rural areas. However, in more developed Asian countries, such as Japan and South Korea, rice consumption per head is steadily declining. In many developing countries outside Asia, where the grain is not a traditional staple food, consumption is growing in line with rising incomes and the availability of improved varieties.

China typically accounts for about 30% of global rice consumption, 138.5m tonnes in 2011/12 (see Table 4.12). In recent years population growth has been offsetting the impact of declining consumption per head as diets diversify. Rising disposable incomes have increased demand for high-quality non-indigenous varieties such as fragrant rice. India is the second largest rice-consuming country, using an estimated 97m tonnes in 2011/12. Large state reserves offset monsoon-related fluctuations in domestic production, and the subsidised Public Distribution System safeguards supplies to the poor. As incomes rise in poorer areas, so does rice consumption.

Rice is the staple food in rural Bangladesh but is giving way to wheat in urban areas. Demand is increasing as the population grows, but consumption varies widely with domestic production and price, and imports sometimes exceed 1m tonnes. As in India, the government operates a public distribution system through which needy people receive rice and wheat.

In West Africa, parboiled rice is widely consumed in cities but demand is sensitive to prices, as imports typically account for about two-thirds of the region's consumption. Rice is also an important food in the Middle East, where imports have supplied rising demand. In Saudi Arabia, consumption has been boosted by immigrant workers and pilgrims.

TABLE 4.12 **Leading rice-consuming countries**[a]

|  | 1995/96 | | 2011/12 | |
| --- | --- | --- | --- | --- |
|  | m tonnes, milled rice | % | m tonnes, milled rice | % |
| China | 130.0 | 34.9 | 138.5 | 30.3 |
| India | 79.0 | 21.2 | 97.0 | 21.2 |
| Indonesia | 33.0 | 8.9 | 39.7 | 8.7 |
| Other East & South Asia | 89.0 | 23.9 | 120.5 | 26.3 |
| Africa | 12.0 | 3.2 | 24.2 | 5.3 |
| Latin America | 14.0 | 3.8 | 18.2 | 4.0 |
| Others | 15.0 | 4.0 | 19.6 | 4.3 |
| Total | 372.0 | | 457.7 | |

a Local marketing years.
**Sources:** US Department of Agriculture; International Grains Council

## Trade: principal players

The international rice market has three main components: the volatile needs of South and South-East Asian producers (Bangladesh, Indonesia and the Philippines); the increasing but more stable requirements of the Middle East; and the price-sensitive markets of West Africa. The leading rice exporters are Thailand, Vietnam, India, Pakistan and the United States, but internationally traded rice accounts for only around 7% of total rice production a year.

Local variation in tastes and purchasing power fragment the market. Preferences include Basmati (fragrant rice from the Indian subcontinent), long-grain rice (as supplied by the United States) and broken rice (mainly from Thailand and Vietnam, but also India, Pakistan and other smaller exporters). Prices vary widely, Basmati being the most expensive and broken grades (especially 100% broken) the cheapest. Most rice is transported in milled form, but this does not store well and has to be bagged for shipment. Freight and handling costs are accordingly higher than for wheat or maize, which are generally shipped in bulk.

Indonesia's needs sometimes dominate the international rice market – in 2011 it bought an estimated 3m tonnes, the largest amount for many years. Some of the purchases appear to be for building up state reserves. The Philippines is another important player in global trade; it was the world's largest importer in 2011. China's imports are almost entirely high-quality fragrant grades, sourced exclusively from Thailand, usually amounting to about 500,000 tonnes annually. However, in early 2012 China procured a large amount (an estimated 900,000 tonnes) of rice from Vietnam, in what appears to have been an attempt to depress domestic rice prices.

The Middle East is a major rice market that is growing as domestic production is limited by lack of water. Imports are mostly high-quality Basmati or parboiled varieties sourced from Thailand, India and Pakistan. The main markets in the region are Iran, Iraq and Saudi Arabia.

Thailand is the biggest rice-exporting country, with exports amounting to 10.6m tonnes in 2011 (see Table 4.13). Preliminary data suggest exports fell to around 6.5m tonnes in 2012, however, following the reinstatement of the intervention scheme (see page 204) and a lack of interest in the government's initial efforts to release reserves. Nevertheless, Thailand is likely to remain the world's largest exporter in the future; it offers a wide variety of types and qualities, and sales are well spread geographically. Vietnam has become a strong competitor in lower- and middle-quality markets.

India's exports are politically sensitive, and for a couple of years before it was removed in September 2011 there was a ban on all exports of non-Basmati rice. Total rice exports in 2012 are estimated at 9.6m tonnes, an increase of almost 50% year on year. Rice is not a staple food in Pakistan, and although consumption is slowly increasing, half of the crop is available for export. Trade is conducted by the private sector, but a state agency helps to arrange government-to-government deals.

American rice exports consist of milled rice (two-thirds) and brown or "rough" rice (one-third). Exports of brown rice, mostly to Mexico and Central America, are increasing, whereas those of milled rice are more variable, depending on the strength of competition from Asian suppliers.

TABLE 4.13 **Leading exporters and importers, 2011**

|  | Exports | | | Imports | |
| --- | --- | --- | --- | --- | --- |
|  | m tonnes | % of total |  | m tonnes | % of total |
| Thailand | 10.6 | 29.5 | East Asia | 11.1 | 30.9 |
| Vietnam | 7.1 | 19.8 | Africa | 11.1 | 30.9 |
| India | 4.8 | 13.4 | Middle East | 7.2 | 20.1 |
| Pakistan | 3.4 | 9.5 | North & Central America | 3.4 | 9.5 |
| US | 3.2 | 8.9 | Europe | 1.6 | 4.5 |

**Sources:** US Department of Agriculture; International Grains Council

## Production and stocks

After falling in the early 2000s, world rice production has resumed its long-term growth, reaching a record 463m tonnes in 2011/12. Most is grown for subsistence, and only around 36m tonnes was internationally traded in 2011/12. Asia accounts for about 90% of global production, but output is increasing in Africa. The high priority given to agriculture by many Asian governments has encouraged private as well as public investment in rice farming, and the use of better cultivation techniques and improved varieties. Improved irrigation has reduced vulnerability to drought, although water is becoming scarcer in some producing areas.

Rainfall – especially summer monsoons – is crucial, as small changes in local harvests can lead to large changes in trade flows. But a shortfall in supplies can usually be made up, as some producing countries grow two or even three rice crops a year. In several countries in Asia, rice farming is coming under pressure from urbanisation and competition from other crops, but the use of high-yielding or disease-resistant varieties has allowed production to grow.

China is the world's largest rice producer, at 140m tonnes in 2011/12 (see Table 4.14). Prices and the supply of fuel, fertilisers and machinery to farmers continue to be subsidised. In India, the summer-sown main (Kharif) crop accounts for about 85% of domestic production; the smaller Rabi crop is planted during the winter months. India has what amounts to two rice economies. In advanced commercial farming, mainly in the north, high-yielding seeds and agrochemicals are used extensively and mechanisation enables harvests to be swiftly and efficiently gathered. However, falling water tables and rising salinity may affect production in the future. Elsewhere, rice cultivation is a means of subsistence and dependent on the vagaries of the monsoon. India produced 104m tonnes of rice in 2011/12.

In Bangladesh, rice occupies three-quarters of the crop area. Three crops are grown annually in parts of the country, but production varies depending on the nature of the monsoon. In some years large imports (primarily on concessionary terms) from India are required. Indonesia and the Philippines are striving for self-sufficiency in rice, but when crops fall short, they can also be large players in the international rice market.

TABLE 4.14 **Leading rice-producing countries**[a]

|  | 1997/98 | | 2011/12 | |
| --- | --- | --- | --- | --- |
|  | m tonnes | % of total | m tonnes | % of total |
| China | 113.0 | 29.2 | 140.4 | 30.3 |
| India | 86.0 | 22.2 | 104.3 | 22.5 |
| Indonesia | 34.0 | 8.8 | 38.0 | 8.2 |
| Vietnam | 21.0 | 5.4 | 25.2 | 5.4 |
| Thailand | 18.0 | 4.7 | 20.0 | 4.3 |
| Other East & South Asia | 76.0 | 19.6 | 90.6 | 19.6 |
| Latin America | 16.0 | 4.1 | 14.9 | 3.2 |
| Africa | 11.0 | 2.8 | 16.2 | 3.5 |
| Others | 12.0 | 3.1 | 13.6 | 2.9 |
| Total | 387 | | 463.2 | |

a Mainly harvested July–December and marketed in the following calendar year.
**Sources:** US Department of Agriculture; International Grains Council

Rice output in Thailand has been rising in recent years as a result of government support and the introduction of new varieties, and stood at 20m tonnes in 2011/12. Water supply is uncertain and floods sometimes damage the crop. In 2011 the government reinstated an intervention scheme, which is proving controversial externally. Under the scheme, farmers are paid a price (known as the intervention or support price) to pledge their crop to the state. International rice prices will therefore be influenced by the timing of sales from government stocks and the price at which they are offered.

Vietnam became a major player in the rice market in the 1990s as a result of intensive efforts to improve farming methods. Half of all agricultural land is given over to rice and, although marginal paddies are being converted to feed crops and aquaculture, production reached 25m tonnes in 2011/12.

The United States is a high-quality rice producer and a major exporter, with an annual crop of around 6m tonnes. Most rice is grown on large farms, which can afford the heavy investment needed, particularly in irrigation. American rice farming would be uneconomical without government support. Almost 75% of the crop consists of long-grain varieties, which are popular in export markets.

Global stocks fell to a low of just under 75m tonnes in 2004/05, but they have been increasing steadily since then and stood at close to 100m tonnes in 2011/12. However, this is only a rough estimate as there is uncertainty about the size of China's stocks. Perhaps more important for the rice market and international prices are the stocks held in the main exporting countries. These have also been increasing in recent years and in 2011/12 stood at a comfortable 35m tonnes, compared with around 20m tonnes in 2004/05, and only slightly less than the total trade in rice in 2011/12.

## The rice market

Rice futures are traded on the Chicago Board of Trade, and there are important exchanges in Thailand, Vietnam and Pakistan. However, much of the international trade in rice is conducted through large trading companies – Louis Dreyfus (France), Archer Daniels Midland (United States), Olam (Indian-owned but Singapore based) – or brokers. Some of the large traders are also involved in rice processing. Many companies are involved in the rice trade, often specialising in meeting the needs of a small market segment. Unusually, buyers are often state procurement companies and the trade can take place on a government-to-government basis.

## Price trends

Traditionally, rice prices (basis Thai white 100% second grade fob Bangkok) were not as volatile as those of some of the other more widely traded commodities, but in 2007 prices started to soar, peaking at around $1,060 per tonne in May 2008. This compares with an annual average of $220/tonne in 2000–05. The price rise was a result of surging demand, falling productivity and natural calamities that devastated major rice-growing areas, but it was exacerbated by government efforts (in India, Egypt and Vietnam) to secure domestic supply by restricting exports. This led to accelerated buying by some importers, notably the Philippines. Prices have since fallen sharply, but

## FIG 4.9 **Rice stocks and prices**

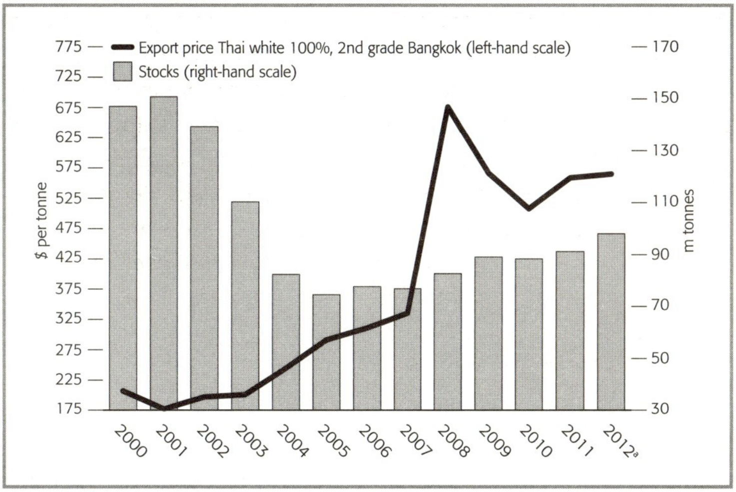

- Export price Thai white 100%, 2nd grade Bangkok (left-hand scale)
- Stocks (right-hand scale)

a EIU estimates.
**Source:** International Grains Council

they remain high by historical standards at an average of $559/tonne in 2011 and $572/tonne in 2012 (see Figure 4.9). In contrast to the strong weather-inspired gains recorded in wheat, maize and soybean prices in 2012, rice prices were weighed down by the increasingly burdensome and bearish nature of Thailand's accumulated intervention reserves.

## The future

- Thailand's intervention scheme is likely to distort the demand and supply fundamentals of the international rice market, as the government will either build stocks when prices are low or offload them onto the market, potentially depressing prices.
- Rice is politically sensitive in much of Asia, and in many countries rice farmers and consumers are a major political force. Accordingly, governments are alert to price fluctuations and are active players in procurement for domestic consumption or export. They are also quick to impose trade restrictions if there are concerns about supply or prices.

- Limited production prospects in the Middle East and a growing market will lead to higher imports. Middle Eastern countries concerned about supplies are also starting to invest in farmland in a number of countries in Africa and Asia.
- Consumption per head will continue to decline in parts of Asia, especially in China, Japan and South Korea, as diets diversify to include greater quantities of meat and other convenience (wheat-based) foods.

# Natural rubber

THE PARÁ RUBBER TREE, native to the Amazon region of Brazil, is the main source of the latex used to make natural rubber. The tree's particular characteristic, making it ideal for commercial cultivation, is that the more the tree is pierced, the more latex it produces. Rubber trees live for about 100 years but are only productive for about 35 years before latex production goes into decline. They start to yield latex about seven years after planting. Like coffee, natural rubber is principally a smallholder crop, and smallholders account for some 70–80% of global production.

## Processes, uses and synthetic competition

To harvest the latex, the trees are "tapped". This involves making an incision in the bark to release the sticky, milk-coloured sap, which is then collected and sent for processing. At the initial processing stage, the rubber is filtered out from the rest of the latex and a hard lump of it emerges. Natural rubber is defined as a natural polymer, or elastomer, and its main component is polyisoprene.

The rubber is then processed to manufacture a wide variety of goods. The sought-after characteristics of natural rubber are that it is stretchy (and retracts to its former shape after stretching) and waterproof. The tyre industry is by far the world's largest consumer of natural rubber, accounting for an estimated 70% of consumption. As well as tyres, a modern automobile has more than 300 components made out of rubber. It is also used to make conveyor belts, footwear, medical instruments, hoses and floor coverings, to name but a few. Furthermore, natural rubber is now being used in soil stabilisation.

Natural rubber accounts for approximately 40% of total rubber consumption, with various types of petroleum-derived synthetic rubber making up the remainder. The two compete mainly on price, but also on slightly different characteristics. Synthetic rubber can improve on some of the qualities of natural rubber in the manufacture of goods, but there are some, such as heavy-duty tyres, where synthetic rubber cannot be substituted successfully for natural rubber. A truck tyre contains about 25kg of elastomer, of which a high proportion (typically about 80%) is natural rubber. Car tyres use much less; Goodyear, an American tyremaker, estimates that about one-third of the 3.5kg of rubber that goes into a typical car tyre is natural.

## Consumption and trade
### Regional trends

Global demand for rubber long ago outstripped supply of the natural variety. By 1986, natural rubber's share of the total elastomer market had fallen to less than one-third. Since then, high prices for oil and synthetic rubber feedstock have resulted in an increase in market share for natural rubber. Natural rubber's share of consumption has remained consistently highest in India and lowest in eastern Europe and the Commonwealth of Independent States owing to the traditional reliance of the former Soviet Union countries on synthetic rubber.

Regional consumption of natural rubber has been changing along with changes in location of industrial production generally. Demand for rubber and other industrial raw materials in China and other parts of Asia, such as India, has been rising. By contrast, demand in OECD countries has been falling, especially in the EU and in North America, where the tyre industries have faced growing competition from imports.

Consumption of natural rubber grew strongly, at an annual average of over 6%, in the five years preceding 2007. However, performance has been mixed since the economic downturn that began in 2008. Consumption contracted by 8.3% in 2009, but this was followed by a robust recovery in 2010. In 2011, the sector was hit hard by the supply problems that beset the wider vehicle production sector, as well as by

TABLE 4.15 **Leading natural rubber-consuming countries**

|  | 1997 | | 2011 | |
| --- | --- | --- | --- | --- |
|  | '000 tonnes | % of total | '000 tonnes | % of total |
| China | 713 | 11.4 | 3,603 | 33.0 |
| India | 572 | 9.1 | 957 | 8.8 |
| Japan | 910 | 14.5 | 753 | 6.9 |
| Other Asia[a] | 1,326 | 21.2 | 2,310 | 21.2 |
| EU | 915 | 14.6 | 1,206 | 11.0 |
| Other Europe & CIS | 163 | 2.6 | 250 | 2.3 |
| North America[b] | 1,175 | 18.7 | 1,165 | 10.7 |
| Latin America | 385 | 6.1 | 582 | 5.3 |
| Africa | 110 | 1.8 | 89 | 0.8 |
| Total | 6,269 | | 10,915 | |

a Includes Australia. b Canada and the United States.
**Source:** International Rubber Study Group

Europe's economic travails and weakening Indian automotive demand. Natural disasters in Japan (the March earthquake and tsunami) and flooding in Thailand caused severe disruption to the global automotive supply chain and thus indirectly led to a 1.2% fall in consumption of natural rubber in that year, according to the International Rubber Study Group (IRSG). However, these were not the only problems faced by the sector in 2011 and, to some extent, in 2012. Consumption was also hampered by the expiration of car purchase incentives, tighter credit conditions and greater substitution of natural rubber with synthetic rubber because of the growing price differential.

China is the world's largest consumer of natural rubber, accounting for 33% of the market in 2011 (see Table 4.15). Japan is still an important consumer, accounting for 7% of global consumption in 2011, despite the relocation of much of its manufacturing to cheaper cost bases such as China. In 2011, Asia accounted for 70% of global consumption, reflecting the region's pre-eminence as a centre of manufacturing, not just of vehicles.

According to *European Rubber Journal*'s annual *Global Tyre Report* for 2010, there are 160 tyre manufacturers worldwide, of which 13 accounted for 71% of the market. The big three – Michelin (France), Bridgestone (United States) and Goodyear (United States) – have just over 40% of the market. They are followed by four medium-sized companies: Continental (Germany), Pirelli (Italy) and Sumitomo and Yokohama (both Japan).

Non-tyre (general rubber products) manufacturing is much more fragmented, with a predominance of small and medium-sized enterprises. But most tyre manufacturers also manufacture non-tyre automotive components such as belting, extrusions and mouldings.

## Trade

Thailand, Indonesia and Malaysia dominate trade in natural rubber, accounting for 81% of global exports in 2011 (see Table 4.16). However, Vietnam has been increasing its output and exports rapidly in recent years, partly in recognition of its proximity to the largest market for rubber, China. Vietnam accounted for nearly 10% of global exports in 2011 and exports grew at a rate of over 30% year on year in 2012. The surge in exports in 2012 reflected efforts 5–10 years ago to develop Vietnam's rubber industry and the long lead time before trees become commercial.

China is by far the largest market and Thailand, in particular, has

TABLE 4.16 **Leading exporters and importers, 2011**

| | Gross exports | | | Gross imports | |
| --- | --- | --- | --- | --- | --- |
| | '000 tonnes | % share | | '000 tonnes | % share |
| Thailand | 2,929.8 | 35.1 | China | 2,665.4 | 30.7 |
| Indonesia | 2,565.8 | 30.7 | EU | 1,663.7 | 19.1 |
| Malaysia | 1,239.5 | 14.8 | US | 1,048.6 | 12.1 |
| Vietnam | 816.6 | 9.8 | Japan | 785.3 | 9.0 |
| Côte d'Ivoire | 226.3 | 2.7 | Malaysia | 667.4 | 7.7 |

**Source:** International Rubber Study Group

been a beneficiary of the growth in China's consumption. Although Indonesia is also relatively close to China, Indonesia traditionally exported more rubber to the United States and this has led to more subdued export growth in recent years as a result of weakness in the American economy. Malaysia, rather surprisingly, is also a large importer of rubber because it has a large number of rubber-using industries. Japan has always been an important market for natural rubber, owing to its large vehicle-manufacturing sector, but imports fell by around 30% in 2009 and imports in 2011 were still 8% lower than in 2007, before the 2008/09 global recession.

## Production

Although rubber trees originated in Latin America, for some time Asia has accounted for the bulk of world rubber production. During the colonial period, the British took seeds from Brazil via the UK to Singapore, India, Sri Lanka and British Malaya, and Belgian colonists took seeds to what is now the Democratic Republic of Congo. Today, Asia accounts for approximately 90% of total production. The three largest producers – Thailand, Indonesia and Malaysia – accounted for 67% of global production in 2011 (see Figure 4.10).

As with all agricultural crops, weather – especially rainfall – is an important factor in the production of natural rubber. A lack of rain reduces latex flow and too much interrupts tapping. In recent years, particularly in Malaysia, production has been hit by labour shortages (tapping is a skilled job but generally less well paid than industrial employment, and rubber farming is more labour intensive than palm oil cultivation) and/or falling profitability relative to other crops (palm oil in particular).

In recent years, Indonesia has been the main driver of natural rubber production growth. Production grew at an annual average rate of 7.5% between 2003 and 2011 and by 9% in 2011 alone, according to the IRSG, although the 2012 crop was affected by adverse weather. In addition, farmers have reduced tapping in response to falling prices.

Thailand remains the world's largest producer of natural rubber, with production concentrated in the deep south of the country, close to the Malaysian border. Production has been growing steadily, at

FIG 4.10 **Natural rubber production, 2011**

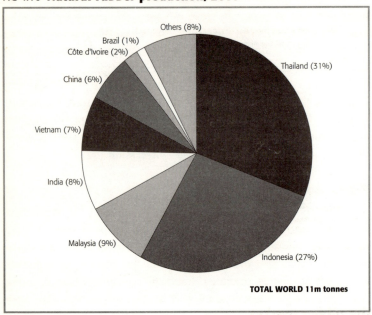

**Source:** International Rubber Study Group

an annual average rate of 2.4% between 2003 and 2011, and output reached 3.4m tonnes in 2011.

Production has also been growing strongly in Vietnam, partly thanks to government support and investment, with exporters targeting the Chinese market. Output surged in 2012, with production reported to be 34% higher in the first nine months of the year. However, there are issues affecting potential growth. In particular, at the end of 2011 Vietnam's Ministry of Finance imposed a tax of 3% on exports of natural rubber to try and encourage local processing.

The scope for adding value to natural rubber is much greater than for many other commodities. Nevertheless, among the major rubber-producing countries, only two – China and India – utilise more than half of their production in the manufacture of tyres and other rubber products.

FIG 4.11 **Natural rubber stocks and prices**

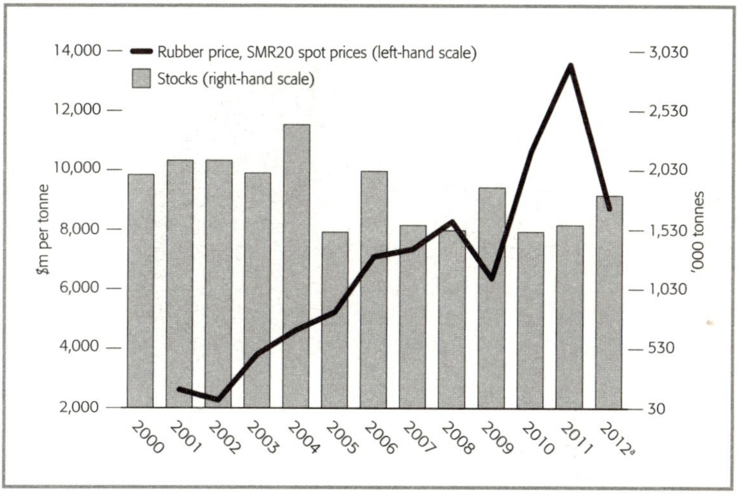

- Rubber price, SMR20 spot prices (left-hand scale)
- Stocks (right-hand scale)

a EIU estimates.
**Source:** International Rubber Study Group

## The rubber market

There are physical markets for natural rubber in Kuala Lumpur (Malaysia), Singapore, London, New York, Tokyo and Guangzhou (China). Contracts with tyre manufacturers account for a large part of trade, which, according to producers, reduces the validity of spot prices in international markets. Contract trading has certainly increased, but the extent to which this has bypassed the open market is unknown (50% is sometimes suggested); nor does the spot price of rubber seem to be less representative of market fundamentals than the spot prices of other commodities. Futures markets in natural rubber operate in Japan, China and Singapore.

Producers of natural rubber have limited control over production (or prices), which is largely influenced by the weather, especially rainfall, and also by the long lead time between planting a tree and it becoming productive. Thus supply cannot respond flexibly to price movements or demand. However, the main producing countries, Thailand, Indonesia and Malaysia, have in the past made efforts to manage supply and in late 2012 they announced a six-month export cap, starting on October 1st 2012, in an effort to put a floor under prices. Prices did not rise significantly in response to the interventionist policy, however, probably because of weak demand. Furthermore, cartels in renewable commodities, in which production forgone is production lost, are notoriously difficult to manage. Nevertheless, the three countries account for a much bigger share of global production than OPEC – just over 70% compared with 40%.

## Price trends

The rubber price has been highly volatile in recent years. Between 2003 and 2008, prices rose at an annual average rate of 25%, reflecting the boom in the global economy and, in particular, strong growth in developing countries involving higher demand for heavy-duty tyres in the mining and construction industries. Prices (Kuala Lumpur basis) subsequently fell by over 26% in 2009 before bouncing back strongly in 2010 (see Figure 4.11), partly because growth in the emerging countries recovered quickly from the 2008–09 global economic slowdown. After peaking in the first quarter of 2011 prices then fell again, reflecting weak demand and concerns about the outlook for growth in China and India. Prices were on a downward trend through 2012 before stabilising and rising modestly in the fourth quarter of the year.

## The future

- The price of crude oil and hence of synthetic rubber will influence both the price and demand for natural rubber.
- Supply cannot react quickly to lower prices because of the time it takes for trees to become productive. Thus a period of low prices could lead to lower investment and planting and supply problems in the future.
- There are clear signs, from the Malaysian example, that the labour-intensive tapping of rubber trees becomes unattractive to farm workers as wages rise and there are increasing opportunities in urban areas. This could lead to rubber production moving to lower-cost countries.

# Soybeans

SOYBEANS ARE A SPECIES OF LEGUME (others include peas, beans, lentils, alfalfa, and so on), originally from East Asia; it is only in the past couple of centuries that they were introduced in other parts of the world. Historically, soybeans have been grown in temperate parts of the world, typically with hot summers, but now they are cultivated in tropical and subtropical parts of the world, particularly India. Aside from being able to sell the beans for consumption, soybean crops improve soil fertility by adding nitrogen from the atmosphere. GM soybeans began to be grown in 1996, and there has been a rapid increase in their cultivation.

The plant has an edible bean that is valued for its nutritional qualities; it is one of the few plants that can provide a complete protein (it contains all eight vital amino acids). A typical bean contains protein (around 40%), oil (about 20%) and carbohydrate (about 30%). The term oilseed is used for soybeans because of their oil content; the price of soybean oil reflects its own market dynamics as well as those of oils from other crops such as sunflowerseed, rapeseed and oil palm.

## Processes and uses

Once the crop has been harvested, the soybeans are exported, sent to a local processor or used directly for human consumption. Globally, 90-95% of soybeans are processed (either in the country of origin or in the importing country), with the remainder being used for human consumption, mainly in Asia but also, to a much lesser degree, in the United States and Europe. The processing of soybeans results in two products: soybean oil and soybean meal. The UN's Food and Agriculture Organisation (FAO) estimates that for every tonne of soybean oil, 4.5 tonnes of soybean meal are produced.

There are three main ways of processing soybeans:

- Solvent extraction. Hexane (a hydrocarbon) is used to leach or extract the oil from soybeans. This is the most common method.
- Continuous pressing. High temperatures and a screw press are used to squeeze out the oil.
- Hydraulic pressing. A mechanical or hydraulic press is used to squeeze out the oil. This is the traditional method.

Soybean meal is used almost entirely for animal feed, with a small percentage (typically about 2%) used to make soy flour and proteins. Most soybean oil (over 90%) is edible oil, with the remainder being used by the biodiesel industry and in the manufacture of products such as soaps, plastics and crayons. It is the most important vegetable oil, accounting for about 20% of global consumption, but it has been losing market share to (typically cheaper) palm oil. The demand for soybean meal for animal feed has been an important factor in soybean oil production and, ultimately, consumption.

## Consumption and trade

### Regional trends

Soybean consumption has soared in recent years reaching 258m tonnes in 2011/12 (see Table 4.17), compared with just 132m tonnes in 1995/96. Growth in consumption has been particularly strong in the developing world, where rising incomes have led to greater meat consumption and thus demand for animal feed. China is now the world's largest soybean consumer, at nearly 71m tonnes in 2011/12. Over the past decade, growth in domestic demand has been fuelled by strong feed production growth. Only tiny amounts of soybeans are fed directly to animals, and food use accounts for only a small proportion of soybean consumption (about 10–15% of the total).

EU consumption of soybeans depends to some extent on European grains harvests, as their use in animal feed increases if the availability of grains is low or prices are high. Imports of soybeans to make oil will also increase if regional output of other oilseeds, rapeseed in particular, is low. Consumption in the United States has been growing steadily in recent years, partly because it has stepped up its exports of meat and partly because of recent demand for soybean oil for biodiesel.

TABLE 4.17 **Leading soybean-consuming countries**[a]

|  | 1995/96 | | 2011/12[b] | |
| --- | --- | --- | --- | --- |
|  | m tonnes | % of total | m tonnes | % of total |
| China | 14.1 | 10.7 | 70.5 | 27.1 |
| US | 40.3 | 30.6 | 47.7 | 18.4 |
| Argentina | 10.8 | 8.2 | 39.0 | 15.1 |
| Brazil | 23.2 | 17.7 | 38.7 | 15.0 |
| EU | 15.5 | 11.8 | 12.7 | 4.9 |
| India | 4.5 | 3.4 | 11.5 | 4.5 |
| Other Asia | 13.4 | 10.2 | 15.2 | 5.9 |
| Others | 9.8 | 7.5 | 22.5 | 8.7 |
| Total | 131.6 | | 257.8 | |

a Years ending September 30th. b Preliminary.
**Source:** United States Department of Agriculture

## Trade

Total trade in soybeans was a provisional 92m tonnes in 2011/12, compared with just 53m tonnes in 2000/01. China dominates trade in soybeans, accounting for 65% of all trade in 2011/12, with imports of 57m tonnes (see Table 4.18), according to the International Grain Council (IGC). China's accession to the World Trade Organisation and the gradual removal or reduction of import tariffs and quotas led to the recent growth in imports. GM food remains a sensitive issue in China, where human consumption of soybeans in the form of tofu is increasing. Each shipment of soybeans to China needs certification, favouring imports from Latin America.

The Indian government seeks to protect and encourage domestic vegetable-oil output, so soybeans can be subject to restrictive trade practices at times. India is involved in both imports and exports of soybeans, depending on the size of the domestic crop.

The EU can be an important import market in years when its own grain or oilseed crops suffer weather-related damage. However, it is also a regular importer of soybeans, accounting for around 10% of trade, and was overtaken by China as the largest importer as recently as 2002/03. EU countries import soybeans particularly for their protein content. However, imports of soybean and soybean meal are constrained by the slow-moving approval process for GM products. The farm lobby is pushing for faster approval, but EU demand for GM-free soybean products is significantly to the benefit of Latin American suppliers.

Brazil has been steadily growing its share of global trade and was the world's second largest exporter of soybeans in 2011/12, with exports of 36.3m tonnes. The United States remained the largest exporter of soybeans in 2011/12, but rising domestic consumption in recent years is constraining exports and Brazil's exports are widely expected to exceed those of the United States within the next couple of years.

Although Argentina is only the world's third largest producer of soybeans, it has a highly developed crushing industry and is

TABLE 4.18 **Leading exporters and importers, 2011/12[a]**

| | Exports | | | Imports | |
|---|---|---|---|---|---|
| | m tonnes | % of total | | m tonnes | % of total |
| US | 38.4 | 41.6 | China | 57.1 | 65.3 |
| Brazil | 36.3 | 39.4 | Rest of Asia | 11.8 | 13.5 |
| Argentina | 7.3 | 7.9 | Europe | 11.5 | 13.1 |
| Paraguay | 3.3 | 3.6 | North & Central America | 4.8 | 5.5 |
| Others | 6.9 | 7.5 | Middle East | 2.3 | 2.6 |

a Preliminary.
**Source:** International Grains Council

the world's largest exporter of soybean meal and oil. This reflects a government policy to encourage domestic processing – the export tax is lower on soybean meal and oil than on raw soybeans.

A few large multinational commodity-trading companies dominate the soybean trade, including Archer Daniels Midland, Bunge, Cargill and Louis Dreyfus.

## Production

Soybean cultivation is highly concentrated: four countries – the United States, Brazil, Argentina and China – account for most of world output (86% in 2011). Historically, the United States was by far the largest producer and exporter of soybeans, but there has been significant expansion of production in Latin America, primarily Brazil and Argentina. In 1995/96, the United States accounted for 47.5% of global production and Argentina and Brazil together for 37%. However, by 2010/11 the position had been reversed, with the US share falling to 33% and that of the two Latin American countries rising to 46.5%. Although the United States remains the largest producer for now, its scope for further expansion is less than in Brazil. Indeed, because of drought, US soybean production may fall below Brazil's in 2012/13.

Soybeans are the second most planted field crop in the United States after maize. Iowa, Minnesota, Indiana and Nebraska in the Midwest are the main growing states. Soybeans are often grown in rotation with maize. There is a close relationship between the two, with farmers often deciding to expand one crop or another in a particular year based on their relative prices. Nearly all the US crop is now genetically modified. Initially, the modifications were made to reduce the need for herbicides and pesticides, but now they are improving the nutritional quality of the soybean.

In Brazil, domestic infrastructure improvements have meant that soybeans are now planted in the huge agricultural expanse of central and western Brazil. Formerly, soybean cultivation was restricted to the south because of proximity to ports. Production reached a record 75.3m tonnes in 2010/11, compared with just 24.2m tonnes in 1995/96. However, in 2011/12 it slipped back to 66m tonnes as a result of adverse weather in 2011 (see Table 4.19).

Argentina's soybean farmers are still near to ports. Production has been growing strongly, increasing from just 12.5m tonnes in 1995/96 to a record 52.7m tonnes in 2009/10, although weather-related problems meant that production slipped to 40.3m tonnes in 2011/12. However, Argentina's domestic consumption is low and as a result it is an important exporter.

A number of countries have started to expand soybean cultivation in recent years, but their output remains small compared with that of the Americas. Ukraine has significantly increased output and is becoming an important supplier to the international market. As soybean is a spring-sown crop, farmers there have been planting it in preference to winter-sown rapeseed, which is often susceptible to winterkill.

China and India have also been trying to increase output in an effort to meet rising domestic demand. In China, soybeans are primarily grown in the north-east, but there are limitations on available land and water. In India, yields are typically low, but production has been growing strongly. However, the soybean crop is entirely summer-sown and therefore dependent on monsoon rains.

TABLE 4.19 **Leading soybean-producing countries**[a]

|  | 1995/96 | | 2011/12[b] | |
| --- | --- | --- | --- | --- |
|  | m tonnes | % of total | m tonnes | % of total |
| US | 59.2 | 47.5 | 83.2 | 35.1 |
| Brazil | 24.2 | 19.4 | 66.0 | 27.8 |
| Argentina | 12.5 | 10.0 | 40.3 | 17.0 |
| China | 13.5 | 10.8 | 13.5 | 5.7 |
| India | 4.5 | 3.6 | 12.1 | 5.1 |
| Paraguay | 2.4 | 1.9 | 4.5 | 1.9 |
| Others | 8.5 | 6.8 | 17.4 | 7.3 |
| Total | 124.7 |  | 237.0 |  |

a Years ending September 30th. b Preliminary.
**Sources:** US Department of Agriculture; national statistics

### FIG 4.12 **Soybean stocks and prices**

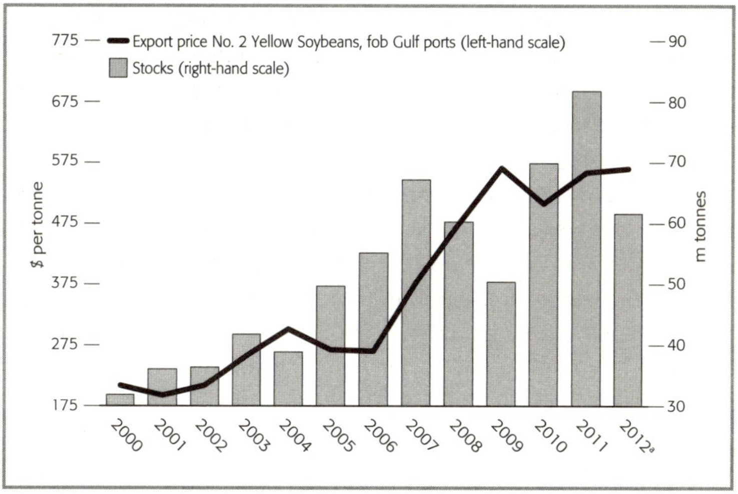

- Export price No. 2 Yellow Soybeans, fob Gulf ports (left-hand scale)
- Stocks (right-hand scale)

a EIU estimates.
**Source:** US Department of Agriculture

## The soybean market

The futures market in Chicago is the main indicator of soybean price changes. Soybeans are also traded on exchanges in South Africa, China, Japan, India and Argentina.

Traders and buyers typically consider soybean prices in relation to the prices of other oilseeds or edible oils, particularly sunflowerseed and rapeseed, as these can be effective substitutes. Sunflowerseed oil typically trades at a premium to soybean oil, but the position can be reversed depending on availability. The relationship between the prices of rapeseed and soybean is more variable, depending on availability, and palm oil traditionally trades at a substantial discount to soybean oil.

## Price trends

Soybean prices were largely in a range of $200–300 per tonne between 2001 and 2006, but a poor crop in 2007/08 (October-September) and a surge in commodity investment led to a sharp increase during 2007/08. As with the majority of commodity prices, soybean prices fell sharply in the final quarter of 2008 and were weak for much of 2009, although they did recover some lost ground. Another poor crop in 2008/09 boosted prices, but a bumper crop in 2009/10 allowed stocks to be rebuilt and soybean prices struggled to make gains, before starting to recover following strong demand in 2011 (see Figure 4.12). In mid-2012 short-dated Chicago soybean futures made exceptional gains as a result of drought in the United States and fears for soybean supply and exports. Spot prices rose to new highs, significantly higher than the recent peak in mid-2008. However, prices started to fall towards the end of the year in anticipation of the arrival of supplies from the Latin American producers in early 2013.

## The future

- Global stocks of soybeans in 2012 were low and a couple of years of good harvests will be needed to bring them back to comfortable levels.
- In the medium term, increased meat consumption in the developing world should sustain growth in soybean demand. This will depend on continued growth in per head income, particularly in China and India.
- The protein in soybeans is a useful addition to vegetarian and vegan diets. However, the presence of trans fats in soybean oil has reduced its popularity in processed foods in recent years.

# Sugar

**SUGAR CANE IS A GRASS** grown in tropical and subtropical parts of the world. It can be cut manually or by machine. It is taken to a processing plant where it is milled and the juice extracted. Sugar beet is grown in temperate parts of the world and is an annual plant with a tuberous root that has a high concentration of sucrose. It can also be harvested manually or mechanically. At the processing plant, the sugar is extracted by diffusion. Sugar cane, the main source of supply, requires more processing than beet and this sometimes takes place in the destination country.

Around 70% of total production is traditionally during October to March, with the peak beet lifting and processing period occurring in October-December, and cane cutting taking place in January-March. Southern hemisphere crops, mainly cane, boost supply in the second and third quarters.

## Substitutes

There are both natural and chemical sweetener substitutes for sugar, although sugar retains about a 70% share of world demand for sweeteners. Chemical sweeteners, such as saccharin and aspartame, as well as an expanding number of synthetic chemical products, are typically much stronger than sugar. High-fructose corn syrup is a more natural alternative to sugar that has been widely adopted in the United States. However, chemical sweeteners are typically less versatile and cannot be used at extremely high temperatures, making them unsuitable for baking. They can also affect taste. Nevertheless, their low calorific value and intensity of sweetness can help with weight reduction or control programmes and make them popular with diabetics. There are also cost advantages in using artificial sweeteners rather than sugar in food processing.

Substitutes for sugar have been widely adopted in the manufacture of soft drinks where taste is more easily masked or in countries where sugar prices are so manipulated that they are price competitive. Technological advances are extending some of the substitutes' properties, gradually enlarging their share of sweetener use, especially in soft drinks.

Chemical sweeteners have been controversial for some time, as there are concerns about their long-term impact on health. In the past decade, more natural sweeteners have emerged to challenge sugar. In particular, Stevia, native to the Americas, has been growing in popularity. Stevia is widely used in Japan, consumption is increasing in the United States, and at the end of 2011 it was given approval by the EU regulatory authorities to be used as a sweetener.

## Consumption and trade
### Regional trends

Consumption of sugar divides between household use and indirect industrial use in soft drinks, confectionery and manufactured foods. Indirect use accounts for over two-thirds of consumption in Europe and North America and over 80% in some East Asian countries. The split in the developing world varies widely, but growth is principally in indirect use, as processed food and soft-drink consumption increases.

Consumption per head ranges from less than 5kg in the poorest parts of Asia and Africa to more than 30kg in Europe, and around 60kg in parts of Latin America. The world average has edged up in recent years, but fell slightly in 2011 to 23.7kg, compared with 24kg in 2010. There is little seasonality in demand.

Between 2001/02 (September–August) and 2007/08, world sugar consumption growth averaged a robust 2.7% a year, but in the four subsequent years consumption growth slowed to just 1.6% owing to supply constraints, weaker global growth and, for the most part, high prevailing prices. In 2012, prices were markedly lower and supply prospects improved, suggesting that consumption growth will have picked up to a stronger 2.3%.

TABLE 4.20 **Leading sugar-consuming countries**[a]

|  | 1995/96 | | 2011/12 | |
| --- | --- | --- | --- | --- |
|  | m tonnes | % of total | m tonnes | % of total |
| India | 14.3 | 12.1 | 24.0 | 14.2 |
| China | 8.2 | 6.9 | 15.0 | 8.9 |
| Other Asia | 21.8 | 18.4 | 26.4 | 15.6 |
| Brazil | – | – | 13.5 | 8.0 |
| Other Latin America[b] | 13.9 | 11.7 | 10.6 | 6.3 |
| EU | 14.2 | 12.0 | 19.3 | 11.4 |
| Africa | 10.1 | 8.5 | 17.3 | 10.2 |
| US | 8.6 | 7.3 | 10.4 | 6.2 |
| Russia | 10.2 | 8.6 | 6.0 | 3.6 |
| Others | 17.0 | 14.4 | 26.3 | 15.6 |
| Total | 118.3 | | 168.8 | |

a Years ending September 30th. b Includes Brazil 1995/96.
**Sources:** International Sugar Organisation; US Department of Agriculture

Indigenous supplies are playing a greater role in meeting new consumption in most countries although some, like China, Indonesia and parts of North Africa, have relied increasingly on imports. India is the world's largest consumer of sugar, at 24m tonnes in 2011/12 (see Table 4.20), although growth in consumption in recent years has been much slower than in China. Consumption in India, though, can vary from year to year depending on the size of the domestic crop and prices.

At around 11kg per year, China's consumption per head is far lower than in industrialised countries, but it has been growing strongly at an annual average rate of just over 7% between 2001/02 and 2007/08. This reflects a rapidly urbanising population with greater access to soft drinks and processed foods containing sugar. Although China is a large producer of saccharin, the government avoids relying too heavily on this artificial sweetener, reflecting unconfirmed reports that it can be damaging to health. The country has also been using more high-fructose corn syrup, but the lack of availability and high price of maize suggest that its use will be constrained.

Demand in the Middle East has been growing steadily in recent years, despite high prices, and in much of Sub-Saharan Africa (apart from South Africa and its sugar-producing neighbours) demand for sugar has long outstripped supply.

## Trade: principal players

Four major players – Brazil, Thailand, Australia and Guatemala – typically account for around two-thirds of world exports, with the rest coming from medium-sized and smaller suppliers, which helps to reduce supply volatility. India and EU can also be important suppliers in years of good harvests.

Around one-third of world production, 32% in 2011, is exported. Shipments grew rapidly during the trade liberalisation of the late 1990s, but have slowed in recent years as demand growth has been concentrated in surplus-producing countries. Exports consist mainly of raws (unrefined cane sugar) and whites (mainly refined from beet but including some refined raws). Raw sugar exports were traditionally dominated by Brazil, Australia, Thailand, Guatemala, South Africa and Cuba, and whites by Brazil, the EU and Thailand and, in good crop years, India. However, a number of countries have developed refinery expertise in recent years, for example the United Arab Emirates, which imports raw sugar and had exports of refined sugar totalling 1.9m tonnes in 2011/12 (see Table 4.21).

Russia, the United States, Japan, South-East Asia, the Middle East, western Europe and China have traditionally been the largest net importers. However, Russia has made some progress in boosting domestic beet supply and is no longer such a large presence in the market, partly because it uses its own stocks when it can, particularly when prices are high. By boosting domestic production, China has also reduced imports by almost 50% since 2004. Indonesia has also made progress on reducing its import volumes but so far has failed to reach its goal of self-sufficiency, while Pakistan has gone from being a net importer to a small net exporter in some years. Efforts by importing countries to reduce their reliance on imports mean that world trade in sugar as a share of production is declining, apart from years in which one of these countries experiences a major crop shortfall.

TABLE 4.21 **Leading exporters and importers, 2011/12**[a]

| | Exports | | | Imports | |
|---|---|---|---|---|---|
| | m tonnes, raw value | % share | | m tonnes, raw value | % share |
| Brazil | 22.2 | 41.8 | China | 4.3 | 8.2 |
| Thailand | 7.3 | 13.6 | EU | 3.7 | 7.0 |
| India | 3.2 | 6.0 | US | 3.3 | 6.2 |
| Australia | 3.0 | 5.6 | Indonesia | 3.0 | 5.7 |
| Guatemala | 1.9 | 3.6 | UAE | 2.0 | 3.7 |

a Years ending September 30th.
**Source:** International Sugar Organisation

## Production and stocks

Over three-quarters of world supply comes from cane, grown mainly in tropical regions of Latin America, South-East Asia, Sub-Saharan Africa and Australia. Cane crops are harvested 12–18 months after planting and cut for up to seven years before replanting. If the weather is good, some countries can harvest more than once a year. The balance comes from sugar beet, which is sown in the spring and harvested from October onwards, mainly in the temperate zones of Europe, the Commonwealth of Independent States and North America. A few countries spanning subtropical and temperate zones, such as the United States and China, produce beet and cane. The contribution of cane to supply has risen sharply in recent years, following steep increases in Indian and Brazilian output and a decline in EU beet production. More recently, the rate of cane sugar expansion has slowed because of competition for the raw material from Brazil's ethanol sector. Furthermore, Russia's efforts to reduce dependency on imports with larger domestic crops is sustaining the size of the global beet crop.

After a nearly 10% drop in global production in 2008/09, almost entirely due to a poor crop in India, sugar production has since grown strongly at an annual average rate of around 5%. Despite lower production in Brazil in 2011/12, global production is still estimated to have risen by 4.9%, as a result of better crops in India, Russia, Europe, Thailand, Ukraine and several smaller producers.

Brazil remains the largest producer of sugar, accounting for 20% of production in 2011/12 (see Table 4.22), and the largest exporter. After many years of mostly relentless expansion, the downturn in Brazil's output in 2011/12 was unexpected but appears to be largely the result of years of underinvestment, especially in the milling sector, rising labour and energy costs, and delays in replanting (extraction rates fall sharply after a few years of cutting the same cane).

India is the world's second largest sugar producer, but annual production can vary enormously depending on the monsoon. In some years India is an important supplier to the global market, but in other years it restricts exports to contain internal prices. For example, India was a net importer of 1.14m tonnes in 2009/10 and a net exporter of 1.67m tonnes in 2011/12.

In the EU, a reform programme designed to be compliant with WTO rules – curbing subsidised output and exports – has resulted in significant restructuring in the industry, which has emerged smaller but more efficient. However, the region is now a net sugar importer. The EU is in a good position to expand beet output with its equable climate, high yields, rapid harvest and modern, efficient processing chains, and the demand is likely to be there if ethanol production expands. However, growing opposition to the use of food crops to make biofuels could curtail this incentive for beet production, although it may indirectly benefit the region's sugar production.

Thailand has significantly increased sugarcane production and milling in recent years, so that by 2011/12 it accounted for 6% of global production, compared with just 2.7% in 2002/03. This expansion is the result of harvest mechanisation and increased milling capacity, and Thailand is now the world's second largest exporter. China typically produces more sugar than Thailand and has also been increasing output, but output still falls short of consumption and the country is a net importer. The government will continue to encourage domestic crop expansion, but suitable land could prove a constraint.

## TABLE 4.22 Leading sugar-producing countries[a]

|  | 1995/96 | | 2011/12 | |
| --- | --- | --- | --- | --- |
|  | m tonnes | % of total | m tonnes | % of total |
| Brazil | 14.0 | 12.7 | 35.2 | 20.2 |
| Other Latin America | 17.0 | 15.4 | 13.2 | 7.6 |
| India | 17.9 | 16.2 | 28.3 | 16.2 |
| EU | 6.8 | 6.2 | 18.9 | 10.8 |
| China | 6.7 | 6.1 | 12.6 | 7.2 |
| Thailand | 6.6 | 5.9 | 10.6 | 6.1 |
| US | 6.3 | 5.7 | 7.6 | 4.4 |
| Russia | 4.5 | 4.1 | 5.5 | 3.2 |
| Australia | 5.1 | 4.6 | 4.0 | 2.3 |
| Others | 39.4 | 35.7 | 38.5 | 22.1 |
| Total | 110.3 |  | 174.4 |  |

a Years ending September 30th.
**Sources:** International Sugar Organisation; US Department of Agriculture

## TABLE 4.23 Leading sugar-producing companies, 2010/11[a]

| Company | Country | Output, m tonnes |
| --- | --- | --- |
| Südzucker | Germany | 4.2 |
| Cosan | Brazil | 4.1 |
| British Sugar | UK | 3.9 |
| Tereos Internacional | Brazil | 3.6 |
| Mitr Phol Sugar | Thailand | 2.7 |
| Nordzucker | Germany | 2.5 |
| Louis Dreyfus | France | 1.8 |
| Thai Roong Ruang Sugar Group | Thailand | 1.5 |
| Wilmar International | US | 1.5 |
| Türkiye Seker Fabrikalari | Turkey | 1.3 |

a Corporate fiscal years.
**Source:** Bloomberg

The largest companies specialising in sugar production are located in producing countries; of the top five, three are European, one is Brazilian and one is Thai. Some of the largest trading companies are also involved in the sugar industry; Louis Dreyfus (France) is the seventh largest producing company (see Table 4.23).

Historically, subsidised production led to high global stocks, which hovered at around one-third of global consumption. India in particular required high stocks to feed a vast and complex distribution system, and the EU and China both maintained stockpiles in an effort to regulate their internal markets. In 2006/07 and 2007/08 there was a massive increase in stocks, owing partly to favourable weather and partly to more efficient cropping, processing technology and productivity. However, two years of global deficits (2008/09 and 2009/10) caused by disappointing crop outturns as well as high demand for cane for Brazil's ethanol industry reversed this comfortable position. Since then improved harvests have enabled some recovery in stocks.

## The sugar market

Transparency in the sugar market has improved hugely as a result of efforts, mainly during the 1990s, to liberalise trade, privatisation and deregulation. However, government policies in some countries still distort domestic prices or prices paid by end-users.

Raw sugar is traded on many agricultural exchanges around the world, but the most quoted or benchmark prices are probably the ICE spot and futures prices. The International Sugar Organisation's ISA daily price is also a recognised benchmark. Prices for white sugar are often benchmarked against NYSE Liffe prices.

## Price trends

World sugar prices were on a long downward trend for much of the 1990s and fell to record lows in the early 2000s. However, the market deficits that started in 2007/08 led to a dramatic run-down in stocks and price rises, so much so that the annual price of sugar rose by an average of 27% in 2008–11, before starting to slide in 2012 (see Figure 4.13). Investor interest in the market has been cited as an important

## FIG 4.13 **Sugar stocks and prices**

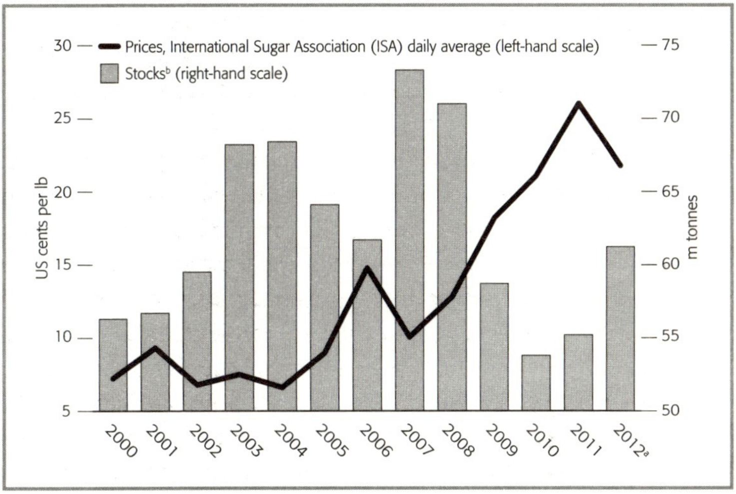

Prices, International Sugar Association (ISA) daily average (left-hand scale)
Stocks[b] (right-hand scale)

US cents per lb / m tonnes

a EIU estimates. b EIU estimates based on ISO data.
**Source:** International Sugar Organisation

factor in the strengthening of prices, but there are others such as years of underinvestment in the sector (because of low prices), rising demand for sugarcane from the biofuel sector, protectionist trade policies and strong economic growth.

## The future

- An extended period of higher world prices provides an incentive for many regions with potential to expand output, including the Commonwealth of Independent States, Southern Africa, South-East Asia, Central America and the Caribbean.
- The United States has removed its tariff on cane-based ethanol imports, which could lead to significantly higher demand for Brazilian ethanol. At the same time, the American government has reduced subsidies on domestic maize-based ethanol production, which, coupled with high maize prices, suggests that imported ethanol from Brazil could be particularly attractive. This would reduce the availability of cane to make sugar and could lead to higher sugar prices. Costly maize also raises the

intrinsic value of high-fructose corn syrup, which helps to bolster sugar prices.

- Sugar consumption, which is often supply-led, weakens but continues to grow during times of high prices. A recovery in supply and a return to lower prices could unleash a rapid acceleration in consumption, particularly in the beverages and manufactured-food industries of developing countries.
- Growing concerns in the developed world, and increasingly in the developing world, about obesity and the rising incidence of diabetes associated with sweet foods (although sweet foods are not always sugar-based) could act as a constraint on sugar consumption.
- Brazil's huge biofuel-powered/hybrid vehicle fleet – and the consequent demand for cane-based ethanol – will remain a constant challenge to the sweetener industry's access to adequate cane supplies.
- Cane (and to a lesser extent beet) can also be used to make biochemicals – acting as a substitute for petrochemicals – and bioplastics. As cane is a renewable input, these industries are likely to grow, putting more pressure on cane suppliers and potentially leading to higher prices.

# Wheat

WHEAT IS A GRASS grown widely throughout the world, but particularly in temperate climates. Certain varieties can, however, cope with widely varying temperatures and levels of rainfall. There are a number of wheat types, each traditionally associated with different products, although modern milling and baking technologies are blurring the distinctions. Some countries have a specific demand for premium (high-protein) milling wheat or for durum (a hard type used to make pasta and couscous). Production of each of these types, being localised, is variable and market prices sometimes diverge significantly from that of average-quality bread wheat. Some high-yielding low-protein types are grown specifically for feed, but bad weather can render any sort of wheat unfit for milling.

## Consumption and trade

### Regional trends

World consumption of wheat grew at an average annual rate of 1.6% between 2001 and 2011. Globally, human consumption per head is falling, but increases in human consumption are still recorded in many developing countries in some cases because of government subsidies, especially in North Africa. In India and Bangladesh massive amounts of wheat and rice are supplied through subsidised public distribution systems.

Population growth and rising sales of flour-based convenience foods underpin world food-wheat consumption. China is now the world's second largest consumer of wheat (nearly 18% of total consumption in 2011/12), after the EU (see Table 4.24). Growth in consumption is largely in developing countries in South Asia, the Middle East, Latin America and North Africa; consumption in the most advanced economies is more or less unchanged. Large amounts of wheat are used for animal feed in Europe and the Commonwealth of Independent States, and the feed industries in some countries in Asia incorporate imported wheat in their compounds when the price is right. In 2011-12 there was significant switching from maize to lower-quality wheat in animal feed because of a lack of availability of maize and soaring prices.

Wheat is also used for industrial purposes, primarily to make starch. An emerging use of wheat, particularly in the EU, is in making ethanol. After rising at a comparatively strong pace in recent years, growth in EU wheat-based ethanol production stalled in 2011/12 as did the wider regional economy. However, assuming some recovery in EU ethanol demand and high crude oil prices, ethanol-related demand should continue to grow. Currently, about 1-2% of global wheat production is used to make ethanol, primarily in the EU.

TABLE 4.24 **Leading wheat-consuming countries**[a]

|  | 2000/01 | | 2011/12 | |
| --- | --- | --- | --- | --- |
|  | m tonnes | % of total | m tonnes | % of total |
| EU | 110.4 | 19.1 | 125.8 | 18.2 |
| China | 107.0 | 18.5 | 121.5 | 17.6 |
| India | 63.3 | 10.9 | 81.2 | 11.8 |
| Pakistan | 20.1 | 3.5 | 23.6 | 3.4 |
| Other East Asia | 29.9 | 5.2 | 42.4 | 6.1 |
| Middle East[b] | 49.1 | 8.5 | 57.2 | 8.3 |
| Russia | 35.1 | 6.1 | 37.6 | 5.4 |
| Other CIS | 30.4 | 5.2 | 42.4 | 6.1 |
| US | 36.3 | 6.3 | 32.1 | 4.7 |
| Others | 97.9 | 16.9 | 126.9 | 18.4 |
| Total | 579.5 |  | 690.6 |  |

a Local marketing years. b Includes Turkey.
**Sources:** International Grains Council; US Department of Agriculture

World consumption of wheat totalled 691m tonnes in 2011/12, a 5.4% year-on-year increase, as high maize prices led to increased use of wheat in animal feed. Human food use accounted for approximately 70% of consumption, animal feed for just over 20%, the industrial sector for 3%, and seed and waste for the remainder.

## Trade: many players

World wheat trade accounts for only 20% of total production. The wheat market, unlike those for barley, maize or soybeans, is widely based geographically. It is almost unknown for a single country to account for more than 10% of total wheat imports.

Countries in the Middle East and North Africa where bread is a staple food are important players in the wheat trade, importing significant quantities, particularly from Black Sea exporters such as Russia, Ukraine and Kazakhstan. Egypt is usually the largest wheat-importing country. Although efforts are being made to increase domestic production, it still falls short of demand, which is sustained at great expense by heavy bread subsidies. Consumption per head is among the highest in the world and rising, with the majority of imported wheat used in the production of subsidised Baladi bread. With high consumption per head and limited production, Algeria is heavily dependent on wheat imports, and Turkey's imports can also be substantial.

India is an occasional purchaser depending on the state of domestic supply and stocks. Pakistan is normally close to self-sufficiency but has to resort to imports occasionally. In Bangladesh, consumption of wheat is growing strongly, helped by the government's open-market sales, which offer wheat at a marked discount to people on low incomes. Domestic production is increasing only slowly, and imports are substantial. Indonesia is a major importer as it produces no wheat and demand for noodles and bakery products is increasing along with economic growth.

The EU is a leading wheat exporter but lacks the high-protein wheat needed in the baking industry as well as high-specification durum wheat. Imports of these types usually total 3m–4m tonnes per year. High internal prices make the EU an attractive market for medium-quality and feed wheat produced in the Black Sea region, although these shipments are subject to import restrictions.

TABLE 4.25 **Leading exporters and importers, 2011**

|  | Exports | | | Imports | |
| --- | --- | --- | --- | --- | --- |
|  | '000 tonnes | % of total |  | '000 tonnes | % of total |
| US | 28,071 | 29.5 | Egypt | 11,650 | 7.6 |
| Australia | 23,041 | 19.8 | EU | 7,369 | 4.8 |
| Russia | 21,627 | 13.4 | Brazil | 7,052 | 4.6 |
| Canada | 17,603 | 9.5 | Indonesia | 6,400 | 4.2 |
| EU | 16,439 | 8.9 | Japan | 6,354 | 4.2 |

**Source:** US Department of Agriculture

With its huge demand, fluctuating production and uncertainty about the exact levels of reserve stocks, China can have a major impact on world wheat markets but it is not a regular importer. Small amounts of wheat are currently imported annually for use in blending with domestic grains.

The United States is always the biggest wheat exporter, accounting for nearly 30% of sales in 2011 (see Table 4.25); no other country can match the range of types and grades it produces and the efficient storage, transport and handling systems keep costs down and enable large amounts to be moved at short notice. The country is the "residual market supplier" and its transparent export prices (closely related to prices on American futures markets) represent a target against which other exporters compete. Although it has not subsidised its wheat exports since 1995, competitors claim that its production subsidies and use of export credits, as well as some aspects of the big American food-aid programme, represent unfair competition. The issue continues to be debated in WTO agricultural negotiations.

With small domestic markets and no production or export subsidies, wheat farmers in Argentina and Australia depend much more on trade than their northern hemisphere counterparts. Some can, however, turn to other products (oilseeds in Argentina and wool or meat in Australia), so output is responsive to world prices as well as to the weather. The Argentinian government attempts to control the market by imposing export taxes and restrictions on the times of year when wheat can be exported.

The traditional five main exporters (Argentina, Australia, Canada, the EU and the United States) accounted for over 90% of world exports in the early 1990s but this has fallen to barely two-thirds of global exports in recent years, following a remarkable increase in sales by Ukraine, Russia and Kazakhstan.

## Production and stocks

As with all agricultural commodities the supply of wheat depends on weather conditions, although investment in the sector – such as fertiliser, pesticides, irrigation and good storage – can also have an effect. There are wide variations in global yields, with the UK, for example, producing an average of 8.4 tonnes per hectare compared with averages of around 2 tonnes/hectare in parts of Russia or North Africa. In general, higher-protein hard wheats, which are grown in a short summer season under relatively dry conditions, have lower yields than other types, while varieties grown for animal feed have higher yields.

The 2012 world wheat harvest was estimated at 650m tonnes, 44m tonnes lower than the previous year's record and fractionally below the five-year average. Weather conditions were not ideal and to meet demand some drawdown of stocks was expected. The EU is the world's largest wheat producer with a crop of 137m tonnes in 2011 (see Table 4.26), of which approximately one-third is grown in France. Other large wheat producers include Germany, the UK, Poland, Romania, Italy and Spain. The EU often produces more than it needs, but wheat remains popular among farmers: it is easy to grow, yields are good, and it is readily marketed. The EU actively supports wheat farming and has taken protectionist measures in the past to prevent cheap imports.

The next largest wheat producer is China, with output of around 118m tonnes in 2011; the Chinese government also actively supports wheat farmers. India's harvests are variable and sometimes it becomes a net importer, but it is the world's third largest producer. Production has increased sharply, from 69m tonnes in 2006 to nearly

TABLE 4.26 **Leading wheat-producing countries**[a]

|  | 2001 | | 2011 | |
| --- | --- | --- | --- | --- |
|  | m tonnes | % of total | m tonnes | % of total |
| EU | 113.1 | 19.5 | 137.4 | 19.8 |
| China | 93.9 | 16.2 | 117.9 | 17.0 |
| India | 69.7 | 12.0 | 86.9 | 12.5 |
| US | 53.3 | 9.2 | 54.4 | 7.8 |
| Russia | 46.9 | 8.1 | 56.2 | 8.1 |
| Canada | 20.6 | 3.5 | 25.3 | 3.6 |
| Pakistan | 19.0 | 3.3 | 24.2 | 3.5 |
| Australia | 24.9 | 4.3 | 29.5 | 4.2 |
| Ukraine | 21.0 | 3.6 | 22.3 | 3.2 |
| Argentina | 15.3 | 2.6 | 14.5 | 2.1 |
| Others | 103.6 | 17.8 | 125.7 | 18.1 |
| **Total** | **581.3** |  | **694.3** |  |

a Mainly harvested July–December.
**Sources:** International Grains Council; US Department of Agriculture

87m tonnes in 2011, helped by increase in area and better yields, as well as attractive government support prices. Storage capacity constraints, however, remain a major problem.

The United States produces a wide variety of types and classes of wheat, each of which is exported as well as consumed domestically. Wheat plantings have generally decreased over the past two decades because of competition from other crops (particularly maize and soybeans), reduced government support (notably the Conservation Reserve Programme) and increased competition in export markets.

Droughts and frost affect wheat production in Russia. To a limited extent this can be offset by increased spring sowings, although farmers often prefer to plant barley rather than spring wheat because of its greater reliability. Nevertheless, the country plays a significant role in the wheat trade. Conditions are similar in Ukraine, where the harvest can be severely reduced by bad weather. The government provides direct price support to farmers and intervenes in markets to maintain supplies of milling wheat for domestic use. Kazakhstan, with a climate similar to Canada's, is a producer of high-protein wheat.

World wheat stocks (measured at the end of each country's respective crop year, and therefore not attributable to a particular date) fell from over 200m tonnes in 2001/02 to only 115m tonnes at the end of 2007/08. This was a major factor behind the rally in prices in that year. The market fulfilled its function, as rising prices stimulated production and, following a series of bumper crops, world stocks had ballooned to 199m tonnes by the end of the 2011 season. Transport improvements and larger supplies from newer exporting countries, such as Russia, mean that the world wheat economy can function smoothly with much smaller stocks. However, the extreme weather-related variations in supply have led to increased market (and price) volatility.

India's food-security policy requires the state to maintain substantial buffer stocks of wheat. China also maintains large stocks, but few other wheat-importing countries carry more stocks than are needed to maintain continuity of supplies on the assumption of uninterrupted imports – typically about six weeks' supply.

## The wheat market

The export price of US No. 2 Hard Red Winter (HRW) wheat (ordinary protein) is usually taken as representative of the market because the wheat is always available and widely traded. Durum (for pasta) and high-protein wheats are much more expensive, while soft varieties for biscuit-making are cheaper. Prices of feed-grade wheats are usually aligned with feed barley and maize. Wheat is traded on the Chicago Board of Trade and the London Stock Exchanges as well as on numerous national and regional exchanges.

As a staple food, wheat can be subject to export restrictions if domestic crops are poor or international prices are high.

## Price trends

In the early 2000s weak import demand and large sales from the Black Sea region kept prices at around $150 per tonne (basis US HRW

FIG 4.14 **Wheat stocks and prices**

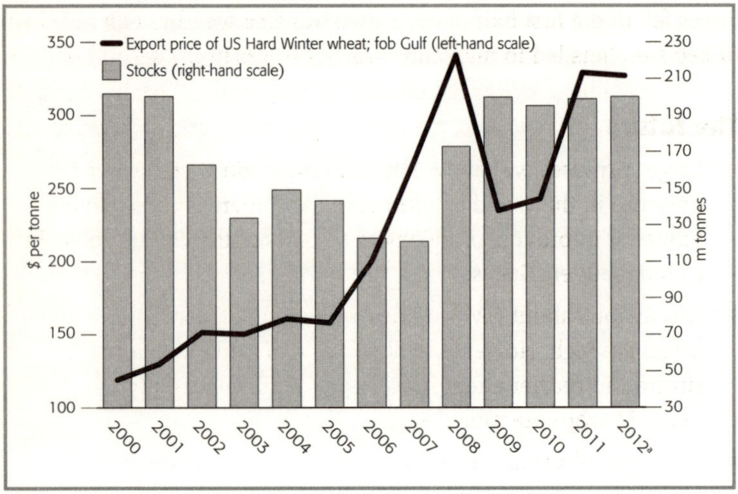

— Export price of US Hard Winter wheat; fob Gulf (left-hand scale)
Stocks (right-hand scale)

$ per tonne / m tonnes

a EIU estimates.
**Source:** International Grains Council

wheat, fob Gulf). A firmer trend set in after mid-2005, and as wheat supplies tightened in 2006–08 the rise accelerated. Governments in some exporting countries (including Ukraine, Russia and Argentina) started to restrict exports, aggravating the global shortage. Aside from the physical market, futures markets in wheat (along with those in other commodities) attracted attention as an alternative to weak bond and equity markets.

Wheat prices peaked in the first quarter of 2008, recording an average of more than $450/tonne in March. The subsequent decline was dramatic: prices averaged just $243/tonne in March 2009, a 46% year-on-year decline, and $191/tonne in the second quarter of 2010. Bumper crops in the northern hemisphere and a recovery in Australian output partly accounted for the fall, coupled with the subsequent increase in global stocks On an annual average basis, prices fell by 31% in 2009 (see Figure 4.14), recovering only slightly in 2010 before a big move up in 2011, partly because of a lack of availability (and the high price) of maize, for which wheat can be a substitute. The average wheat price in 2012 was broadly unchanged from 2011, but this masked considerable variation during the year. Prices fell in the first half of 2012, then adverse weather in a number of key suppliers led to markedly stronger prices in the second half.

## The future

- Large surpluses will allow Russia to maintain a significant presence in the world export market and there is considerable scope for improving productivity in parts of the Commonwealth of Independent States.
- Discussions about GM varieties will continue, particularly when prices are high. However, aversion to GM is likely to remain strong and further attempts to improve the availability of non-GM crops are more likely.
- Shortages of water will limit growth in wheat production, especially in China and other rapidly urbanising and populous developing countries.
- Growth in food use will remain sluggish and mainly concentrated in developing countries in Asia, particularly India, and Latin America. In the longer term, food-wheat consumption growth may begin to slow as more meat is included in diets in parts of Asia and North Africa.
- The use of wheat as feed is linked to pricing and availability. The EU and Russia will remain big users, but processors in other countries could switch back to maize and other products.

# Glossary

# Glossary

Cross-references are in **bold**.

| | |
|---|---|
| *Acid leaching* | A method for extracting metals from ores using an acid-based solution, usually sulphuric acid. |
| *Alloy* | A mixture of two or more metals which has different chemical properties from the metals it is made from. It is typically made by melting the metals and mixing them when they are in liquid form. The mixture then hardens to form the alloy. |
| *Austenitic stainless steels* | The most common type of stainless steel, containing 16–25% chromium and a nitrogen solution as well as nickel. Austenitic steels are particularly resistant to corrosion. |
| *Backwardation* | A market is said to be in backwardation when **futures** prices are lower than spot prices. |
| *Bayer process* | A process used to extract aluminium oxide (or alumina) from bauxite, which involves washing the bauxite in caustic soda. The acid dissolves the oxides of aluminium and silicon but not the other components of bauxite, which can be separated and removed as waste. Carbon dioxide is then bubbled through the solution. The carbon dioxide forms a weak acid that neutralises the caustic soda from stage one, |

allowing the aluminium oxide to form, but leaving the silicon in solution. The aluminium oxide is then heated to a high temperature to remove any water.

*Brownfield development* — Enhancement of sites where other mines and infrastructure already exist. Such sites are typically quicker and cheaper (less capital outlay) to develop.

*Carbon capture and storage (CCS)* — A process of capturing carbon emissions, usually produced by a thermal power plant, and storing them where they will not enter the atmosphere.

*Carryover* — The amount of a good produced in one year that is not consumed and goes into stocks.

*CIF (cost, insurance and freight)* — In shipping, if a price is quoted in CIF terms, the seller will pay all the costs involved in bringing the good to an agreed port, including insurance.

*Coal bed methane (CBM)* — Natural gas that is extracted from coal seams or beds (called coal seam gas in Australia). Extraction is by drilling into the rock formation containing the coal seam, but a number of different technologies are used depending on the nature of the coal bed. **Fracking or hydraulic fracturing** is one method that can be used.

*COMEX* — Commodity Exchange Inc, a division of the **New York Mercantile Exchange** (NYMEX), which in turn is owned by CME Group.

*Commonwealth of Independent States (CIS)* — Created in 1991 following the collapse of the Soviet Union, its members are Azerbaijan, Armenia, Belarus, Georgia, Kazakhstan, Kyrgyzstan, Moldova, Russia, Tajikistan, Turkmenistan, Uzbekistan and Ukraine.

*Contango* — A market is said to be in contango when **futures** prices are higher than spot prices.

| | |
|---|---|
| *Derivatives* | Financial instruments whose values or prices are a function of (or are derived from) one or more underlying assets such as commodities, equities and exchange rates. They are typically contracts between two parties that agree the terms of the derivative investment. |
| *Electrolysis* | In mining, the use of an electric current to break down an ore into its constituent components. |
| *Euronext-LIFFE* | The subsidiary of Euronext that trades **futures** and options contracts. It resulted from a takeover by the Amsterdam-based Euronext electronic exchange of the London International Financial Futures and Options Exchange (LIFFE). Euronext merged with the New York Stock Exchange (NYSE) group in 2007 and NYSE Euronext was created. |
| *Exchange-traded fund (ETF)* | A fund that holds a specific set of underlying assets, for example a commodity index. Shares in an ETF trade on a stock exchange like a regular corporate share. |
| *Exogenous* | In economics, a factor outside the variables being considered. |
| *Fair trade (or fairtrade)* | An organisation or movement that aims to help farmers and workers in developing countries by seeking better prices for their goods and better terms of trade, or by improving working conditions. Sustainability is also an important goal. |
| *Ferronickel* | An **alloy** containing nickel (typically 35%) and iron (typically 65%). |
| *Fiat currency* | Currency or paper money that has no intrinsic value issued by a government or state. |

| | |
|---|---|
| *Fracking or hydraulic fracturing* | The process of fracturing shale rocks to release natural gas or oil. It involves drilling and injecting fluid at high pressure into the rock formation. |
| *Futures* | A futures contract is an agreement between two parties (the seller and buyer) to buy or sell a particular asset at a certain price at a future date. In the commodities world, the market originally evolved as a way for producers to lock in a certain price for their good when it is produced (and so enable them to budget and agree a price that would cover costs by some margin). For commodity consumers – often manufacturing companies – it means they know the price of their future inputs, which again helps with budgeting. |
| *Genetically modified (GM)* | When genetic engineering has been used to alter the DNA of plants, usually in an effort to make them more productive or resistant to disease or extreme weather conditions |
| *Hall-Héroult process* | The principal process used to produce aluminium from alumina. Alumina is dissolved in cryolite to lower the melting point, and then aluminium is produced by the electrolysis of molten alumina in what is called a Hall-Héroult cell. The cell is a carbon-lined reaction vessel which acts as the cathode, with carbon anodes dipped into the alumina-cryolite electrolyte. |
| *Hedging* | A method used by investors to protect themselves from potential losses on another financial transaction. This usually involves taking an offsetting position in a related security, often by buying **futures** or options contracts. |

| | |
|---|---|
| *Horizontal drilling* | Traditionally, the only way to extract natural gas and or oil was by drilling a vertical well. Horizontal or directional drilling is a new technology for drilling a curved well to reach a target that is not directly beneath the drill site. This has enabled the drilling of areas that were previously considered inaccessible. |
| *Hydrometallurgical process (HP)* | Removing metals from their ores by a series of chemical processes, starting with leaching (when solutions, usually acid, are used to separate the components of the ore). |
| *Imperial smelting process (ISP)* | The traditional method used to refine lead and zinc. Ore concentrates containing lead, zinc and possibly other metals are fed into a furnace, and in the process lead and zinc are reduced into metal. ISP has lost favour in recent years as it is energy intensive. |
| *Intercontinental Exchange Inc (ICE)* | An American company that operates a web-based stock exchange. Historically, ICE was focused on energy products and it still has an extensive presence in commodity markets, but it now also offers a wide range of other products. In late 2012, it reached an agreement to buy NYSE Euronext, and this is now awaiting regulatory approval. |
| *Latin America* | Includes South America, Mexico, Central America and the Caribbean countries. |
| *Liquefied natural gas (LNG)* | A clear liquid that is created when natural gas is cooled to around −160°C. The gas can then be transported easily in liquid form and converted back to gas when it reaches its destination. |
| *London Bullion Market Association (LBMA)* | A wholesale (or **over-the-counter**) market for gold and silver, based in London. Its clients include central banks, miners, refiners, traders and fabricators. |

| | |
|---|---|
| *Margin requirement* | The minimum amount a buyer must deposit in the form of cash or eligible securities as collateral for an investment in **futures** or options. |
| *Marginal cost* | The change in a producer's total cost resulting from a one unit change in output. |
| *Monopsony* | A market where there is only one buyer but many sellers. All the market power is with the buyer, who can then set the price. |
| *Natural-gas-to-liquids (NGLs)* | Liquids that are extracted from natural gas, usually in a natural-gas processing plant. The most common examples are ethane, propane, butane and isobutene. |
| *Nearby futures* | **Futures** contracts that are close to their expiry date. |
| *New York Board of Trade (NYBOT)* | A physical commodities exchange in New York. It is now called ICE Futures US following its takeover by **Intercontinental Exchange** in 2007. |
| *New York Mercantile Exchange (NYMEX)* | A commodity futures exchange owned by CME Group. Most trading on NYMEX is now electronic, but there is still a small open outcry operation or physical trading floor. |
| *Organisation of Petroleum Exporting Countries (OPEC)* | An organisation set up in Baghdad in September 1960 by representatives of Iran, Iraq, Kuwait, Saudi Arabia and Venezuela to co-ordinate opposition to cuts in prices posted by multinational oil companies. Its role has evolved and OPEC now seeks to maintain prices within a target range by balancing the global supply of oil with demand. It operates a loose system of production quotas. |

| | |
|---|---|
| Original-equipment (OE) battery | A battery that is made by an independent supplier, not the original manufacturer of the good that the battery runs. It is often a replacement battery. |
| Over-the-counter (OTC) market | A market where there is no official exchange or trading floor and transactions are carried out by telephone or through an electronic platform. OTC markets are traditionally less regulated. |
| Quantitative easing (QE) | An unconventional monetary policy adopted by central banks when conventional policies, such as changes in interest rates, have not been effective. There are a number of different types of QE, but it is an expansionary policy aiming to increase the domestic money supply and kick-start economic growth. |
| Remelt ingot | A product of aluminium refining. It is siphoned from the potlines in smelters without being alloyed or purified and then poured directly into moulds to form other aluminium products such as standard ingot. Remelt ingot is traded as a commodity in its own right |
| Renewable Fuels Standard (RFS) | The mandated minimum requirements of biofuels to be used in American transport fuels. |
| Shale gas | Natural gas that is found in shale (fine-grain sedimentary) rock formations. |
| South America | Excludes Mexico, Central America and the Caribbean countries. |
| Sovereign wealth fund (SWF) | A fund created by a government that has excess cash and no debt. In the case of commodities, such governments typically have high levels of commodity export earnings. To avoid creating inflationary conditions in the domestic economy or massive currency appreciation, governments lodge the excess earnings in funds, which typically invest abroad in a diverse range of assets. |

| | |
|---|---|
| Starter-lighting-ignition (SLI) battery | A lead-acid storage battery. |
| Superalloy | An **alloy** with exceptional properties, in particular strength or resistance to corrosion, used extensively in the aviation industry. Most superalloys contain some nickel or cobalt. |
| SX-EW (solvent extraction and electrowinning) | A process in which smelting is replaced by leaching, allowing refined metal to be produced at the mine without further processing. It is usually used with copper found in oxides and has become increasingly popular in recent years, partly because it costs less. |
| Tight gas | Natural gas that is found in extremely impermeable, hard rock. |

# Sources of statistical information

### BP Statistical Review of World Energy
An annual publication of BP, a UK-based energy company, containing a wide range of data on energy market fundamentals, prices and trends.

### EIU (Economist Intelligence Unit)
Part of The Economist Group, the EIU provides extensive forecasting and advisory services across countries, industries and commodities (see www.eiu.com and www.store.eiu.com). Its commodity coverage involves in-depth analysis of the 25 major global commodities, including 14 energy and industrial raw material commodities and 11 agricultural commodities. Monthly reports are published on each commodity with analysis of trends in the market and two-year forecasts of consumption, production, stocks and prices.

### International Cocoa Organization (ICCO)
An intergovernmental agency established in 1973 with headquarters in London. Its membership includes cocoa producing and consuming countries. Initially, it aimed to influence prices and supply of cocoa, but attempts to manage the market largely failed and now it focuses on sustainability and fair trade practice in the cocoa market. The ICCO is an important source of statistical information on cocoa.

### International Coffee Organization (ICO)
An intergovernmental agency established in 1962 and based in London. It initially tried to manage prices and supply in the global

coffee market, but now it focuses its efforts on promoting the development of a sustainable coffee economy. The ICO collects and publishes information on all aspects of the coffee economy and is an important source of statistical information on coffee.

### International Copper Study Group (ICSG)
An intergovernmental organisation or forum based in Lisbon, Portugal, where governments, the mining industry and copper consumers discuss issues related to copper. The ICSG seeks to increase transparency in the global copper market and is an important source of statistical information on copper.

### International Cotton Advisory Committee (ICAC)
An intergovernmental organisation founded in 1939 in Washington, DC, involving cotton producers and consumers. The ICAC undertakes research into the global cotton economy and market and is an important source of statistical information on cotton.

### International Energy Agency (IEA)
Based in Paris, the IEA was founded in the 1970s as a response to the oil price shocks and focused its efforts on ensuring supply. It still focuses on ensuring supply in oil-importing countries, but it has expanded its remit to include all forms of energy and other areas associated with energy including economic development and the environment. The IEA also seeks to reach out to non-members, both consuming and producing countries. Its 28 members are all members of the Organisation of Economic Co-operation and Development (OECD).

### International Grains Council (IGC)
An intergovernmental forum for co-operation in grains trade. It was established by the Grains Trade Convention (GTC) and oversees or monitors the implementation of the GTC. The IGC is an important source of statistical information on cereals, rice and oilseeds.

## International Lead and Zinc Study Group (ILZSG)

An intergovernmental agency founded in 1959 to provide information and research on the lead and zinc markets, to monitor the international trade in lead and zinc and to try to resolve any issues. It is based in Lisbon, Portugal, and operates under the auspices of the UN. The ILZSG is an important source of statistical information on the global lead and zinc markets. Its membership accounts for about 85% of the world's consumers and producers of lead and zinc.

## International Nickel Study Group (INSG)

An intergovernmental agency established in 1990 and based in Lisbon, Portugal. Its members include major nickel consuming, producing and trading countries. The aim of the INSG is to provide information on the nickel market and to discuss and try to resolve any issues.

## International Rubber Study Group (IRSG)

An intergovernmental agency established in 1944 and based in Singapore. The IRSG publishes research and statistics on the global rubber (including synthetic rubber) industry.

## International Sugar Organization (ISO)

An intergovernmental agency based in London with 85 members. The ISO is dedicated to researching and providing statistics on the global sugar, sweetener and ethanol industries. It administers the International Sugar Agreement and once had a price-controlling function, including export quotas, but this was ineffective and was abandoned.

## International Tin Research Institute (ITRI)

A non-profit making agency, based in the UK, representing the tin industry. Its members are mainly miners and tin refiners. The ITRI aims to promote the use of tin by contributing to technical research and commercial development. It also collates statistical information on the tin industry.

## The International Wool Textile Organisation (IWTO)

An association of national organisations from some 20 member countries involved in combing, scouring, processing, and so on. The secretariat is based in Belgium. The IWTO's functions include research, data compilation and arbitration of members' disputes.

## Johnson Matthey

A UK-based multinational chemicals and precious metals company that publishes research and data on precious metals markets.

## The Silver Institute

A non-profit international association founded in 1971 and based in the United States. Its members range from mining companies to refineries, traders and jewellers. The Silver Institute seeks to promote the use of silver but also provides useful data on demand and supply trends in the silver market.

## US Geological Survey (USGS)

A department of the US Ministry of the Interior. The USGS collates and publishes impartial scientific information.

## World Bureau of Metal Statistics (WBMS)

An independent and commercial source of data on metals founded in 1947 and based in the UK.

## World Gold Council (WGC)

A non-profit organisation founded in 1987 and based in the UK. Its 23 members are leading gold-mining companies. The WGC promotes the use of gold in all sectors, and also provides research and detailed data on supply and demand of gold as well as on gold investment trends.

# Index

Page numbers in *italics* indicate figures and tables.

## A
Abu Dhabi National Oil Company (ADNOC) 154
acid leaching 245
Africa
  aluminium 33
  cocoa 166, 167, 169–170
  coffee 176
  copper belt 46
  cotton 180, 182
  crude oil 149, 151, 152
  gold 58
  maize 193, 194, 197
  natural gas 136, 137, 139, 141
  rice 201, 203, 205
  rubber 211
  sugar 226, 227, 227, 228
  tin mining 106
  wheat 236, 237, 239
Agreement on Textiles and Clothing (ATC) 180
Alcoa 37, 37
alloys 245 *see also* superalloys
aluminium 29
  bauxite reserves 29, 30
  consumption trends 31–32, 32
  international trade 32–33, 33
  major companies 37
  market trading 38
  outlook 39–40
  price trends 38–39, 39
  production 30, 33–36, 35
  stock levels 36, 39
  uses 29, 30–31
Aluminium Bahrain 37
Aluminium Corporation of China *see* Chalco
Aneka Tambang (Antam) 94
Anglo American 95
Anglo American Platinum 72, 76
animal feed
  maize 191, 193, 194
  soybeans 218
  wheat 236, 239
Archer Daniels Midland 165, 206, 221
Argentina
  maize 194–195, 195, 196, 197
  soybeans 219, 220–221, 220, 222, 222
  wheat 238–239, 240
  wool 187, 188
artificial sweeteners 225–226, 227
Asia
  cocoa 166

copper 44
cotton 181
crude oil 149, 151, 151, 155
lead 81
maize 193, 197
natural gas 137, 139, 141, 143, 144
rice 200, 201, 203, 204, 205
rubber 211, 211, 213
soybeans 219, 220
sugar 226, 227
tin 101, 106
wheat 236
austenitic stainless steels 245
Australasia, natural gas 137, 139, 141
Australia
aluminium 29, 30, 33, 33, 35
coal 126, 128, 129, 130, 131, 132
copper 42, 47
cotton exports 180
gold mining 57, 58
lead 79-80, 83-84, 83, 84, 85
natural gas production 142
nickel 91, 95-96, 95, 97
silver production 67
sugar 228, 229, 231
tin 101, 102, 106
wheat 238-239, 238, 240
wool 186-187, 187, 188
zinc 112, 113, 116, 117, 118
Australian Wool Exchange (AWEX) 188
automotive industry *see also* tyre manufacturing
aluminium use 31, 39, 44
copper use 43, 44
lead batteries 81, 88-89
palladium use 74, 75-76
platinum use 70, 71, 74
rubber use 209, 212

zinc use for galvanised steel 114, 120
AWEX Eastern Market Indicator (EMI) 188

## B

backwardation 20, 21, 245
Bangladesh
cotton 179, 180
rice 201, 204
wheat 201, 235, 237
Barry Callebaut 165
batteries
lead 80-81, 86-87, 88
nickel 92
tin 104
zinc 113
bauxite 29-30, 30
Bayer process 245
Belgium
cocoa imports 166
coffee imports 174
lead exports 83
wool consumption 185
BHP Billiton 37, 46, 48, 67, 85, 95, 96
biofuel production 150
maize 192
soybeans 218
sugar 230, 233-234
wheat 236
BlackRock 68
Blommer 165
Boliden 118
Bolivia
silver production 67
tin 101, 102, 105, 106-107, 107
zinc reserves 113
Botswana, copper mine production 48
BP 153

*BP Statistical Review of World Energy* 253
Brazil
  aluminium 29, 30, 32, 35
  cocoa 164, 168
  coffee 172, 173, 174–175, 174, 175
  cotton 179, 182
  crude oil production 157
  ethanol 229, 232, 233
  maize 192–193, 193, 195, 195, 196, 197
  nickel reserves 91
  rubber production 214
  soybeans 219, 220, 220, 221, 222
  sugar 227, 228, 229–230, 229, 231
  tin 101, 102, 104, 107
  wheat imports 238
  zinc consumption 115
Brent Blend oil benchmark 157–158, 159
Bretton Woods system 60
Bridgestone 212
British Sugar 231
bronze 101, 103, 104
brownfield development 246
Bunge 221

## C

Cameroon
  cocoa 166, 168
  coffee 176
Canada
  aluminium 32, 33, 33, 35
  copper production 47
  crude oil 148, 152
  gold mining 58
  lead production 84, 85
  natural gas consumption 139
  nickel 91, 93, 94, 95, 97
  wheat 238, 240
  zinc 113, 116, 117, 118
carbon capture and storage (CCS) 135, 246
carbon emissions 34, 127–128, 138, 145
Cargill 165, 221
Caribbean, cotton consumption 179
carpets, wool demand 185
carryover 246
Central America
  coffee production 175
  crude oil reserves 149
  natural gas 137, 139, 141
  rice imports 203
  soybean imports 220
central banks, demand for gold 54
Chalco (Aluminum Corporation of China) 33, 37, 37
chemical industry
  nickel use 92
  palladium use 75
  platinum use 71
  tin use 103, 103
Chile
  copper
    exports 45, 46
    production 46, 47, 47, 48, 49
    reserves 42
  silver production 67
China
  12th five year plan 130, 134, 182
  aluminium
    bauxite reserves 29, 30
    consumption 31, 32
    exports 32, 33
    production 33–34, 35, 36, 37, 40
  coal
    consumption 127, 128
    imports 129
    production 129, 130, 131

reserves 126
coffee consumption 173
copper
   consumption 44, 45
   imports 45, 46
   production 41, 47, 47, 48, 49
   reserves 42
   state reserves 50
cotton 179–180, 179, 180, 181, 182, 184
crude oil 148, 151, 151, 152
GM food 219
gold 55–56, 56, 57, 58
industrialisation 7, 17
lead
   consumption 81–82
   production 83, 84–85, 84, 85, 86
   reserves 79–80
maize 192, 193, 194, 196, 197, 197
natural gas consumption 138–139, 139, 145
nickel 91, 92, 93, 93, 96, 97
overseas investments 12
platinum consumption 70
power generation 127, 134
rice 200, 201, 202, 204, 205
rubber 210, 211, 211, 212, 214, 214
scrap 97
self-sufficiency 11
shale oil 156
silver production 67
solar-powered energy 65
soybeans 218, 219, 219, 220, 222, 222
steel industry 8, 90, 92, 99–100
sugar
   consumption 227–228, 227
   imports 228, 229
   production 230, 231
   stock levels 232

tin
   consumption 104, 105, 111
   international trade 105, 106
   mine production 107
   refined production 107–108, 109
   reserves 102
wheat 236, 238, 239, 240, 241
wool 186, 186, 187–188, 187, 190
zinc
   consumption 114, 115
   imports 115, 116
   production 116, 117–118, 117, 118
   reserves 112, 113
   stock holdings 119
China Power Investment Corporation 37
CIF (cost, insurance and freight) 246
CIS (Commonwealth of Independent States) 246
   cocoa consumption 166
   crude oil consumption 151
   natural gas 137, 139, 141
   rubber consumption 211
   wheat consumption 236
clothing
   cotton use 178–179
   wool use 185, 190
coal 125
   consumption 127–128, 128
   international trade 129, 129
   market trading 132–133
   outlook 134–135
   price trends 133–134, 134
   production 129–132, 131
   reserves 125, 126
   uses 126–127
coal bed methane (CBM) 136, 146, 246

cocoa 163
  consumption 165–166
  international trade 166–167, 166
  market trading 168–169
  price trends 169, 170
  processing 14, 164–165, 164
  production 167–168, 168
  stock levels 168, 169
  uses 164–165
Codelco 46, 48, 49
coffee 171
  consumption 172–173, 173
  international trade 173–174, 174
  market trading 176
  outlook 177
  price trends 176, 177
  processing 171–172
  production 174–176, 175
  stock levels 177
collateral return 20–21
Colombia
  coal 129–130, 129, 131, 132, 134
  coffee 174, 175, 175
  COMEX see New York Commodity Exchange
commodity indices 9, 22–23, 25
Commonwealth of Independent States see CIS
construction industry
  aluminium use 31
  copper use 42–43, 43
  lead use 80
  zinc use for galvanised steel 114, 120
contango 20, 21, 246
Continental (tyre company) 212
copper 41
  consumption trends 44–45, 45
  international trade 45, 46
  market trading 50–51
  mining constraints 47–48
  outlook 52
  price trends 51–52, 51
  production 41–42, 46–49, 47, 49
  reserves 42, 42
  stock levels 48–50, 51
  uses 42–44, 43
corporate risk 18
Cosan 231
Côte d'Ivoire
  cocoa 164, 166, 167, 168, 169
  coffee production 175
  rubber 212, 214
Cotlook A index 182
cotton 178
  consumption 178–180, 179
  international trade 180–181, 180
  market trading 182
  price trends 183–184, 183
  processing 178
  production 181–182, 182
  stock levels 183
  uses 178–179
crack spread 158
crude oil 147
  consumption 149–152, 151
  international trade 152, 152
  major companies 153
  market trading 157–158
  outlook 160
  price trends 10–11, 158–160, 159
  production 153–157, 155
  refining 147–148
  reserves 148–149, 149, 153, 154
  uses 147, 149–150
Cuba
  nickel reserves 91
  sugar exports 228

## D

demand, price effects 14–15
demand curve 15
Democratic Republic of Congo (DRC)
   copper 46–47, 48
   tin mining 106
dentistry, metal use in 55, 70, 75
derivatives 247
developing countries
   changing food consumption 185, 191, 200, 218, 234, 235–236
   commodity demand 7
   processing profits 14
   windfall revenue 13
DRC *see* Democratic Republic of Congo
Dubai Aluminium 37
Dutch disease 13

## E

Economist Intelligence Unit (EIU) 253
Ecuador, cocoa production 168
Egypt
   maize imports 195
   wheat imports 237, 238
elasticity of demand 14–15
electrical and electronics industries
   aluminium use 31
   copper use 43
   gold use 54–55
   lead use 80
   palladium use 75
   tin use 102, 111
   zinc use 114
electrolysis 247
EM Vinto 109
equilibrium price 14
equity markets 24–26
Eramet 95
ETFs (exchange-traded funds) 23, 247
   copper 50–51
   gold 54, 60
   palladium 77
   platinum 70, 72
   silver 66, 68
ethanol
   maize 192
   sugar 230, 233–234
   wheat 236
Ethiopia, coffee 173, 175
ETNs (exchange-traded notes) 23
Euronext-LIFFE 247
Europe
   aluminium 31, 33, 34, 36, 40
   coal consumption 128, 128
   cocoa 164, 165–166
   coffee consumption 173
   copper 44, 45, 48, 49
   cotton 179, 179, 181
   crude oil 148, 149, 151, 152
   ethanol 236
   lead 81–82, 82, 84, 85, 86
   maize 193, 193, 194, 195, 196, 197
   nickel 92, 93, 97
   natural gas 137, 138, 139, 141, 144
   rice imports 203
   rubber 210, 211, 212
   soybeans 218–219, 219, 220, 220
   sugar 226, 227, 228, 229–230, 229, 231, 232
   tin consumption 104, 105
   wheat 236, 236, 237, 238, 239, 240
   wool consumption 185, 186
   zinc 114, 115, 116, 117, 118
European Commission 19
exchange-traded funds *see* ETFs
exchange-traded notes *see* ETNs

exogenous 247
ExxonMobil 153, 154

**F**
fair trade 247
ferronickel 247
fiat currency 247
fibres, man-made 178, 184, 185
Finland, nickel exports 93
floating liquefied natural gas (FLNG) 138
food security 11–12, 19, 241
fracking 248
France
   aluminium consumption 31, 32
   cocoa 164, 166
   coffee imports 174
   maize production 196
   natural gas consumption 139
   tin imports 105
   wheat production 239
Freeport-McMoRan Copper & Gold 48, 49
Fresnillo 67
futures 20–21, 248
   crude oil 157–158
   gold 61, 63
   investment return 20–21
   market size and regulation 19
futures price curve 20, 21

**G**
G20 19
galvanising 113–114
Gazprom 140–141
Gejiu ZiLi 109
GCC *see* Gulf Co-operation Council
genetically modified (GM) crops 248
   cotton 181
   maize 193, 194–195, 195–197
   soybeans 219–220, 221
   wheat 243
Germany
   aluminium 31–32, 32, 33
   coal 126, 129–130, 129, 131
   cocoa 164, 166
   coffee imports 174
   copper imports 46
   crude oil imports 152
   lead, international trade 83
   natural gas consumption 139
   nickel imports 93
   tin imports 105
   zinc imports 116
Ghana
   cocoa 164, 166, 167, 168
   Cocobod 169
   gold mining 58
Glencore 117
global poverty 19
GM *see* genetically modified crops
gold 53
   consumption trends 55–57
   futures 61, 63
   inflation hedge 61–62
   market trading 59–61
   mining constraints 57
   outlook 63–64
   price trends 61–63, 62, 69
   production 57–59, 58
   reserves 53
   uses 54–55, 55
Gold Corp 67
Gold Standard 60
Goldman Sachs commodity index 25
Goodyear 212
Grupo Mexico 49
Guangxi China Tin 109

Guatemala, sugar exports 228, 229
Guinea, bauxite reserves 29, 30
Gulf Co-operation Council (GCC) 34-35
Gulf Oil 153

## H
Hall-Héroult process 248
Handy & Harman silver price 68
hedging 18, 26, 61-62, 248
Henry Hub benchmark 143, 144
Hidalco Group 49
Hindustan Zinc 117, 118
horizontal drilling 249
HP *see* hydrometallurgical process
Hubbert, M. King 10-11
hydraulic fracturing 248
hydrometallurgical process (HP) 112, 249

## I
Iceland, aluminium production 34
Impala Platinum 72, 76
imperial smelting process (ISP) 113, 249
income elasticity of demand 15
India
    aluminium 29, 32, 35
    coal
        consumption 128, 128
        imports 128, 129
        production 129, 130-131, 131
        reserves 126
    coffee 174, 175, 175
    copper consumption 44, 45
    cotton 179, 180-181, 180, 182
    crude oil 148, 152
    gold consumption 55, 56
    lead 80, 82, 85
    maize exports 195
    natural gas consumption 139, 140
    platinum consumption 70
    rice 201, 201, 203, 203, 204, 205
    rubber 210, 211, 214, 214
    silver consumption 65
    soybeans 181, 219-220, 219, 222, 222
    sugar
        consumption 227, 227
        exports 228, 229
        production 229-230, 231
        stock levels 232
    wheat 235, 236, 237, 239-240, 240, 241
    wool 186, 187
    zinc 113, 115, 117, 118, 118
Indonesia
    bauxite exports 40
    coal 129, 130, 131, 131
    cocoa 164, 166, 168
    coffee 173, 174, 175, 175
    copper 42, 47
    cotton imports 180
    gold 56, 57, 58
    nickel 91, 94, 95, 99
    rice 201, 202, 204, 205
    rubber 212, 213, 214
    sugar 227, 228, 229
    tin
        exports 105, 110-111
        mine production 106-107, 107
        refined production 108, 109
        reserves 101, 102
        stock exchange reference price 109
    wheat imports 237, 238
inflation hedging 26, 61-62
Intercontinental Exchange Inc (ICE) 249

International Cocoa Organisation
  (ICCO) 253
International Coffee Agreements
  (ICAs) 176
International Coffee Organisation
  (ICO) 253-254
International Copper Study Group
  (ICSG) 254
International Cotton Advisory
  Committee (ICAC) 254
International Energy Agency (IEA)
  254
International Grains Council (IGC)
  254
International Lead and Zinc Study
  Group (ILZSG) 255
International Nickel Study Group
  (INSG) 255
International Rubber Study Group
  (IRSG) 255
International Sugar Organisation
  (ISO) 255
International Tin Agreement 110
International Tin Research Institute
  (ITRI) 255
International Wool Textile
  Organisation (IWTO) 256
Iran
  crude oil reserves 148
  natural gas 136, 139
Iraq, crude oil 148, 156
Iraq National Oil Company (INOC)
  154
Italy
  aluminium 31, 32, 33
  coffee imports 174
  copper imports 46
  gold consumption 56
  lead imports 83
  natural gas consumption 139
  nickel imports 93
  wool consumption 185
  zinc imports 116

## J

Jamaica, bauxite reserves 29, 30
Japan
  aluminium 32, 33
  coal 128, 129, 132-133
  coffee 173, 173
  copper 45, 45, 46, 48, 49
  cotton consumption 179
  crude oil 148, 152, 152
  gold consumption 56
  lead 82, 85
  maize imports 195
  natural gas consumption 139
  nickel 93, 97
  rubber 211, 212, 213
  sugar 226, 228
  tin 104, 105
  wheat imports 238
  wool consumption 186
  zinc 115, 118
Japanese Steel Mills (JSM) 132
jewellery-making
  gold use 54, 55, 55, 56
  palladium use 75
  platinum use 70, 71, 71
  silver use 65, 66, 66
Jiangxi Copper 49
Jinchuan Group 49, 95
Johnson Matthey 256

## K

Kazakhstan
  coal 126, 131
  copper reserves 42
  cotton production 181
  lead exports 83

wheat 239, 240–241
zinc 113, 116
KGHM Polska Miedz 67, 85
Koba Tin 108
Kondratiev, Nikolai 8–9
Korea Zinc Group 118
Kuala Lumpur Tin Market (KLTM) 109
Kuwait Petroleum Corporation (KPC) 154

**L**
Latin America 249
   copper consumption 45
   crude oil 151, 152, 155
   maize 193, 197
   rice 201, 205
   rubber consumption 211
   sugar 226, 227, 231
   wheat consumption 236
LBMA (London Bullion Market Association) fixing price 60, 68
lead 79
   consumption 81–82, 82
   international trade 82–83, 83
   market trading 86–87
   outlook 88–89
   price trends 87–88, 88
   production 79, 83–86, 113
   quality 86–87
   reserves 79–80, 80
   stock levels 88
   uses 80–81
liquefied natural gas (LNG) 137–138, 142, 143, 144, 145, 249
LME (London Metal Exchange) 36, 38, 50, 86–87, 97–98, 108, 119
LNG see liquefied natural gas
London Bullion Market Association (LBMA) 249

London Metal Exchange see LME
Lonmin 76
Louis Dreyfus 206, 221, 231

**M**
maize 191, 228
   consumption 191, 192–194, 193
   international trade 194–195, 195
   market trading 198
   outlook 199
   price trends 198–199, 198
   production 195–197, 197, 221
   stock levels 197, 198
   uses 191–192
Malaysia
   cocoa processing 164
   rubber 212, 213, 214
   tin 102, 105, 108, 109
Malaysia Smelting Corporation (MSC) 108, 109
margin requirement 20–21, 250
marginal cost of production 14, 250
market-clearing price 14
market risk 18
medicine, metal use in 55, 70, 71
Metallo-Chimique 109
Mexico
   coffee 173, 175
   copper 42, 47
   cotton consumption 179
   lead 80, 82, 83, 84, 85, 85
   maize 193, 193, 194, 195, 197
   silver production 67
   zinc 113, 117
Michelin 212
micronaire 182
Middle East
   aluminium production 33, 34
   crude oil 151–152, 151, 152
   natural gas 136, 137, 139, 141

rice 201, 202, 203
soybean imports 220
water supplies 12
wheat 236, 236, 237
Minara Resources 95
mining constraints 47–48, 57, 67, 107
Minmetals Australia 117
Minsur 108, 109
Mitr Phol Sugar 231
monopsony 250

# N

National Balancing Point (NBP) 144
National Iranian Oil Company (NIOC) 154
national oil companies (NOCs) 153
National Oil Corporation (Libya) 154
natural gas 136
   consumption 138, 139
   market trading 143
   outlook 145–146
   price trends 143–145, 144
   processing 137–138
   production 140–143, 141
   reserves 136–137, 137
   uses 138
natural-gas-to-liquids (NGLs) 157, 250
nearby futures 250
Netherlands
   aluminium 33
   cocoa 164, 166
   exchange-rates following natural gas find 13
   zinc imports 116
New Caledonia, nickel 91, 95, 96
New York Board of Trade (NYBOT) 250

New York Commodity Exchange (COMEX) 50, 246
New York Mercantile Exchange (NYMEX) 50, 250
New Zealand, wool 187, 188
NGLs *see* natural-gas-to-liquids
nickel 90
   consumption 92, 93
   international trade 93, 93
   market trading 97–98
   outlook 98–100
   price trends 98, 99
   production 90, 94–97, 95, 97
   reserves 90, 91
   stock levels 99
   uses 91–92
Nigeria, cocoa 166, 168
Nigerian National Petroleum Corporation (NNPC) 154
NOCs *see* national oil companies
Nordzucker 231
Norilsk Nickel 76, 94, 95
Norsk Hydro 37
North America
   crude oil 149, 151
   natural gas 137, 139, 141
   palladium production 76, 76
   platinum production 72
   rice imports 203
   rubber consumption 210, 211
   soybean imports 220
   sugar consumption 226
North American Free Trade Agreement (NAFTA) 179
North Sea oil fields 157
Norway
   aluminium 33, 34, 35
   nickel 93, 97
nuclear power 134, 135
Nyrstar 118

## O

Olam 206
OPEC (Organisation of Petroleum Exporting Countries) 12, 153–154, 155, 250
original equipment (OE) battery 251
OTC (over-the-counter) markets 19, 60, 251

## P

packaging industry 31, 103, 111
Pakistan
    cotton 179, 182
    rice exports 203, 203
    sugar trade 228
    wheat 236, 237, 240
palladium 75
    consumption 75
    market trading 77
    outlook 78
    price trends 77–78, 78
    production 76, 76
    uses 75–76, 75
palm oil 213, 218, 223
Pan American Silver 67
Paraguay, soybeans 220, 222
peak oil theory 10–11
Peru
    coffee production 175
    copper 42, 46, 47
    gold mining 57, 58
    lead 80, 83, 84, 85
    silver production 67
    tin 101, 102, 105, 106–107, 107, 108
    zinc 113, 116, 116, 117
Petra Foods 165
Petróleos de Venezuela SA (PDVSA) 154

Philippines
    nickel mine production 94, 95
    rice 202, 204
Pirelli 212
platinum 70
    consumption 70–71
    market trading 72
    outlook 74
    price trends 73–74, 73
    production 71–72
    uses 70–71
plumbing
    copper use 42–43, 43
    tin use 102
Poland
    copper 42, 46, 47
    gas exploration 142
    silver production 67
portfolio diversification 24–25
power generation
    coal use 126, 127, 131, 134–135, 150
    copper use 44
    gas use 138, 145, 150
    oil use 150
price determination 12, 14–17
price elasticity 14–15

## Q

Qatar
    aluminium production 34
    natural gas 136, 142
quantitative easing (QE) 251
    and attractiveness of gold 63

## R

rapeseed oil 219, 223
recycling 11
    aluminium 35–36, 39
    copper 41–42
    gold 58–59

lead 86, 88
nickel 96–97
platinum 71
silver 66–67
tin 107–108
zinc 118
regulation 19
remelt aluminium ingots 251
renewable energy systems 44, 64, 65, 134, 145
Renewable Fuels Standard (RFS) 192, 251
resource nationalism 11, 13
resource-rich countries, downsides 13–14
rice 200
   consumption 200–201, 201
   government interventions 204, 205, 207
   international trade 202–203, 203
   market trading 206
   outlook 207
   price trends 206–207, 207
   production 204–206, 205
   stock levels 206, 207
   uses 200
Richards Bay Coal Terminal 132
Rio Tinto 37, 37, 46
roll return 20
rolling mechanism 23
Rosneft 154
rubber, natural 209
   consumption 210–212, 211
   international trade 212–213, 212
   market trading 215–216
   outlook 216
   price trends 215, 216
   production 209, 213–214, 214
   stock levels 215
   synthetic competition 210

   uses 209
Rusal 37, 37
Russia
   aluminium 32, 32, 33, 33, 35
   coal 126, 128, 129, 129, 131–132, 131
   copper 42, 46, 47, 49
   crude oil 148, 152, 156
   gold 56, 58
   lead reserves 80
   natural gas 136, 139, 140, 140–141
   nickel 91, 93, 94, 95, 97
   palladium 76, 76, 78
   platinum production 72, 72
   power generation 131
   silver production 67
   sugar 227, 228, 229, 231
   tin 102, 104
   wheat 236, 238, 239, 240, 240
   wool consumption 186

## S

S&P 500 index 25
S&P GSCI 22, 25
saccharin 227
Saudi Arabia
   aluminium production 35
   crude oil 12, 148, 156
   gold consumption 56
   natural gas consumption 139
   rice consumption 201
Saudi Arabian Oil Company (Aramco) 154
Schumpeter, Joseph 8–9
scrap *see* recycling
security of supply fears 11–12
self-sufficiency, national 11–12
Seven Sisters 153
shale gas 137, 141–142, 146, 251
shale oil 149, 152, 155–156

Shandong Xinfa Aluminium and
  Electricity Group 37
Shanghai Futures Exchange 50
Shell 153
Sherritt International Corp 95
silver 65
  consumption 65-66
  market trading 68
  mining constraints 67
  outlook 69
  price trends 68, 69
  production 66-67, 67
  uses 65-66
The Silver Institute 256
Singapore
  crude oil refining 148
  tin exports 105
solar energy industry 64, 65
solder alloys 102-103, 103
South Africa
  aluminium production 35
  coal 128, 129, 130, 131, 132
  gold mining 57, 58
  maize 194
  palladium production 76
  platinum production 71-72, 72
  sugar exports 228
  wool production 187, 188
South America 251
  crude oil reserves 149
  natural gas 137, 139, 141
  tin production 108, 109
South Korea
  aluminium 32, 33
  coal 128, 129
  copper 45, 46
  lead 82, 83, 85
  maize imports 195
  natural gas consumption 139

nickel consumption 93
tin 104, 105
zinc 115, 116, 118
sovereign wealth funds (SWFs) 13, 251
Soviet Union
  aluminium consumption 32
  wool consumption 185
soybeans 217
  consumption 218-219, 219
  international trade 219-221, 220
  market trading 223
  outlook 224
  price trends 223-224, 223
  processing 218
  production 181, 196, 221-222, 222
  stock levels 223, 224
  uses 217-218
Spain
  lead imports 83
  maize production 196-197
  zinc 116, 118
SPDR Goldshares 60
speculators 19, 63, 98, 158
spot return 20
starch industry 192, 236
starter-lighting ignition (SLI) battery 252
steel industry 91, 92
  China production 8, 90, 99-100
  galvanised 113-115
  production 96-97
  stainless steel 90-91, 99
  US production 8, 115
stevia 226
stock levels, price effects of 16
storage costs 22
structured products 24, 158
Südzucker 231

sugar 225
   consumption 226-228, 227
   international trade 228, 229
   market trading 232
   outlook 233-234
   price trends 232-233, 233
   production 225, 229-232, 231
   stock levels 232, 233
   substitutes 225-226, 227
Sumitomo Metal Mining Co 49, 95
Sumitomo Rubber Industries 212
sunflowerseed oil 223
superalloys 91-92, 252
supercycles 8-10
supply, price effects 15-16
Suriname, aluminium 29
SWFs *see* sovereign wealth funds
SX-EW (solvent extraction and electrowinning) 41, 252

**T**
Taiwan
   coal imports 129
   copper 45, 46
   lead consumption 82
   nickel consumption 93
   tin consumption 104
   zinc consumption 115
Tajikistan, cotton production 181
Teck Resources 85, 117
Tereos Internacional 231
Texaco 153
Thai Roong Ruang Sugar Group 231
Thailand
   cotton imports 180
   rice 202-203, 203, 205, 205, 207
   rubber 212, 213-214, 214
   sugar 228, 229, 230, 231
   tin production 108
Thaisarco 108, 109

tight gas 137, 146, 252
Timah Persero Tbk PT 108, 109
tin 101
   consumption 104-105, 104
   international trade 105-106, 105
   market trading 108-109
   mining constraints 107
   outlook 111
   price trends 110-111, 110
   production 102, 106-109, 107, 109
   reserves 101, 102
   stock levels 108, 110
   uses 102-104, 103
tinplate 103, 103
Tongling Nonferrous Metals Group 49
trading exchanges, historical perspective 18-19
transport industry
   aluminium use 31
   copper use 43
   crude oil use 150, 160
   natural gas use 138
   steel use 114
Turkey
   bank gold reserves 57
   coal consumption 128
   cotton 179, 180
   gold consumption 56
   wheat imports 237
   wool consumption 185, 186
Turkiye Seker Fabrikalari 231
Turkmenistan
   cotton production 181
   natural gas reserves 136
tyre manufacturing 209, 210, 212, 215

**U**
Uganda, coffee production 175, 176

UK
  cocoa processing 164
  natural gas 139, 142
  scrap 96–97
  wheat production 239
  wool 186, 187
Ukraine
  coal reserves 126
  maize 195, 197
  soybean production 222
  wheat 239, 240–241, 240
United Arab Emirates (UAE)
  aluminium production 34, 35
  gold consumption 56
  oil reserves 154
  sugar 228, 229
United States (US)
  aluminium 31–32, 32, 33, 34, 35, 36
  coal
    consumption 127, 128
    exports 128, 129
    production 129–130, 131
    reserves 126
  cocoa 164, 165, 166
  coffee 172, 173, 174
  copper
    consumption 44, 45
    imports 46
    production 47, 48, 49
    reserves 42
  cotton 179, 179, 180, 181, 182
  crude oil 11, 148, 152, 152, 156
  ethanol 192, 233
  gold 56, 58
  lead
    consumption 81–82
    imports 83
    production 83, 84, 85, 86
    reserves 80
  maize
    consumption 192, 193
    exports 194, 195
    production 195–196, 197
    stock levels 197
  natural gas 138, 139, 141–142, 143, 144
  nickel 92, 93
  power generation 127–128, 134
  rice 203, 203, 205–206
  rubber imports 212
  scrap 96–97
  shale oil 152, 156
  soybeans 218–219, 219, 220, 220, 221, 222
  steel industry 8, 115
  sugar 227, 229, 231
  sugar substitutes 225–226
  tin 104, 105
  wheat 236, 238, 238, 240, 240
  wool consumption 185, 186
  zinc
    consumption 114–115, 115
    imports 116, 116
    production 116, 117, 118
    reserves 113
Uruguay, wool production 187, 188
US Commodity Futures Trading Commission (CFTC) 19
US dollar exchange rates 16, 52, 61, 62
US Geological Survey (USGS) 256
US No. 2 Hard Red Winter (HRW) wheat benchmark 241
Uzbekistan
  cotton 180, 181, 182
  wool consumption 186

V
Vale 94, 95, 96

Vedanta 117
Venezuela
  bauxite reserves 29
  crude oil reserves 148
Vietnam
  bauxite reserves 29, 30
  coffee 174, 174, 175, 175
  rice 203, 203, 205, 205
  rubber 212, 212, 214, 214
Volcan Compañía Minera 85
Votorantim 118

**W**
weather phenomena 167, 170
West Texas Intermediate (WTI) oil benchmark 157-158, 159
wheat 235
  consumption 235-237, 236
  genetically modified (GM) crops 243
  international trade 237-239, 238
  market trading 241
  outlook 243
  price trends 241-243, 242
  production 239-241, 240
  stock levels 241, 242
Wilmar International 231
windfall revenue 13
wool 185
  consumption 185-186, 186
  market trading 188
  outlook 189-190
  price trends 188-189, 189
  production 186-188, 187
  stock levels 189
  uses 185
World Bureau of Metal Statistics (WBMS) 256
World Gold Council (WGC) 256

**X**
Xstrata 48, 85, 94, 95, 96, 117

**Y**
Yokohama Tire Corporation 212
Yunnan Chengfeng 109
Yunnan Copper Group 49
Yunnan Tin 109

**Z**
Zambia, copper 42, 45, 46-47, 46, 47, 48
Zimbabwe
  palladium production 76
  platinum production 72, 72
zinc 112
  consumption 114-115, 115
  international trade 115-116, 116
  market trading 119
  outlook 120-121
  price trends 119-120, 120
  production 112, 116-118, 117, 118
  reserves 112, 113
  stock levels 120
  uses 113-114